Jill Benton has written extensively on the works of Naomi Mitchison. During the research for this biography, she spent many hours enjoying the company of Naomi Mitchison and her family. She is an Associate Professor at Pitzer College in Claremont, California, and together with her husband, Al Schwartz, has three children.

NAOMI
MITCHISON

A Biography

Jill Benton

Pandora
An Imprint of HarperCollinsPublishers

Pandora Press
An Imprint of HarperCollins*Publishers*
77–85 Fulham Palace Road
London W6 8JB

First published in hardback by
Pandora Press in 1990

This edition published in 1992

10 9 8 7 6 5 4 3 2 1

A CIP record for this book is available
from the British Library

ISBN 0 04 440862 5

Printed in Great Britain by
HarperCollins Manufacturing, Glasgow

For
KATY, CHRIS, AARON
and
AL

Contents

List of Illustrations

Acknowledgements

I wish to thank Naomi Mitchison for granting permission to quote from her private papers and published works and for her enormous generosity. I am grateful to many people for talking with me about Naomi and her world: to her children – Dennis Mitchison, Murdoch Mitchison, Lois Godfrey, Av Mitchison, and Val Arnold-Forster; to her friends – Elizabeth Longford, Louise Annand, Roderick MacFarquahar, Mary Munro, Jemima McLean, Robert and Chrissie Paterson; and to others whose voices are heard in this book. Thank you to Dorothy Sheridan for permission to quote from her edited version of Naomi's Second World War diary, *Among You Taking Notes. . .*; to the Trustees of the Tom Harrisson Mass Observation Archive, the University of Sussex, and Curtis Brown Limited, London for permission to quote from the manuscript of Naomi's diary and from essays; to the Harry Ransom Research Centre the University of Texas at Austin, for permission to quote from letters and manuscripts in the Naomi Mitchison papers; to the Fondren Library, Rice University, for permission to quote from Naomi's letters held in the Julian Huxley papers; to the Department of Manuscripts, the National Library of Scotland, for permission to quote from letters and manuscripts in the Haldane papers; to David Doughan, the Fawcett Library, City of London Polytechnic, for his librarianship; to Daimid Gunn, on behalf of the Gunn Family, for permission to quote Neil Gunn; to Donald Smith for sharing his doctoral dissertation, *The Poetry and Fiction of Naomi Mitchison*, written for the University of Edinburgh; to John Shelton for his photographic assistance.

This biography has been made possible by a Graduate Research Grant from the University of California in San Diego, by a Woodrow Wilson Grant in Women's Studies and by two Humanities Summer Research Grants from Pitzer College. Thank you to Roy Harvey Pearce for introducing me to the work of Naomi Mitchison, to Dale Spender and Philippa Brewster for providing the opportunity to write her biography, and to Al Schwartz for invaluable help editing this book in its various versions, for good advice and for kindness.

Introduction

This book is about Naomi Mitchison, a remarkable British writer whose life of literature, politics and social experiment spans the twentieth century. It is not a conventional biography for its subject is still very much alive. Now in her nineties, she writes daily, acts politically, runs her estate in the Mull of Kintyre, rides the London underground, and regularly treks to her Bakgatla tribe in southern Africa.

Naomi Mitchison celebrated her 90th birthday twice in November 1987, once in a grand fête in the prestigious Haldane Room at University College in London and again in Edinburgh at the Scottish Arts Council, bagpipes wailing, gathered friends of a lifetime singing to their bonny 'Nou', as intimate friends tend to call her. She twinkled, hunched shyly, and bowed her head to praise and honour. In the decade past she had received honorary degrees from the University of Stirling, the University of Strathclyde and St Anne's College in Oxford, plus an OBE, the Order of the British Empire, from the Queen. In her 90th year, Naomi's mannered voice and softly wrinkled image, blue eyes hooded, smiled into British households, televised by BBC specials dedicated to her fame. She is a prominent writer, socialist and feminist politician, and advisor to a Botswanan chief.

Best known for her novels, Naomi Mitchison has been a literary pioneer several times over. She was the first woman writer in the English speaking world to revise mythology and history from a woman's point of view, anticipating by a half-century the recent wave of such literature and adding her voice to the exploration of the theme of female quest. The best known of this genre is *The Corn King and the Spring Queen*, published in 1931. Her brave political novel, *We Have Been Warned*, published in 1935, identified the contradictions which plagued the uneasy upper-middle class alliance of communism, socialism and feminism. It was the only work of its kind. Naomi shifted literary ground during the Second World War, to become an influential writer in the Scottish Renaissance, her novels uniquely blending Celtic mythology and socialist politics. Later, her science fiction novels were among the first by women writers to present androgynies, sexual alternatives to conventional dualism and heterosexuality. Translated into many languages, *Memoirs of a Spacewoman* (1961) predates science fiction written by Doris Lessing and Ursula LeGuin. Her writings on Botswana in the 1960s, 1970s and 1980s have been banned by the South African government. Her complete bibliography contains over 1,000 publications.

Old age does not stop Naomi. Slinging her lightly packed bag over her shoulder in the style of contemporary student travellers, she journeyed once again in 1988 to visit her Bakgatla tribe. It is blistering hot, dry and dusty in Mochudi in the Kalahari, not an inviting habitat for most 91 year olds. But outside of Great Britain, Mochudi is her home.

I last stayed with Naomi at her Scottish estate for a week in the summer of 1988. She seemed healthier and younger than I remembered from four years before. Her house was alive with visitors.

Entering the living-room of Carradale, a baronial manor isolated on the Mull of Kintyre, Naomi balanced a tray laden with lacquer cups and sherry for her guests, the usual summer gathering of family, friends and fans. Interested, articulate, she reigned, spreading her diaphanous skirt, pleated and etched with blue-green peacock feathers. Her son, Murdoch, and his wife, Rowy, were reading by the fire. They had come up from Edinburgh where he is a Professor of Biology and she, a historian. Grandson, Josh, was practising laboured French with London friends he had brought to meet his Grannie. On a flanking couch chatted film-makers who have negotiated rights to *Memoirs of a Spacewoman*. There were two young women with small children: one was a scholar of French Carolingian history and literature, the subject of Naomi's current writing project; the other was visiting from Naomi's far-away tribe in Botswana.

Each morning Naomi unearthed salad potatoes from her garden, then boiled and peeled them for her hungry guests. She washed mud from her hands before writing, preferring to scribble and type at her living-room desk surrounded by murmuring conversation. She once interrupted the murmur to read Carolingian Latin aloud, laughing at its crudity. While no one but Naomi seemed to understand the joke, we received the gesture as a gift. Naomi was working, fully focused on the project at hand.

Several years ago during one of our early meetings, Naomi bent over my hand, cradling it in hers, reading the prophetic lines of my palm. 'Och,' she exhaled, signaling that she was about to deliver a Scottish irony, 'it's shorter than I thought.'

'Oh?'

'Yes, your line of imagination is very short, far shorter than mine,' she said, droll and teasing. At that time in 1982, when I was living with her in London and before she lived with me in California, neither Naomi nor I foresaw that I would one day write her biography – where it might be to her advantage that I lack the story-teller's gift of embellishment.

I come to Naomi's life as a passionate student of literature unabashedly respectful of any writer who can spin engrossing tales of fictive truth; but I come also as a woman especially bent on honouring the lives of those accomplished women writers short-changed by literary history. Familiar as Naomi Mitchison's name might be in England and Scotland, it is little known elsewhere – even among literary scholars. Yet she has written beautifully, bravely and prolifically for more than seventy of her more than ninety years.

I make no claim for this biography as the whole truth. No biographer can fulfil that promise. But Naomi Mitchison does deserve to be honoured by an honest rendering of her life and work. That is my aim. No doubt, Naomi will take issue with what I have written. She was neither asked to read nor to approve this final version of how I see her personal life and public accomplishments. Naomi might prefer that her own well-turned version of herself pass on to posterity. She has, after all, shaped her long and fruitful life into diaries and memoirs, which I urge readers to explore for themselves.

Finally, I want to connect Naomi Mitchison's story to those obstacles encountered by generations of strong, literate women. Her life, idiosyncratic and exotic in many ways, nevertheless covers the entire curve of Scots–English history and culture in the twentieth century. The challenges and trials she faced are those experienced by women who have struggled for an independent voice throughout this century. By shedding light on Naomi Mitchison's life and works, I hope to contribute some understanding to the experience of women everywhere struggling for their voice.

1

First Worlds
1897-1909

Naomi Mary Margaret Haldane was born to Louisa Kathleen née Trotter and John Scott Haldane in the home of her maternal grandparents in Edinburgh on November 1, 1897; she was the younger of two children. Naomi and her older brother Jack grew up in a financially comfortable family of considerable public stature. The Trotters were wealthy and had generations of military and administrative service in India behind them. But it was clearly the Haldane line that dominated Naomi's family experience. As far back as the thirteenth century, Haldanes were Lords of Gleneagles, earning respect by guarding the Scottish Lowlands from Highland raiders. Haldane family roots run deep through some eight centuries of political, religious and intellectual Scottish history.

Naomi was surrounded by an extended family of highly achieving people. Her father, John Scott, revolutionised the science of physiology; her Uncle Richard, a powerful Liberal political leader and Secretary of War, was Lord Chancellor at the beginning of the First World War and then again after; Elizabeth, Naomi's Aunt Bay, wrote books on Descartes, Hegel and George Eliot, and became the first woman in Scotland ever to be appointed Justice of the Peace; Naomi's older brother by five years, John Burdon Sanderson, Jack to the family and J. B. S. to the world, was not outdone. He excelled in several fields – physiology, biology, chemistry, mathematics and genetics; his mathematical formula is still the basis for forecasting genetic changes.

Layered into this family's productivity were its traditions and especially the Haldane obligations impressed upon Naomi as she grew up. Her remarkable paternal grandmother, Mary Elizabeth Haldane née Burdon Sanderson, who died aged 100, when Naomi

1

was in her late twenties, would bid her children and their progeny to her bedside each New Year's Eve. There they were asked to evaluate the family's accomplishments of the past year and expectations of the year ahead. Only Haldane 'blood' relatives were invited – Naomi, her father, her brother, Aunt Bay, Uncle Richard, another uncle, William and his children. Naomi's mother and other non-bloodline relatives were not called. Granniema's New Year's ritual exemplifies the pervasive sense of Haldane pride and purpose running through Naomi's childhood and early adult years. A single word, 'Suffer', is the Haldane motto imprinted above the family coat of arms. 'Suffer' is carved in the family's marble burial monument at Gleneagles, in the wooden panels above the hearth in Granniema's Cloan mansion and in the garden wall of Naomi's childhood home in Oxford. Along with a sense of family pride and purpose, a Haldane was expected to pay the price of sacrifice, to 'suffer' in quest of accomplishment.

Naomi grew up living in two places. During the school year, she lived in Oxford, first in a modest home on St Margaret's Road, then after 1906 in a house of more than twenty rooms on the banks of the river Cherwell, off the Banbury Road. Summer months and most holidays were spent mainly at Cloan, Granniema's baronial Scottish mansion adjacent to the ancient Haldane lands at Gleneagles. Now over 94 years old, Naomi continues to make these pendulum swings from the heart of England, now London, to the edge of the Scottish Highlands, now Carradale.

The newly married John and Kathleen Haldane moved to Oxford in 1887, ten years before Naomi's birth and five years before Jack was born. Uffer, as first Jack then Naomi called their father in baby-talk, launched his eminent career in the physiological laboratory of his uncle, John Burdon Sanderson. Uffer became a Fellow, then a Reader at New College. Politically liberal and humanitarian, his significant scientific achievements were usually linked to concern about unhealthy conditions for workers, including the effects on miners of toiling in foul air and high temperatures. Uffer's interest in the working conditions of coal and tin miners led to important discoveries regarding the physiology of respiration. Specifically, he investigated suffocative gases encountered in coal mines and wells, inventing new means for overcoming the danger of colliery explosions. His research in pure physiology, published in collaboration with J. G. Priestley, showed how the regulation of breathing is determined by the sensitivity of the respiratory centre of the brain to variations in the amount of carbon dioxide in the blood, accounting for automatic adjustments of breathing which occur with changes in body activity.

After the First World War, his health deteriorated because he had experimented on himself in his rush to invent the mask that was used to protect soldiers from poison gases.

Uffer's scientific work was his consuming interest. He seldom took time away, eschewing holidays. His work was an everyday part of Naomi's life in her Oxford home where Uffer conducted many of his experiments in the laboratory he built there. The early twentieth century was still a time when scientists could house their own laboratories. Uffer and his assistants experimented with the effects of gases on the physiology of breathing. It was dangerous work, particularly when they experimented on themselves. Occasionally the young Naomi was called into the laboratory where she was instructed to watch the experimenter, who was usually her father. If he fell over unconscious, she was to tug him out of the experimental chamber and perform artificial respiration. Although she does not recall being put to the test, the request itself made a lifelong impression upon her. Through his work, Uffer imbued Naomi's childhood with the importance of experimentation in pursuit of scientific and ultimately human progress. Naomi would take her father's perspective to a rather different turn. Experimentation became a way of conducting her life in pursuit of her art and of her relationships, political and intimate, as well as in pursuit of the self she was to become.

Kathleen Haldane, whom Naomi and Jack fondly nicknamed Maya, began life in Oxford on less firm ground than her husband. Uffer, after all, had his work and his colleagues. Oxford was an entirely unfamiliar environment for Maya. Edinburgh, at 10 Randolph Crescent, had been her main childhood home, but also the hotels and spas in Europe and England. Maya's politics were passionately Tory and imperialist, which meant that Oxford's social circle was far too liberal for her taste. She immersed herself in the Victoria League, an organisation devoted to promotion of the British Empire, becoming well-known as a lecturer for the League in the Oxford area. Completely certain of her political views, Maya sought yet another security: land. The handful of acres that encircled Cherwell – the large, newly built, comfortable though aesthetically cumbersome house in Oxford – were cultivated as a Scottish estate. There were gardens and chickens, pastures and cows. She ran a small dairy, among the first in Oxfordshire to be free of tuberculosis bacteria.

Maya was certain enough of her political mind to extract a promise from Naomi's father before she would marry him; Uffer agreed not to discuss his Liberal political opinions at home. As a result, Maya thought she had a free hand to influence the political thinking of her

3

children. She could not have been more surprised by the outcome. Her insistence that nation and empire were one – the keystone of her patriotism – translated into brotherhood, human equality and internationalism in her daughter and son. Naomi, as an adult, became a Labourite socialist; Jack, a Communist.

Even without words, the thrust of Uffer's rational Liberalism had centuries of Haldane social and political involvement to give depth and force to his actions, the kind of force that would move through the carefully held boundaries of what was actually said. While Uffer abided by his prenuptial agreement regarding liberal political talk, his conduct clearly expressed his humane convictions. Both Jack and Naomi were influenced, for example, by Uffer's socialising with coal miners at home. One young miner aroused Naomi's compassion by sharing his life story with her while they were canoeing: 'It started making holes in quite a lot of my assumptions'.[1] Miners were frequent guests in the Haldane home because of Uffer's work. Fishermen were also included in the Haldane household. Uffer had conducted experiments in Cornwall, where Sennen Cove became a traditional Easter retreat for Maya and her two children.

The occasionally charged political undercurrents in Naomi's Oxford home at times replicated the currents of national politics. One such disruption at the turn of the century was sparked by the Boer War in South Africa, particularly the British policy of herding Afrikaner women and children into several camps where poor nutrition and sanitation led to epidemic and death. Maya never understood why Uffer did not see it her way. She writes about this in her memoir, *Friends and Kindred* (1961), which she wrote in her nineties. Maya describes attempting to explain to Uffer what she considered to be the obvious necessity of these camps: Afrikaner guerrillas had to be prevented from receiving support from their families. She recalls that Uffer refused to listen to her: 'It seemed as if he were deliberately closing his mind to any reasoning on the matter, and could only talk about "inhumanity" and "starving" women and children'.[2] Her own quotation marks suggest continuing frustration sixty years later. Wrong-headed as Maya's views might have been, she never backed away from her beliefs even in her position as a minority of one in her own home, as she had been in the extended Haldane family from the beginning.

It must be added that, while Maya did not succeed in tailoring her children's political views, neither Jack nor Naomi made lives entirely in line with their vowed commitments to ideologies of equality. Jack's biographer, Ronald Clark, reports that Jack was frequently overbearing and even cruel to his subordinates. Jack was comfortable living in social hierarchies. When he emigrated to India in later life, he embraced the caste system.[3] As for Naomi, she has at times portrayed society as a barnyard pecking order. 'Status', she once wrote, ' – essential for all gregarious animals, essential in the farmyard. I knew it and would always know it'.[4] Naomi, as we shall see, could peck with the best.

Despite Uffer's liberal convictions and humane actions, he was usually not an outspoken exponent of causes. Temperamentally, he avoided conflicts. His good work took precedence over all else. Indeed, Uffer was famous in Oxford for his consuming involvement in his experiments. He would appear for supper, eat silently and quickly, then disappear into his laboratory. On occasion he would forget about dinner altogether, even at times when Maya had invited guests. House guests have commented on Uffer's inclination to be withdrawn. According to Gervas Huxley, a visitor at Cherwell in 1914, the 'Prof', as he was frequently called in Oxford, was kind, gentle, slightly stooping and silent.[5] Nevertheless, Uffer's influence on the household was powerful if not always obvious to visitors. Like the pervasive smell of chloride and pungent gases coming from his home laboratory, his impact was not quite visible but always sensed by his daughter.

Uffer brought to Naomi the adventure of science. An atmosphere of inquiry permeated the Haldane house as thoroughly as did the gases that escaped from the laboratory. Naomi haunted the lab although she never understood the gas analysis apparatus. She would pet the experimental mice, sometimes retrieving one from its hiding place under a bench; she would chat with the lab assistants; she would wash equipment. Oxford students crowded into her home for her father's mentorship and company. At teatime Uffer would sometimes be absentmindedly pleasant to as many as a dozen students. Scientists, both local and foreign, sought the warmth and companionship of the Haldane home, an atmosphere which, according to accounts of house guests, was produced largely by Maya's hospitable hands and welcoming mien. In her second memoir, *All Change Here: Girlhood and Marriage*, Naomi remembers this home-society of scientists: 'There were not only the regular workers, but my old love Teddy Boycott. . .and then Barcroft and the Copenhagen physiologists, the hours of talk going on in the study and the smell of pipe smoke coming out'.[6]

Naomi idolised her father as she was growing up. In *Small Talk* she records that she always associated security and safety with him, his lap a haven, especially when she could tuck a finger in his ear. In her fiction she describes heroes and heroines who suffer for the welfare of their communities just as she perceived Uffer to be doing. Naomi once told me that as she has grown older, she often dreams about her father. He is invariably rescuing her. Naomi continues to revere Uffer as she did when she dedicated her book *The Moral Basis of Politics* (1939) to him a couple of years after he died. In acknowledged reference to Xenophon's praise of Socrates, she wrote of her father: 'when I consider both the wisdom and nobility of the man, I find it beyond my power not to have him in mind, or having him in mind, not to praise him'.[7]

The young Naomi learnt to be scientifically observant, a skill that has stood her in good stead through a long lifetime of writing. By the age of 11 she was a competent field botanist who wanted to be a scientist when she grew up. This was not to be; she never pursued the education necessary for a career in science, nor was she ever encouraged to do so.

Although Naomi felt unfairly cut off from what she later recognised to be the privileged male scientific mode of her family, she was not cut off from the supportive yet demanding influence of Granniema at Cloan. Upon receiving Naomi's letters of botanical observation, Granniema would ask for yet more description and then demonstrate exactly how Naomi might turn a phrase more effectively. Naomi was eager to please her grandmother, suggesting that the elder was also a tactful editor. In her memoirs Naomi is quick to acknowledge that her Haldane grandmother was centrally important in her venture as a writer.

Cloan itself was a significant context for Naomi's development generally. Under Granniema's presence, the Scottish mansion was as intellectually alive as Naomi's Oxford home. It was the place for the sturdy, thick-set Haldanes to gather. It was there that Naomi mainly came under the sway of Uncle Richard, Aunt Bay and their intellectual and political companions. It was at Cloan, moreover, that Naomi would find the most agreeable religious experience of her long life. On Sunday evenings members of the family laid aside their reading in favour of prayer, cushioned benches hastily arranged by status for servants – the cook, the butler, Uncle Richard's chauffeur and all the staff down to the kitchen maid. Senior men of the family, her father and eventually her brother when Uncle Richard was not there, intoned a chapter from the Bible and improvised a prayer, Presbyterian style. On the piano Aunt Bay picked out hymns chosen by Granniema. As long as religion was in the hands of her beloved family, practised in the familiar drawing-room furnished with comfortable chintz chairs and plush purple benches, Naomi could be contentedly Protestant. However, church Presbyterianism offended her. In her first memoir, written after several decades of bitter experience of what she considered the blighting religious climate of the Highlands, she reports that as a child she thought Presbyterianism altogether 'ugly' – its building, its decoration and its congregation.[8] Her aesthetic repulsion was backed by her mother's opinion that religion was fit only for servants. She brought up Jack and Naomi as agnostics. One can see why Christian prayer did not protect Naomi from her nightmares.

From among the many intellectuals and politicians passing through life at Cloan, Naomi chose in her memoirs to pay particular homage to Andrew Lang, who, although in his seventies, became her friend and confidant when she was 9 years old. She had many other alternatives both at Cloan and in Oxford. One supposes she might have chosen Robert Baden-Powell, close friend of the Haldanes, who as founder of the Boy and Girl Scout Movements influenced generations of children, or failing that she might have chosen her godfather, Samuel Alexander, the elderly, patriarchally bearded philosopher, author of *Space, Time and Deity*, who conceived of the world as a single cosmic process in which there periodically emerges higher forms of being. But Naomi preferred Andrew Lang, a renegade academician.

Lang was an import into the English intellectual scene, a last representative figure of the Scottish Enlightenment. In his heyday, he had been an influential London literary critic. He was also among the founders of modern anthropology, combating conventional historical philology with his comparativist theories of totemism; he gathered folk and fairy tales (which Naomi read); he wrote a major history of Scotland plus a history of British literature; and he wrote historical novels, making his young friend Naomi a gift of *The Monk of Fife*, his novel set during the time of Joan of Arc's martyrdom. By the time Lang entered Naomi's life, however, he had lost his public glamour. He had already begun to talk about ghosts as though he believed in them; people, including Naomi's family, were laughing at him.

But it was to Lang that Naomi confided her special secret. Not even her mother knew it, and Naomi was expected to share everything with her mother. Naomi felt isolated at times in the rational Haldane world:

My brother had the irrational streak, but he would have thought it inappropriate to share it with me. I could not speak to him, still less to parents or teachers. It would never have entered my mind to speak to a doctor. I could not have mentioned things to my other classmates, who would either have laughed or thought less highly of me as a competitor or leader.[9]

And what was Naomi's awful secret? She had nightmares – yet, perhaps, they were not nightmares and were something else. As a child she was deeply uncertain. For one thing she was not always asleep when these 'Powers of Evil' visited her: 'In this state I was held, unable to move, while something rushed by or through me. . .apparently taking with it some part of my thinking and will'.[10] The result of these visitations for Naomi was private alarm and distress.

Nor were these traumas, which increased in frequency as Naomi grew into young adulthood, relegated to night and darkness. A monster, uncharacteristically invented by Aunt Bay, who was usually sweet-tempered and considerate, was thought to inhabit a tower room at Cloan, there to frighten Naomi and her cousin Graeme. Other places at Cloan alarmed her, and so did some bad patches in the glen near it. Certain mirrors terrorised her. She found herself worshipping a rock. As a small child, she beat her head rhythmically on occasion in order to propitiate her tormentors.

At least Andrew Lang did not tease her as apparently some Haldanes did. Naomi remembers being haunted by an eye gouged from a cooked sheep's head and presented to her in fun by Uncle Richard. She claimed that family teasing would only drive her into deeper terrors. Lang sympathised and even encouraged her to see fairies although she thinks she may not have told him the more frightening parts of her experience. Lang was so keen to encourage Naomi's psychic imagination that he invited her to attend the doctoral dissertation defence of one of his students at Oxford, a young man who wished to prove the existence of fairies. She was becoming Lang's expert on the subject.

Naomi recalls many fantasy episodes. One is a childhood memory of helping reapers in a cornfield while visiting Cloan. In typical Haldane fashion, she had been given the task of gleaning for old ladies in a nearby poorhouse, her sheaf to be transformed into a bag of oatmeal. Half a century later, Naomi tells her story as if it actually had happened to her: 'Then I met a brown hare and we went off and kept house (marriage as I saw it) inside a corn stook with six oat sheaves propped around us'.[11] In this same description Naomi carefully points out that in Celtic mythology hares are signs of fertility. She relishes the association. In her poem, 'The House of the Hare', the first in her collection of poems from the Scottish period of her life, *The Cleansing of the Knife* (1983), Naomi suggests that her fantasies were private sources of freedom and art:

> And the thing that happened to me
> The day that I went with the gleaners,
> The day I built the corn-house,
> That is not built with prayers,
> For oh I was clean set free,
> In the corn, in the corn, in the corn,
> I have lived three days with the hare.

Hitting incantatory rhythms, a favoured beat, Naomi associates herself with symbols of sex and fertility set against organised religion; it frees her.

Naomi played with her hare in the same way that she dammed streams and concocted glorious beds of flowers for passing fairies. One might note, however, that this description of childhood play with the hare did not actually take form until Naomi, well into her seventies, wrote *Small Talk* (1973). Even the poem was written in later life – at the very earliest when Naomi, in her forties, was living in Scotland. In both the poem and the account in her memoir she synthesises folk and psychological archetypes, as well she might given her prior experiences. Servants at Cloan had filled their receptive charge with tales of hauntings and second sight, the stuff of Scottish folk culture and magic. Andrew Lang corroborated these stories, adding some of his own, many of which may still be read in his essays in turn of the century editions of the *Encyclopaedia Britannica*. In addition to these accounts from true believers, by the time Naomi was a young woman she had read all twelve volumes of James Frazer's *The Golden Bough*, which broadened and formalised her knowledge of mythology. Finally settling in Scotland during the Second World War, it seemed to her that C. G. Jung had got it right in his theory of collective archetypes. Both hare and corn are key symbols in Frazer's anthropological mythology and Jung's archetypal psychology.

None of Naomi's plentiful, precociously detailed and complete childhood diaries hints at this private netherworld of terror and magical incantation. These diaries, she reports in her memoirs, were written for school competitions and public perusal. In them she describes all the mundane matters which could be understood: parades of soldiers, people met, adventures, botanical observations and drawings. She left out the Terrors for fear that revelations would bring down on her head some new torture at their hands. Left out, as well, are the fantasy stories Naomi had begun to tell herself, the seeds of future fictions:

> I think, but with no real certainty, that the stories had no real background in time or place and that they involved long conversations which gave me great pleasure to devise; some may have risen from books I read; it is also possible that some may have been a dip into a changed state of consciousness. If this was so, it is quite possible that I might not remember unless I could get back into that particular 'high'.[12]

Reviewing these early years of inner imaginings, Naomi herself remains uncertain about their objective nature, but she is sure that she had these experiences. Locating her descriptions of these terrors in *Small Talk* and *All Change Here* with accounts of her ill health, she implies that these bewildering experiences might have been caused by bouts of fevers and whooping cough, by surgery to remove tubercular glands, and, following that, by a head concussion. In later life she was able to duplicate, unpleasantly, her childhood terror through experimenting with the mind-altering drug mescalin.

Naomi's mother was as unaware of her daughter's secret terrors as she was of her fantasy worlds, but not out of disinterest in Naomi's inner life. In *All Change Here* Naomi confides that Maya wanted more of her than she was prepared to give, which is to say, her secrets: 'Above all I must tell everything I did, if possible, everything I thought'. Maya did seem to require a good deal from her daughter. When 11-year-old Naomi broke her leg, she brought Naomi's bed into her own bedroom, where it stayed for seven years. As Naomi recalled to me, she learnt to avert her eyes in order not to see Maya remove her stays. In Naomi's memoirs she surmises that Maya had used her to discourage sexual relations with Uffer. Apparently Uffer had left to Maya's domain the explicit arrangements for all Naomi's upbringing – not just in political matters. When Maya wanted to keep Naomi near, she did. It is true, in any case, that her mother seemed to give no thought to providing space for Naomi's emergent womanhood. One of Naomi's first tasks in achieving creative voice would be to escape from what she perceived as her mother's intrusive domination. Exploring forbidden worlds would be her mother tongue.

It was as if Maya considered Naomi merged with herself. In Maya's own memoir, *Friends and Kindred*, she seldom mentions Naomi as an independent person. Situation after situation is described in which she and Naomi have identical experiences – from being loved by their pet 'Polly' to sitting in the surf of Cornwall. Maya entitles one chapter 'My Son', but does not devote even a separate page to her daughter who by 1961 had long been a famous writer.

Perhaps, living so closely under her mother's wing and scrutiny, Naomi became an expert at keeping secrets not only from Maya but from us all. Her three volumes of memoirs reveal a preoccupation with secrets. *Small Talk: An Edwardian Childhood* (1973) and *All Change Here: Girlhood and Marriage* (1975) shout every secret she can remember keeping from her mother. These memories of childhood and adolescence, augmented by diaries and letters, are trustworthy sources, rich in textual detail and observation – thick sociological tapestries woven with revelations of body, fantasy, nightmare and guilt. But her story blurs as she begins to chronicle her first years of marriage. Naomi's lifelong habit of keeping secrets becomes fully evident in her last memoir, *You May Well Ask* (1979), in which she proposes to answer questions about crucial years in her political, social and intimate relationships in the 1920s and 1930s. Instead of answers, she obfuscates by avoiding chronology and blotting out details, writing her truths in too generalised albeit tantalising terms. The details are found securely wrapped in large envelopes lodged in Naomi's bedroom desk at her Carradale house. These letters and photographs from husband, friends, lovers, and some written by Naomi herself, tell a story of experiment, struggle, joy and suffering to which she merely alludes in *You May Well Ask*, contours sketched but not fleshed out.

The strains and tensions that characterise Naomi's adult fiction were set in place and tautly wound in her childhood. Her parents, Uffer and Maya, were locked in subterranean political conflict, pitting class privilege against social justice. Naomi experienced the strains of being pulled between the scientific rationalism of the Haldane world view and the irrational, to Naomi magical, aspects of her own deeply private experiences. Yet another tension would trouble Naomi's up-bringing and pervade her art. For much of her childhood, Naomi was raised with boys and educated to think, behave and compete like a boy herself; none the less, she was expected to mature into an Edwardian lady, subduing her competitiveness and abiding by unwritten feminine codes governing decorum and conduct in the British upper middle classes.

For the first decade of her life Naomi thought that she was like the boys who surrounded her – with only some slight differences. The first boy in her life was her brother Jack, whom she nicknamed 'Boy', often turning it into 'Boydie', short for 'Boy-dear'. Then there were Jack's friends whom she preferred to her own.

At home, Jack was the main recipient of Uffer's explicit scientific training: 'it was the scientific excitement that came through most to my brother with a small spill-over to me', wrote Naomi.[13] Boy grew up to be a world-famous scientist. He began his training in his father's home laboratory, was a Fellow at Cambridge and then headed the Department of Genetics at University College in London. Following his disillusionment with Communism in the 1950s, he continued his work in India where he was to die.

Because Jack was five years older, Naomi had to scramble to keep up with him. They would have most in common during Naomi's adolescence and young womanhood. Nevertheless, both their childhood diaries recount adventures in which they mutually participated, parallel play though it may have been. They went on botanical hikes, climbed mountains, swam. Together they skinned a woolly caterpillar to make a fur rug for Naomi's dolls' house. It shrivelled up, an unsuccessful experiment. More dangerously, they laid out lines of gunpowder and then lit them. Naomi did not especially like her dolls; she remembers gutting one in pursuit of scientific curiosity. Sometimes Boy and Naomi would play trains, manufacturing collisions. Sometimes they would build castles and forts with their building blocks 'which we garrisoned with lead soldiers and then fired at with the spring-loaded artillery whose wooden projectiles could make a real dent, in time bringing the whole thing satisfactorily crashing down'.[14] Naomi was allowed to help Jack, though sometimes he pushed her away in anger. Jack's fury, for which he became well-known in adulthood, did not daunt Naomi. Despite the occasional violence of their fantasy-play, she considered Jack a part of the everyday world and a hedge against the Powers of Evil which tormented her in secret:

> Often he teased me till my temper went and I stamped and screamed, feeling furiously helpless. I hated him for minutes and then suddenly it was all over. This wasn't the kind of thing which really worried me. This was alive.[15]

In her memoirs Naomi suggests that Jack had been a major love of her life. Her love – a passionate mix of envy, competition and admiration – was an open secret informing the themes of incest which occur again and again in Naomi's novels. Her first, *The Conquered*, and most stories and novels written in the 1920s and 1930s including her major work, *The Corn King and the Spring Queen* (1931), pivot on unresolved attractions and conflicts between brothers and sisters. In *The Conquered*, for instance, the sister kills herself for her brother's sake, freeing him to travel into the wide world to suffer, to adventure and to mature.

There were grounds for envy. Perhaps because he was male, perhaps because he was five years older, perhaps because he was unusually gifted, Boy was granted freedoms denied Naomi. For instance, in 1906, when she and Boy were accompanying their father in his deep-sea diving experiments for the Admiralty off the Kyles of Bute, Jack, then 14 years old, was allowed to descend into the watery depths, bubbles rising from his breathing apparatus. While under water, alone, his suit began to leak at the sleeve-cuffs. Rather than signal for help, he adjusted the pressure himself; he was eventually pulled to the surface with a suit half-filled with water. Boy was a hero in the eyes of his father and the crew. Naomi was wildly jealous of Jack's privileged freedom which had given him a chance to display courage in the face of danger; and she was envious, as well, of the attention he received. Longingly she wrote in her diary: 'I wish I were a boy'.

Besides her brother, Naomi's schooling contributed substantially to her boy-shaped early world. She had the unusual experience of attending a private preparatory school for boys. Maya had chosen it for her daughter, feeling so strongly about Naomi's attendance that she chose to live in Oxford itself rather than out in the countryside where more acreage would have appealed to her Scottish landowning desire. Maya may have had unfulfilled dreams that she wished for her daughter. As a young woman, she had wanted to be a doctor of medicine. Later, Maya thought herself a feminist, supporting the principles of suffrage and equality for women in the professions. Most certainly she wanted a good education for her daughter. As long as Naomi was young enough not to arouse sexual attention, she would be well-educated according to the highest standard available for young British boys of her class.

In the Oxford Preparatory School, soon to be renamed Dragon School, Naomi learnt the usual reading, composition and arithmetic. She participated in Shakespearian productions, which she adored. She also studied Latin, enjoying a gentleman's Classical education, the lack of which was rued by Virginia Woolf and other women of letters of her generation who felt sorely excluded from cultural discourse. Latin influenced Naomi's choice of time period when she began to write historical novels. Her first novel which she wrote in 1922, *The Conquered*, was based on her schoolgirl reading in Latin. She wrote about Vercingetorix, the admired Celtic rebel whom Caesar describes having conquered in his *Chonicles*.

More than subject matter made the progressive Dragon School a special circumstance for a girl. There Naomi was encouraged to be as competitive as a boy, or nearly so. She revelled in the tumble of competition and the public rewards for her excellence. When her formal education ended, she mourned keenly the passing of this atmosphere of contest which she came to believe had motivated her performance:

> There would have been little incentive to write a diary without competition and the almost certainty of getting a prize! I missed the school prize givings, the hall filled with parents who probably did one credit and one's proud walk up to the platform. . .[16]

Along with the boys in school, Naomi swung Indian clubs for drill and learnt gymnastics. She remembers swinging upside-down on the rings. Although she was bad at tops, she enjoyed the different games of marbles, confessing, 'I got very fond of some of the glassies and there was a terrible thrill in putting them into danger of being captured'.[17] Unlike many Edwardian girls, she was learning to take risks. Naomi was excluded from some male activities, but not from many:

> Most of the time I was either the only girl at a boy's school or the only girl but one, and the other either much older or much younger. But I didn't know or understand other girls – I felt I was a boy who unfairly was not allowed to play rugger (and had no wish to play cricket).[18]

When not in school, Haldane played with her friends, Richards, Rankin, Carline and Smyth – they surnamed each other as young men in public school would do. They played Devil-in-the-Dark, 'groaning and flashing lights at passers-by out of the hedges, delighted if they ran. . .'.[19] The evident pleasure Naomi took in rough-and-tumble play with boys shines in her memoirs of old age. Some of their games were intellectual; they wrote and acted their own plays. They also built forts, sometimes in the ditches of new house sites, sometimes in the thick shrubbery of a garden.

It would be a mistake to claim that Naomi entirely side-stepped the restrictive upbringing that was the lot of most Edwardian girls. Naomi's clothes, for example, were many layered and cumbersome, and became more so with every year that passed. Nor, as we have noted, was she allowed to join her schoolmates in all their activities. Even though one of Naomi's instructors at the Dragon School wanted her to participate in his Blue Dragon cruise, she was not allowed to go. Nor was she permitted to have a bicycle because of her mother's vague fears that it would harm her daughter's sexual organs. So we can see lurking in the wings restrictions which became increasingly noticeable with each passing year.

There were nevertheless occasional compensations. Instead of playing rugger, she and Jack Slessor, who was lame, rowed on the Cherwell. Eventually they formed a literary club and wrote a play, a whodunit. Instead of riding a bicycle, Naomi was given a pony and taught to ride side-saddle. She thinks the pony was a gift to salve her disappointment at not being allowed to participate in a community-wide historical pageant of Shakespeare. She speculates in her memoirs that her mother did not want her exposed to the common people of Oxford. Later in life Naomi analysed her experience. She concluded that class consciousness, the assumption of privilege and exclusiveness, was an important aspect of becoming a lady 'by instinct'.

As she thought back on this episode in her first memoir, Naomi realised that little girls were expected to like ponies, although she would have preferred performing in the Oxford community play. For a 10 year old, riding side-saddle was hardly an unprecarious business. Once falling from her pony, she was dragged for a distance, breaking her leg, cracking several ribs and spraining her neck. It was not all that easy to become a lady. The doctor who predicted that she would never run again did not consider Naomi's determination. Not only would she run, she would dance Scottish reels when she was 80 years old.

But at the age of 12 Naomi had a difficult trial to endure. She was wrenched from Dragon School and her days of thinking herself a boy were rudely ended. Blood had stained her blue serge knickers. Menstruation took Naomi by surprise; she had not been prepared by any biological instruction whatsoever. Nor did Naomi understand exactly why menstruation meant that she had to be exiled from her beloved Dragon School. Henceforth, it was her lot to be a girl, a stay-at-home with a well-meaning but badly prepared governess, Miss Blockey, for a teacher. Naomi writes: 'It was all very discouraging and I acquiesced in it, as indeed in other discouragements, but no doubt resentments and determinations built up inside'.[20]

In her decision to remove Naomi from school, Maya's commitment to feminist principles of suffrage and education for women was at odds with her class attitudes, its code of conduct for girls and its conservative politics. Ironically, something similar would happen to Naomi on the political left in the 1930s when her feminism clashed with the politics of socialism and communism. Apparently feminism rubbed against the ideological grain of both right and left.

Female blood, red, staining and assigned troublesome meaning by her mother, ended Naomi's formal education in 1909, marking an important turning point in her life. It flowed hard on the wounds of other felt misfortunes. Jack left home and their playroom for Eton in 1907 when she was 10; a year later she fell from her pony and was consigned to her mother's bedroom. Naomi writes: 'In her room and in that bed I stayed and dreamed into adolescence', a way of saying, we might add, that she shared 'this least nice of the rooms at Cherwell' with her mother until she was released, aged 18, into marriage.

If Naomi was to achieve personal independence she would have to do it for herself. She would receive little help from her family. Eventually, but not immediately, she connected her loss of delight and of male options at the Dragon School, as well as her meek acceptance of rules and subsequent despondencies, with Maya's narrow loyalty to class and ladyhood.

2
Girlhood and War
1910–1915

When Naomi was 13, she and her brother carpeted the front garden of Cherwell with cages for 300 guinea-pigs, sometimes more. Naomi remembers having frequent conversations, chittering and squeaking as she bent close to the creatures locked in their hutches. She may well have been commiserating with them.

Pulled out of Dragon School because she had started to menstruate, Naomi could no longer pretend that she was a boy. Unavoidably she was a girl, expected to become a lady, caged by rules of class and gender. The restrictions were difficult to abide especially since she could so clearly measure the liberty she had lost in losing her 'boyhood'.

Denied a complete formal education at Dragon School, relegated to the second-rate tutelage of Miss Blockey, Naomi's first task was to scramble up an education for herself, indeed to scramble up a self she could value. In that scramble she never lost sight of her standing relative to her older brother. Year by year she remembers calibrating her loss of footing in comparison to Jack, her generic 'Boy'.

The chasm between Jack's education and Naomi's was widening. While Naomi was at home being tutored along with three other girls – Miss Blockey was at her best when she played the piano while Naomi chanted poetry and danced – Jack had all the resources of western civilisation at hand. After two years of Classics at Eton, backed by his father who rejected the headmaster's accusation that his son was a 'mere smatterer', Jack turned to science, winning prizes in physics, biology and chemistry. Enrolled at New College in 1911, about the time Naomi began to keep guinea-pigs, he immediately published his first article in genetics and, then, unexpectedly veered away from science, again with his father's blessing. At the end of Jack's first year he switched from mathematics and biology to the Greats, in which he eventually took a First. Curiously, J. B. S. Haldane never took a degree in the sciences, for which he would eventually be hailed. Rather he learnt Latin, Greek, French and German and how to write well, a talent he turned to good purpose in his readable essays about scientific discoveries. His was a tough act to follow. But Jack was the one with whom Naomi most proudly and keenly competed, while she herself was being groomed for Edwardian ladyhood and a good marriage.

Picture them as teenagers – he was 19 and she, 14 – on one of their long hikes in the pastures around Oxford or in the glens above Cloan. Jack was an imposing figure, over 6 feet tall and thick; Naomi was diminutive, barely 5 feet tall, with corn silk hair flowing in waves over her shoulders. He loomed over her. They capped verse, an exercise which required an opponent to quote a line of poetry beginning with the same word as the last word of a line of poetry quoted in challenge. Sometimes to make the game easy they would cap by merely using the initial letter of the last word of the presented line of poetry. Mind would tumble over mind. Both siblings were hot in the fray, memorising vast quantities of verse in preparation for their competition, both to declaim long passages of it flamboyantly in conversation all their lives. When she was older, Naomi recalled that Jack tended to win in the dead languages, while she eventually triumphed in modern tongues.

The guinea-pigs in the front garden were there for genetic experiments initiated by Jack and carried forth in collaboration with his little sister. Jack and Naomi were especially enthusiastic about animals with unusual characteristics. She had high hopes for a strain of pink guinea-pig to be derived from a new acquisition; but she was cheated. Pink dye washed off. Sixth toes were coveted, and ears with unusual dents elated them. For several years Naomi and Boy, sometimes with the help of their house guest, Aldous Huxley, raised guinea-pigs, keeping records of colour, brindling, hair length and whorls. Almost immediately they found that their results did not coincide with Mendelian projections. They were observing, as Naomi would know in retrospect, what would be called linkage and cross-over. Naomi and Jack extended their experiments to fast-breeding mice and rats, which eventuated in Naomi's first published work, a scientific article about colour inheritance in rats.

Naomi continued her observations of guinea-pigs until she was 17, even during the war when she was a volunteer auxiliary nurse at London's St Thomas's hospital for several months in 1915. Her interest and ability in making such scientific observations transferred into a talent for observing human situations as well: 'If I was anything, it was a good observer, not only of guinea-pigs and wild plants, but also of people. . .'.[1]

As she was moving to young adulthood, Naomi's passion for observing the life and lives around her differed from her scientifically trained older brother. Like Jack she observed guinea-pigs to learn about genetics, but she also yearned to discover the very essence of the guinea-pigs' world, their experiences, even the 'language' they used. She would try to imagine herself into their skins. Indeed Naomi believed that she had mastered their chitter-squeaks enabling her to talk to her guinea-pigs and they to her.

Naomi did not become another Haldane scientist even though she could muster the cool objectivity that permitted her to cut open dead and pregnant creatures in order to note the characteristics of their unborn. She was a girl, categorising herself as did her family – and, for that matter, as did western culture – by strict opposing paradigms of reason versus emotion: 'I would be caught out, made to say something silly and – yes, feminine. For there was certainly an overtone of male superiority and reasonableness, as against female passion and irrationality. . .'.[2] Naomi received little in the way of direct scientific training: 'Did I ever become educated? If so, only accidently and occasionally, with a few questions filled in during odd times in the lab, or perhaps talking with distinguished guests'.[3]

Was Naomi uneducated? No. She was reading day and night. Although she does not credit it in her memoirs, she ranged as freely over culture as did her brother in the more formal settings of Eton and New College. Given Naomi's temperamental rejection of assigned readings, it may have been of some intellectual and artistic benefit to have left school. Sir Walter Scott had already been ruined for her there. On her own, she read the works of Kipling, H. G. Wells, Stevenson, Walpole, Poe, Swinburne, Coleridge, and although she claimed to be bored by Henry James, she remembers *The Turn of the Screw* as a terrifying experience. She had already read Plato and Frazer. She taught herself history, philosophy and sociology, but needed help that she did not receive in mathematics.

However, in Haldane terms Naomi's education in the *belles-lettres* seemed not to count as part of the serious business of life. It was merely the expected accoutrement of self-defined highbrows within the upper middle classes, a circle of families sometimes called Britain's intellectual aristocracy. The circle included such families as the Darwins, Huxleys, Arnolds, Wedgwoods, Trevelyans and Haldanes. Naomi would be proud to call herself a highbrow all of her life.

Naomi became fluent in French, acquired some German, memorised vast quantities of English verse, wrote and produced plays and exercised her skills of observation. Underneath these cultivations, she continued to be haunted by her terrifying dream and psychic life and to submit to a variety of mysticisms, or as she called them, altered states of consciousness. Overlaying these cultivations, she acquiesced to her mother's demand that she be a proper lady, 'sometimes rebelling a bit, but never quite enough'.[4]

Naomi stopped playing boy games altogether. She and the three other girls who shared her governess would fantasise that they were captives. These were Naomi's first girlfriends. She found them alien, her memoirs suggesting some shame about their group fantasies. They tied one another up; they were in bondage and they were sacrificial. Naomi, innocently enough, played bondage with her friend Frances Parkinson until they were 16 years old, suggesting, perhaps, a connection to the larger social, psychological and sexual realities of their lives.

When Naomi was 14, her fantasy about bondage and sacrifice brought on a formative aesthetic experience. She had been sent to France with Miss Blockey to work on her French. In Le Havre, living with a French family, Naomi read tedious four-page swatches of Dumas and Victor Hugo; she was put off these writers for life. In Rouen, her head swimming with images of Joan of Arc bound to a stake by soldiers, her senses opening to the jewelled and penetrating hues of the stained glass windows in Rouen Cathedral, she felt a kind of ecstasy: 'I drank and drank in the colours of the glass, twined myself into the traceries, quite unable to express any of it'.[5] When she did express herself in memoirs written a half-century later, she used words like 'riot' and 'explosion' to describe the sensual assault. Naomi spent a lifetime seeking aesthetic highs. She once told me that she exulted when she felt herself dying as she swooped in a small plane over the brink of the Grand Canyon in the United States; there she experienced another riot of colour and the relish of violence accompanying her momentary fear. She was 86 years old.

Naomi recalls another death-like moment. She was touring a coal pit where miners revered her father whose work with poison gas and human physiology was saving their lives. Dressed in black and wearing a miner's lamp, she went down into one of the deep pits, Bentley's near Doncaster. Dropping into the deep shaft, then walking with the teasing miners along the face, hearing a lone voice singing in the murky reaches, 'was as exciting as Rouen'.[6] The darkness, vertigo and this camaraderie with workers formed a contrasting experience.

In Rouen Naomi was moved by light and colour. In Doncaster, it was the plunge into darkness followed by comfort of near and protective human bodies which touched her deeply.

Meanwhile Naomi remembers that her own inner life, that underneath world of terror and propitiation of forces and indescribable furies, continued unabated. She kept these terrors to herself, doing her best to keep the monsters in abeyance. They would grow dim when she immersed herself in activity that was either aesthetically or communally fulfilling.

Unfortunately, Naomi remembers her day-to-day adolescent life as more oppressive than fulfilling. Instead of gaining more freedom as she grew older and more responsible, Naomi reports in her memoirs that she grew less and less free. Her skirt hems grew longer; her hair was wound up on her head, kept in place with elaborate combs; she was chaperoned and, if left to walk by herself, cautioned to avoid certain streets, ostensibly because she might encounter a man. Hansom cabs were forbidden. When she was not accompanied by Miss Blockey, Maya was by her side, sometimes with weary patience as when they roamed the best places to find wild flowers, sometimes with enthusiasm, especially if there were young men in tow, for, according to her daughter's jaundiced memory, Maya relished promoting her notions of Empire with the Oxford undergraduates.

Naomi's clothes, she recounts in her memoirs, were not chosen for attractiveness or for style and never because they matched her colouring. Instead, the bolts of Liberty material sewn into dresses by a dressmaker at home were chosen for Naomi according to the rule of class:

> What seems in some way oddest about this is that instead of thinking what was prettiest or would suit one best, the essential was to wear the right clothes for one's station in life. The curious word 'suitable' was one which was often employed: 'dainty', 'graceful', 'elegant', and so on were for upper-class clothes, 'useful' for the lower orders, though I think 'hardwearing' would be employed for men's tweeds at all levels. Clothes accentuated class divisions and of course one was uncomfortable if one dressed out of fashion, unless that is one had deliberately broken with the range of class custom.[7]

There were seductive compensations for this lady-learning. Naomi had special dresses, such as the long, white silk georgette she wore for her first Old Dragon dinner and for Boy's last Commemoration ball. She was allowed to come out temporarily for an allowance of two balls for which she was given dancing lessons and instructions in proper behaviour.

Naomi paid for these privileges. The cost was in selfhood. She did not brush her own hair, she had no money of her own, she did as she was told. For instance, one of Boy's friends was known to be Jewish. Maya instructed Naomi not to choose him when she was picking sides for the games they played at parties. Once he was the remaining person and it was Naomi's turn to choose. Their eyes locked; in misery she could not speak: 'was I to disobey Maya's explicit instructions?' She obeyed. Even though Naomi does not say so in her memoirs, it seems clear that, implicitly, she was being groomed for marriage. Certainly, she was not being educated to earn a living for herself. She was allowed her hobbies; however, special tutors were not brought in to add discipline and rigour to her intellectual ventures. Mainly, she was left to define her own pursuits.

In 1913, when Naomi was 16, the Huxleys arrived in Oxford. Trev Huxley, who lived down the way from the Haldanes on Banbury Road, welcomed his younger brother, Aldous, who was preparing for Balliol, having cut short his education at Eton when stricken with a cornea disease that left him blind for eighteen frightful months. Now, somewhat better, reading with a powerful magnifying glass, he was augmenting what he had already learnt tediously by braille. When the school term began, Aldous joined his cousin Gervas and their friend, Lewis Gielgud, in college.

Together these young men frequented the Haldane home. Maya was warm, friendly and adored, remembered especially for her tolerant understanding of young people. Many confided in her. According to Gervas Huxley, it was in the Haldane home that he and his companions mingled with lovely young women, Naomi and her friends. It was a rare and appreciated opportunity.[8] Aldous, Gervas and Lewis brought with them a taste for dramatic performance which they had acquired during their days together in preparatory school at Hillside. Naomi began to write plays for them. Temporarily, she was one of the boys, their equal through her scriptwriting and the creation of imagined worlds.

Her first play, *Saunes Bairos: A Study in Recurrence*, was performed in 1913 when she was 16 years old. A photograph of cast members appended to a privately published edition shows Trev, Gervas, Aldous, Lewis, Naomi, Jack, Jack's close friend Dick Mitchison and several others. Too soon, some would die in war. In *All Change Here* Naomi lingers over this photograph:

There is Hartley the chief priest, whose dark and regular features fluttered my heart, killed two years later, and Gerald Boswell the snow-guard who sang my song '. . .and all the land lies far below, Below the snow-line and the snow, The snow-line changing never,' walking up and down with his spear, making up the tune which I remember as lovely: killed too. Moss Blundell who drew brilliant cartoons of us all: killed in the same year.[9]

As a piece of juvenilia, *Saunes Bairos* is remarkably good. In it Naomi strikes many of the keys she would sound again and again in her fiction: a sister wins mental competitions over her twin brother and by so-doing manages to overcome cultural repression. There is an encircling barrier of snow-covered mountains, a barrier protected by social and religious laws and this barrier must be crossed in order for the girl, and people in general, to be free. Typically, Naomi uses the grist of her everyday life in this play. Her guinea-pigs are its inspiration. The inhabitants of Saunes Bairos not only raise guinea-pigs, but they breed them for genetic reasons as well. It is a mythical account of a point in Indian history of British Guinea when a small community has lost faith in the old laws based on magic; they have turned for leadership to a manipulating priesthood. Actually, Naomi is transcribing Frazer's *The Golden Bough*. But she complicates her myth with a good deal of theorising about genetically engineered master races. She is examining her mother's imperialism, and although she seems to give lip service to its eugenicist policies, she undermines the spoken content of the play with a dramatic reversal: the characters who escape from Saunes Bairos are not representatives of the genetically chosen race of the play; instead, one is a peasant girl and another a blind boy – perhaps inspired by Aldous, but played by Dick Mitchison. They escape over forbidden snow and across barriers of law and restriction, away from the master race.

In Gervas's memoirs and Aldous's biography, the next group performance in late spring of 1914 is vividly and nostalgically remembered. In their memories it was a golden moment, the last of an age before it shattered on rocks of war. Apparently, Maya had organised a particularly jolly picnic on the Cherwell after the play. The weather was sweet and unseasonably warm. Everyone was hilariously happy.[10]

The group performed two plays, *The Frogs* by Aristophanes and Naomi's *Prisoners of War*, a psychologically curious, rather depressed piece in which the daughter of a king sacrifices a prisoner of war in an ill-fated attempt to save her mother's life; the mother dies, the prisoner dies, the battle is lost and on that note the play ends. The sacrificed soldier is played by Dick Mitchison; Naomi is the daughter of the king; the king is played by her brother.

Two young men were in love with Naomi Haldane in 1914. Within a year she would know of one of them. He was Mitch, Jack's friend Dick Mitchison. The other was Gervas Huxley, who announced his love fifty years later in his autobiography, *Both Hands* (1978).[11] Gervas' story corroborates Naomi's memory of what she calls highbrow courting. It was marked by a kind of intellectual bantering. According to her, there was nothing physically sexual about it. Gervas reports that he was thrilled simply to be near the object of his desire.

In the summer of 1914 Mitch invited Naomi boating. Out on the water of the Cherwell the two lapsed into companionable silence. In photos as a young man Dick appears tall with gentle eyes and soft lips. He was five years older than Naomi, preparing for the bar, having already left Oxford with a First in Greats. Naomi recalls that they had stopped rowing and were bobbing on the flow of water. On an impulse she spoke. She told Mitch about her netherlife of terror and nightmare. He did not laugh at her or attempt what she considered to be the grown-up habit of reasoning with her. He listened carefully and commiserated. Naomi thinks that she was probably the only one in her household who had failed to notice that he was in love with her. Nor did she know that by sharing her private fears, those dark visitations with which she had lived since childhood, she was transferring some of their mesmerising power to a living person, someone she came to think would buffer her against their attacks.

Dick did not propose marriage on this outing, although Naomi would have considered herself old enough to have received his suit. In 1988 when Naomi and I bent over a photograph taken of the cast of *Prisoners of War* and *The Frogs*, I suggested that she looked like a very young girl. Naomi replied that she is absolutely certain that my remark would have offended the young woman in front of us, who she remembers would have considered herself altogether grown-up. We agreed, at least, that the 17-year-old Naomi in the photograph appeared to be brooding.

If all had gone as expected in the summer of 1914, and there was good reason for Naomi to foresee her entire life at that time as all was so stable and unchanging, then she might have looked forward to a long courtship, time in which to grow up, then a large wedding surrounded by friends and family. That was in July; by the end of August the war had started and all changed, which accounts for the name of Naomi's memoir of this period, *All Change Here*. She and her generation stepped out of an Edwardian train into one thundering towards modernism.

Naomi recalled that the beginning of the war felt exciting. All of the young men she knew were rushing off to become soldiers. It was upsetting to be a girl and be left out of the fun. 'Fun', she thinks, was Maya's expression for it. Few foresaw the devastation ahead; in 1914 Naomi and her friends assumed that the war would be short and they they would win. As if to prove to future generations how ignorant the world was of the modern mechanised war that was to be waged, Mitch, now Dick to Naomi, was sent as a Second Lieutenant to the Queen's Bays, where he was trained to lead cavalry charges. Her brother Jack went with the family territorial regiment, the Black Watch.

It did not take long for the initial euphoria to evaporate: 'Then the casualties began. Inexplicably we were not winning and our friends began to be killed: really killed so that we would never see them again'.[12] In her memoir Naomi devotes a poignant chapter to letters from school friends, teachers and members of her family who were in the war. Letter writer after letter writer stops writing. She came to believe that Dick and Jack survived the war because they were badly wounded and spent large portions of it recovering.

Significant changes in Naomi's life were only partially wrought by the beginning of the war: Aldous Huxley came to live with the Haldanes, there to be a major influence on Naomi, as she would acknowledge in early autobiographical accounts.[13] Almost blind, Aldous could not go to war. He had recently suffered an even more awful loss. His 25-year-old brother, Trev, had hanged himself in August – perhaps because he had not performed well in his exams, perhaps because he had fallen in love with a young woman from an 'inappropriate' class. The pressure on the Huxleys, in fact on all boy-children of this class within a class, was enormous. Naomi asserts that it was simply expected that everyone in their crowd would earn Firsts. Not that she did. She never sat for college exams.

Aldous was lanky and thin, over 6 feet 4 inches, sweet, witty, both vulnerable and self-contained. Naomi remembers wanting constantly to kiss him; she was 17 and he, 21. There were no kisses.[14] Aldous read with his magnifying glass, played syncopated jazz rhythms on the piano, drew pictures and took upon himself the guidance of Naomi's reading, most memorably *Tom Jones*, which had been forbidden by her mother. He introduced her to French symbolist poetry. They talked incessantly. He brought a new aesthetic dimension to her life and, if one is to judge from their fiction writing in the next decade, he shared with her a tendency to disassociate ruthlessly from pain and emotion.

In January 1915, Naomi's father was urgently called by Uncle Richard, now Lord Chancellor. He departed immediately for the front in France, charged with identifying a ghastly poison gas that was killing soldiers. Uffer requested that his son Jack be called out of the battlefield to help him; together they breathed the gas, noting its deadly physiological effects. Harmful as that gas was to their lungs, Naomi thinks it may have saved Jack's life. While with Uffer, the Third Battalion of the Black Watch was destroyed in a suicidal charge at Richebourg L'Avoue. Desperately trying to rejoin his regiment at the end of that battle, Jack was wounded but not killed.

Returning to Oxford, Uffer went furiously to work inventing a mask that would protect from mustard gas. Naomi recalls that everyone helped. She and Aldous shredded their woollies for absorbant material. Tension ran high; with each minute that passed a man died horribly. It took Uffer two days to invent a mask that worked.

Sadly, Uffer was not officially commended by the British government, nor was he asked to participate on any government committees consulting about gas warfare. Politics washed over him in the wake of Uncle Richard's trouble. The governing Liberal Party, for whom Richard Haldane had successfully served as Secretary of War and Lord Chancellor over the preceding years, formed a coalition government in May 1915; Uncle Richard was not included in the new cabinet. His German university education had tainted him. Some members of the public foolishly suspected that the Haldanes could be traitors; Uncle Richard's political enemies did not miss their chance. He was out for the time being, only to re-emerge in the 1920s as a senior statesman for the Labour government.

At first, it seemed that life would go on as usual for Naomi, merely with new activities of Red Cross classes and lessons in folding bandages. But this illusion of sameness was short-lived. All was different. At the beginning of the summer of 1915 she prevailed upon her parents to let her go to London where she worked in St Thomas's Hospital as a volunteer auxiliary nurse, a VAD.

Volunteer nursing at St Thomas's was Naomi's first experience of hard work and it was her last experience labouring in what, in normal conditions, would have been a wage-earning job. She learnt how to make beds, to empty bedpans, to bathe the bodies of men, to walk as though running; she learnt to work until she was exhausted and then beyond. Deeply impressed, she witnessed pain, both the pain of disease and the gangrenous pain of war wounds. Once she remembers fainting. But only once, for the head nurse was furious with her.

For a young woman whose environment had progressively restricted her exposure to life, and especially to life as it was led by working people, this new contact must have been both exciting and shocking. In her memoirs she writes that she had never even been in a hospital with large rooms filled with beds; people of her class were cared for in private hospitals. She had never been in a situation where she was not respected as the daughter of J. S. Haldane. Here she learnt to stand whenever a doctor entered a room and learnt to bite her tongue when sternly reprimanded for visiting her guinea-pigs on the terrace, territory forbidden to VADs. If Naomi felt any pleasure in her new freedom – after all, she was now alone in London and unchaperoned, although living with the family of a friend from Oxford – then this freedom must have been associated with new obligations to adults in a hierarchy which gave her little status. Leaving home to take a job would not be Naomi's path to adulthood.

Before the summer's end, Naomi caught scarlet fever apparently from infected milk served at the hospital. She was sent home to Oxford and put in quarantine, which meant that Aldous could not live with the Haldanes when he returned at term. Instead, he began to socialise in Bloomsbury circles, soon to make friends with D. H. Lawrence. Again healthy, Naomi did not return to St Thomas's in London. She divided her time between volunteer work at the local hospital in Oxford and academic studies, to which she applied herself half-heartedly. She had passed some exams which were equivalent to university entrance exams and had enrolled as a home student at what was to become St Anne's college. Her education was desultory: there was little academic supervision and no tutorial system; degrees were not the goal. Naomi's judgement: 'Women's higher education was still rather new and unorganised'.[15] She sat in on physiology lectures and resumed her study of botany; she enjoyed dissecting animals and drawing plants, but not much more. Even though her girlfriend, Frances Parkinson, was pursuing a course of study and would take an Oxford degree, this was not Naomi's path towards independence. She was, in fact, still sleeping in her mother's bedroom.

In autumn 1915 Naomi was invited to Frolbury Manor in Surrey, one of Dick Mitchison's family homes. His mother and hers had already talked with each other; a marriage had been arranged, although Naomi reports she knew nothing of it. Dick Mitchison was a good match; he was well-educated, promising and wealthy, money having being accumulated by Dick's grandfather who had founded the

Bank of New Zealand. At Frolbury, Dick asked Naomi to marry him and, although she accepted, she remembers being panic-stricken; she abruptly terminated her visit to the Mitchisons. At home in Oxford Aldous asked her to describe love to him; she could not and came to believe by the time she wrote her memoirs that she failed because she had not actually been in love with Dick, although she had been too inexperienced to know it. Then why did she marry?

Naomi accounts for her desire to marry in clichéd terms; she says she would have accepted the first proposal from any officer in uniform. Perhaps it is true that war and uniform might momentarily drop barriers that separate men and women, although never completely. Some might think it patriotic to marry soldiers who are about to put their lives on the line for their country. Maya did. However, the operative word in Naomi's apology is 'officer'. In the First World War officers in the British military were gentlemen recruited from public schools. We might speculate that Naomi also thought marriage would bring her independence, a seemingly easy, even arranged, avenue of escape from her mother.

There may have been warning signs which Naomi overrode. Naomi remembers that she did not enjoy kissing Dick. She lost her engagement ring, a Mitchison family heirloom; ill-fitting, it slipped from her finger into the Cherwell where no amount of frantic diving and mud-sifting could turn it up. Dick reminded her of her brother. She recalls that her worries over her decision to marry brewed in her imagination with alarming images of trench warfare: 'the duck boards over the sucking, stinking mud, the bodies of friends frozen onto the wire, tatters of uniform and human flesh'.[16]

During the few months of her engagement, Naomi recalls that she was not as strictly chaperoned as before, but still restricted. She and Dick were allowed to walk the streets of London where they alternated between treating themselves to sweets and remarking on the unfair disparity in wealth they were observing; however, she was chastised for 'compromising' herself by dining in public with Dick at Simpson's. They were scolded by both their families for this breach in class etiquette. When she took Dick to Cloan to introduce him to Granniema, she had to ride in a separate train. Perhaps Naomi thought marriage would put an end to this surveillance.

Again writing the script, Naomi pushed for an early wedding date, initiating a troubled relationship with her future in-laws who wished to slow progress toward marriage in order to give time, according to Naomi, for planning a proper wedding. Naomi would have nothing of it. By mid-February, a couple of months after she became 18, she was

Mrs Mitchison. Granniema supported her from Cloan: if she wanted a civil service, if this is what Naomi's conscience dictated, then this principle must stand. That was the Haldane way.

Naomi's perceptions of the Mitchisons come in different shades over the years – from her earliest experiences with her intended in-laws to her later sensibilities coloured by decades' experience with sons and daughters-in-law. Recounting her early encounters with Dick's parents, she judges herself harshly: she thinks that she was inconsiderate, lacking compassion for their differences. She writes: 'I might so easily have been nicer to his parents. But I wasn't'.[17]

Part of the trouble, according to Naomi, was that the Mitchisons lived more lavishly than the highbrow Haldanes. They maintained two homes in London as well as Frolbury. Frolbury itself was large and spacious, with terraces facing south, a small wood, and several green-houses, one of which produced huge cinnamon-smelling carnations for Naomi's hair. There was an army of servants to care for valuable furniture, paintings and china. Naomi recalls that she was awed by both the circumstance and the social expectations of Dick's mother and her sisters. But she was not submissive. In retrospect, she came to see how she must have disturbed them. By their standards Naomi might have been thought to lack social sensibilities. They must have despaired at her lack of style. For instance, Dick's mother gave her an elegant suit of black velvet with a creamy crêpe de Chine blouse and a stylish hat. Typically, Naomi succumbed to the dress-up aspect of costuming herself, but refused to wear the high heels that would have finished the effect: 'I didn't mind dressing up, but nobody was going to get me out of my clodhopping "sensible" shoes into high heels, nor would I take any extra trouble over doing my hair in a more attractive way. I must have been singularly irritating'.[18] Not only was she irritating; she was rejecting.

Their wedding was an austere affair, a civil ceremony, Naomi wearing a black wool skirt and green silk blouse; Dick, his uniform. Naomi recalls that it suited her to sacrifice luxuries. Perhaps she enjoyed goading Dick's mother who would have taken great pleasure, Naomi thinks, in providing a splendid gown. She was holding true to form, learning to shape the ingredients of her life according to her own design. This marriage may have been arranged; nevertheless, she could design costume and setting, set the pace, write the script.

At the end of that week of wedding leave Dick returned to the war front in Flanders; Naomi returned to her parents' keep.

3

War into Marriage
1916-1925

The First World War put an odd shape to the early years of Naomi's marriage. Everything around her was changing drastically except her own life, or so it seemed to her.

Three years after her marriage she was still living with her parents in Oxford, where, after her fashion, she had continued her education in science at St Anne's. Mostly she was compliant, meaning to do what she considered the right thing. In her memoirs Naomi reflects on this time in her life: 'Well, there I was, a married woman, but still tied up with a host of attitudes, some of which I accepted, while others I questioned; but not enough to take really abrasive action'.[1] Naomi was treated like a girl at home. For instance, Lewis Gielgud, back from war recovering from a bad wound, asked Naomi to come to May Day carols at Magdalen and to share breakfast afterwards. Just as before her marriage, she was to be chaperoned; her mother sat in the bow of the canoe as Naomi, who remembers being deeply resentful, paddled. Naomi was not yet in control of her social life. Even her hair was still being brushed for her. It was the same with money. She had none of her own, although provisions had been made in her marriage contract for Naomi to receive £250 annually from her parents (£400 would have been sufficient for most families of four at that time). However, for reasons that were neither explained to Naomi nor queried by her, this stipend did not materialise for three years, roughly coinciding with Dick's return at the end of the war.

Lewis was not the only friend in Oxford recovering from wounds. Jack had been wounded as well. Naomi remembers being relieved to have her brother near although he brought the war vividly home. His muddy kilts were real and so were the lice in their

30

seams. Naomi began to develop a political sense as the war came to her: 'And our friends went on getting killed and I saw my father and mother both weeping for them. What was it all for? The younger people at least had begun to discount the patriotic rubbish which we had fed on in the beginning. I heard about the League of Nations Society. Surely that was an idea that made some sense?'[2] Aldous's older brother Julian had put Naomi on to the League of Nations Society enabling her to think, perhaps for the first time, in political terms not established by her mother.

Meanwhile, Naomi's brother-in-law, Dick's brother Willie, was killed in battle.

Dick Mitchison was transferred to Signals from what was left of the Queen's Bays. There would be no more cavalry charges in this war. As it turned out, the transfer almost killed him. While motorcycling behind the lines, he was mowed down by a French military vehicle and, assumed dead, he was left in a ditch at the side of the road.

Dick's skull was fractured, but he was still alive. Naomi recalls learning of it while in London with Jack. She received the news from Dick's distraught parents when she came in with her brother from a matinée performance of the Bing Boys.

Coincidently, Naomi had come to London from Oxford on her way to meet Dick for a few days of holiday in Paris. During this war, it was still possible for civilians to move easily behind the lines. In the face of this grisly turn of events, she joined Dick but not according to their holiday plan. Instead, accompanied by Dick's father, she was transported to Northern France to Dick's hospital in Le Treport. It was grim.

There Naomi remembers being told that Dick was not likely to live, and if he did, he would be intellectually impaired. Dick did survive; moreover, his mind was acute enough to pass the bar exam a couple of months later.

But none of this was certain in the first weeks of his hospitalisation. Naomi recalls spending a couple of hours each day with him; she was allowed to nurse him because of her VAD experience in London. In her memoirs she describes Dick's pain and delirium and her exhaustion. He often fought against restraint, nor did he always recognise Naomi, once even accusing her of 'molesting' him with a kiss, not recognising that she was his wife. Another time he expressed outrage because he thought that his nurse had stolen his wife's wedding rings. It was Naomi who wore the rings. Dick did lose memory of some events occurring before the accident, so that

Naomi had the painful task of retelling him that his good friend Geoff Wardley had been killed.

Dick's wartime brush with death was deeply disturbing to Naomi; it was also fateful in her development as a writer. This was her first encounter with the suffering and near death of someone with whom she was intimate. She was uncertain and fearful of the outcome and one of her initial responses was to bind her anxiety with writing. Naomi's diary takes the attitude of a meticulous but somewhat detached observer. She describes her father-in-law, people she meets, conversations, the hospital, Dick's deliriums. She, herself, is just another person to be described. Her diary reads like the narration at the beginning of a novel. Naomi is the main actor, not in the sense of aggrandising herself but rather as a character to whom things happen that require actions in response. At the same time, she steers clear of describing her emotions. For instance, she does not describe her nervousness and terror upon arriving at the hospital to see Dick for the first time; instead, she presents the scene in starkly objective terms:

> I wait outside, while Sister goes in, leaving the door ajar. Suddenly a voice, so strong and familiar I can hardly believe it. 'What, my wife? Bring her in at once, Sister.' I go in. It is a small white cheerful room, a bed with a silk quilt. Dick, looking very well and normal, but for a very unshaven chin: 'Hullo Nou!' Sister leaves us for a few minutes. I try not to talk or let him, but he, talking rather too loud, asks questions, is very cheerful, moves his head about, is sorry he is such a wretched sight but he can't get his shaving things. There is a slight smell of paraldehyde. . .[3]

For much of her life, when confronted with deep distress, especially in the face of death, Naomi would keep a diary. These records detail the surface of things, conveying compressed pain through enactment rather than through description of emotion.

In 1917 Dick arrived in London to recuperate from his head wound. While on sick leave he passed his Bar Finals exam, proving to everyone's relief that his brain had not been permanently damaged. For the first time since they had married a year earlier, he and Naomi spent an extended period getting to know one another. They rented a house in Scotland that autumn and he tried to teach her to shoot. She recalls not liking it, preferring her dress up game of 'Nebuchannezar', as Naomi was wont to spell it. It is a variety of charades in which players, intending to impersonate an author or an aspect of a book, dress from chests full of costumes. Naomi and Dick began to discover their differences during this Scottish retreat.

Dick was a bon vivant, fluent in French and Italian, relishing excellent food and wine, having spent stretches of time as a youth in Southern France with his family. She, on the other hand, had an ascetic streak through her Haldane and Calvinistic heritage; rich sauces and expensive wines were slightly distasteful, even sinful for her. Ordering in a fine restaurant bored her, as she remembers in *You May Well Ask*. Naomi preferred scribbling in a notebook while Dick pleased his appetites.

Naomi writes in her memoirs that all was not well with their early marriage. Their sex life was a distressing problem. All that summer Naomi felt depressed and ran a low-grade fever: 'I got little or no pleasure, except for the touch of a loved body and the knowledge that for a time he was out of the front line. The final act left me on edge and uncomfortable. Why was it so unlike Swinburne?'[4] Their problems were hardly surprising. Naomi's knowledge about matters sexual was largely derived from observing guinea-pigs; she had not let Maya help her out, reporting in retrospect that whatever help her mother might have had to give would have been misinformed. And her husband Dick's sexual knowledge, especially of human physiology, was slight as well. For instance, when they married, he did not know that females menstruated. He thought, for some biological reason, that they had headaches once a month. When Dick had asked his regiment doctor for information before marriage, he was brushed off, told he would know soon enough.

Returning to Cherwell to live with her mother and father when Dick again took his place on the war front, this time in Italy, Naomi – sexually inexperienced as she may well have been – was pregnant. She gave birth to Geoff in Oxford in 1918.

Naomi remembers that all her childbirthings frightened her. She had been told that she would have a tough time giving birth because the broken leg from her pony-riding days had left her pelvic bone distorted. She reports that actual labour was always more painful than she had expected and she was always given chloroform for the last clutch. Many of Naomi's later fictional characters talk about the pain of childbirth:

> . . .she was sufficiently sure that when the time came and she was whimpering under the grip and relax and tighter grip of the pain

whose quality she remembered so well, people would say it came of having got into the shadow of Erif's bad luck. Well, the other women must be given something to say, some excuse for her hating pain so much![5]

In the mid-1930s, Naomi would have one of her fictional female heroes conclude that women would gain less than men from a socialist revolution. In *We Have Been Warned* Dione says to her husband: 'I'm not so far from *praxis* as you are, Tom, after having had four children; modern medicine hasn't got far enough to prevent childbirth being devilishly alike for all women'.[6] Naomi had her share of *praxis* by 1933; she had given birth to six children before she wrote the novel in which that passage occurs.

Naomi does not dwell on pregnancy and lactation in her memoirs so that it might be easy to overlook the fact that she was pregnant three-quarters of the time between 1918 and 1925, giving birth to four of her children, and this while producing two novels and a volume of short stories: *The Conquered* (1923), *When the Bough Breaks, and Other Stories* (1924), and *Cloud Cuckoo Land* (1925). The most we learn of her pregnancies is that she liked to costume herself in dresses that emphasised her swollen belly or that she would read while she nursed her babies. Naomi's mothering experiences are poignantly described in her fiction where passages glow with sensual joy. She wrote in stark contrast to other women writers in the 1920s and 1930s – such as Storm Jameson, Winifred Holtby and even Virginia Woolf for all her desire to write otherwise – who tacitly obeyed literary injunctions against presenting women's biological realities. For instance, she describes Erif Der, the female hero of *The Corn King and the Spring Queen*, nursing her child:

By and bye he began to give little panting, eager cries of desire for food and the warmth and the tenderness that went with it. Erif's breasts answered to the noise with a pleasant hardening, a faint ache waiting to be assuaged. Their tips turned upward and outward, and the centre of the nipple itself grew velvet soft and tender and prepared for the softness of the baby. She unpinned her dress and picked him up and snuggled down over him on to a heap of cushions. He moved his blind, silly mouth from side to side eagerly. For a moment she teased him, withholding herself; then, as she felt the milk in her springing towards him, she let him settle, thrusting her breast deep into the hollow of his mouth, that seized on her with a rhythmic throb of acceptance, deep sucking of lips and tongue and cheeks. Cheated, her other breast let its milk drip in large bluish-white drops on to his legs, then softened and sagged and waited. For a time he was all mouth, then his free arm began to waver and clutch, sometimes her face, sometimes a finger, sometimes grabbing the breast with violent, untender little soft claws. She laughed and caught his eye, and the sucking lips began to curve upward in spite of themselves. He let go suddenly to laugh, and her breast, released, spurted milk over his face.[7]

This exquisitely rendered sensuousness in a mother's life was written during the time Naomi was nursing her son Avrion in 1928.

As the war neared its end in 1918, Dick and Naomi made plans to meet in Italy for a short holiday. Neither her parents nor her parents-in-law had paid the slightest heed to what she remembers as her sulky wish to make her way to Perugia alone; they had insisted on hiring an older woman to accompany her on the ferry to Dieppe and on the train thereafter. Cleverly calculating class inhibitions, Naomi jumped from first to third class on the ferry, ditching her unwanted chaperone who did not think to search for her there, where all the fun was anyway, or so Naomi thought.

She recalled that she could hardly wait to see Dick, for she had sent him a copy of Marie Stopes' *Married Love*, an early sex manual that had taken her breath away. She thought that if she and Dick used just a few simple techniques their love-making might be altogether more satisfying. She reports in her memoirs that it actually did get better.

Naomi enjoyed every moment of her holiday: 'I felt suddenly and gorgeously free and grown-up. This time I really escaped and by my own wits'.[8] Naomi was 20 years old. She and Dick roamed the narrow, cobbled streets of Perugia. Then, on her way back to England by herself, she met up with Lewis Gielgud and Gervas Huxley in Paris. Revelling in her freedom, she took a hotel room and stayed for several days even though she was expected home. She, Lewis and Gervas romped; they walked 'round the Place de la Concorde heaped with captured guns and cannon, a real old triumph, and the statues of Metz and Strasbourg garlanded with roses and chrysanthemums and the French crowds tossing with glory and excitement'.[9] The final push of the war had been made in October 1918; the day of Armistice was near. Naomi received a telegram ordering her home. She obeyed.

Still, by travelling alone, Naomi had made a point to herself. She had gone against the codes of class and gender and seemed none the worse for it. Indeed, she felt exhilaration. Naomi's somewhat perverse courage would increasingly come to characterise her life, both the way in which she lived it and the way she wrote about it. Eventually, she would relish undermining conventional systems of twentieth-century thought, experiencing delight when she used her wit and strong, analytical mind to jump traces.

Because her memoir *All Change Here* lacks chronology, Naomi does not make clear that she was already a mother, having given birth to Geoff before taking the trip to Perugia. In fact, she had left her 6-month-old in Maya's capable charge. Upon returning, Naomi wrote to her friend Julian Huxley affectionately about her baby:

> Geoff – little pig – had completely forgotten me, but is getting reconciled to me now; he's huge & strong & rushes about the room on all fours; he's also taken to chattering all the time; it sounds like Russian & one always knows when he's in mischief, because he looks round and squeaks & grins at one – it wouldn't be fun otherwise![10]

The war over, Naomi and Dick bought a house on Cheyne Walk in Chelsea where they lived between 1919 and 1923. There was room for Geoff, for the already expected next baby and for servants: a cook, a nurse and a parlour maid.

In 1919 Naomi gave birth to her second child, Dennis. She returned to Cherwell and her mother's care for Dennis's birth, as she did in 1922 for the birth of Murdoch, her third child in five years.

Although mistress of her own house, Naomi did not feel grown-up, as she herself asserts in her memoirs. Whenever she could, she returned to her parent's Oxford home. Maya, with her daughter's blessings, took charge of the babies leaving Naomi free to socialise with her Oxford companions, Gervas and Lewis. Another Oxford attraction was Jack, whom she always wanted to be near. He was working as a scientist and Fellow of New College until 1923 when he left to teach in Cambridge, soon to marry Charlotte Burghes in 1926, a choice that pulled him away from Naomi in unexpected ways.

Dick suffered from bouts of 'melancholy' and headaches during their first decade of marriage. These were attributed to his head injury, but Naomi told me from the distance of a half-century that she thinks he was psychologically depressed. Apparently, he was especially anxious about having enough work in his law practice. For the first several years there was not much income from this source. But it must have been more a matter of professional recognition than of money. It actually made little material difference to the young

Mitchison family, for Dick had already inherited enough stock and directorships to support his family well.

In her memoirs Naomi confesses that routine adult responsibilities overwhelmed her during these first years of homemaking. She was even frightened by her servants. She did not know how to cook, nor did she know how to make her cook prepare food properly. If the cook was discovered drunk, it was Dick who had to deal with her. Naomi hated doing accounts and did not really have to do them in order to budget. There was plenty of money to live comfortably, buying furniture, china, silver and such, whenever they were wanted.

Dick's parents offered generous gifts, which were always accepted. In the early 1920s they gave Naomi and Dick two holidays: first, they sent the young couple to the Riviera to cure Dick's winter cough; at another time, they hired a car and chauffeur to drive Naomi and Dick from Vienna through Czechoslovakia to Hungary. Dick and Naomi took frequent holidays. Together with Jack, they explored Tunisia, crossing from Marseilles. At another time, without Dick, Naomi and Jack walked the countryside of Southern France.

In her memoir of this period, *You May Well Ask*, Naomi defends her early married way of life. She points out that women of the 1920s and 1930s were given a breather from homemaking expectations and that many flooded into the professions and the arts. If she had not had servants and leisure, she would not have had the energy or the time to write. She has a point. Nevertheless, to have servants would be philosophically troublesome to the socialists that Naomi and her husband would become. As long as she and Dick chose to maintain class and have children, servants were essential for allowing Naomi time to be a writer, or so Naomi rationalises as she pleads her case.

But, not yet socialist, the issue for Naomi – just 23 years old in 1920 – was how to balance her expanding social life with her ever-pressing urge to write. Sometimes the twain would meet. A play she wrote, *Barley, Honey and Wine*, served as an excuse to bring the old gang together along with new faces. Dick, Jack and Naomi had roles, as did Julian Huxley and H. T. Wade Gery, a classical scholar in Oxford. Several letters to Julian testify to Naomi's avid involvement in her project. She wanted Julian to reassure his wife Juliette: 'Tell her you've got no love-making at all! I've got to do most of it, and Wade Gery (whom I love) simply won't kiss me in the least convincingly!' In another letter detailing Julian's costume requirements, Naomi jokingly complained: 'That little swine, Basil

Murray, has chucked us for Zeno; some idiot is taking him round the Mediterranean, on a yacht, free; he produced a quite hopeless substitute, so we are getting Jack Gielgud, who can, at least, act well, to take it'.[11] Jack was Lewis's younger brother, better known to the world as John Gielgud. The play itself was set in Marob, the imaginary Scythian country so important in Naomi's future opus, *The Corn King and the Spring Queen*.

It appears that playwriting was no longer enough to sate Naomi's appetite for writing, but finding time to write was another matter for a mother of three boys under the age of 4. In 1922 in the little London garden between Cheyne Walk and the Embankment, Naomi pushed a baby pram containing Murdoch and wrote her first novel, *The Conquered* (1923). With a board fixed precariously to its handle, the pram was her desk.

Never slight or delicate, solidly in place on well-rooted ankles, photographs of Naomi during this period show that she was sensuous, almost beautiful, with abundant sun-streaked hair bound conventionally in braided swirls over each ear on either side of broad cheekbones, with brooding blue eyes, and an innocent, though perhaps seductive mouth. In her costume on those warm summer days pushing a pram, she would have enjoyed the freedom of the fashionable Isadora Duncan look, soft material clinging in the breeze to thighs and partially exposed calves – all draped over an unconstrained torso. The fashion heralded new freedom for women in the 1920s, that decade immediately after British women had attained the vote. Naomi relished the freedom.

In 1923 she, Dick and their three children moved from Cheyne Walk to their River Court house on the Mall in Hammersmith; they would make it their major home until the Second World War. They brought with them a cook, a housemaid, a parlour maid, a nurse and a butler, one of Dick's army friends – which, Naomi notes, prefigured the erosion of class barriers in the Mitchison upstairs–downstairs configuration.

Their Hammersmith neighbourhood, bordered on three sides by a loop in the Thames, had a distinctive social character lingering from the nineteenth century when William Morris made it headquarters for his Kelmscott Press, for his craft workshops and for his socialist organisations. It was here that the working people of Hammersmith had mingled with artists, intellectuals and politicians; the mingling continued into the 1920s and 1930s when working-class friends from the Mitchisons' Labour constituency became part of their social circle of politicians and artists. But by no means was the Mitchison home the only class melting-pot in Hammersmith; a few short blocks away on Hammersmith Terrace, the writer Joe Ackerley welcomed his friend E. M. Forster among other artists to parties with Hammersmith policemen, one of whom, Bob Buckingham, became Forster's long time intimate companion. Naomi was welcome at Ackerley's, there to cement her friendships with other intellectuals, some of whom, like Gerald Heard and Forster, were also homosexual. Hammersmith had much in common with the more visible Bloomsbury. Members of both communities had an intellectually and socially coherent sense of themselves although it seems that the Hammersmith crowd was more politically active and less cruelly excluding.

Hammersmith was a good place to raise children, mixing country with city, and it had lots of artists to make life interesting: A. P. Herbert, the writer, and his wife Gwen lived down the street. Their children and those of the Mitchisons were frequently in each other's homes. Julian Trevelyan, the artist, was nearby and a friend; another artist, Gertrude Hermes, soon to divorce, was a neighbour, ready to start her lifelong friendship with Naomi. This was Naomi's milieu. However, lest one gives the wrong impression, this was not a bohemian move to the margins for Dick and Naomi. They bought a huge house, a historical landmark, the 1680s' home of the Queen Dowager Catherine of Braganza, which was rebuilt in 1808. Large as it was, the Mitchisons added even more rooms, whole apartments for servants.

Overlooking a tremendous sweep of the Thames, their house, River Court, had the balanced charm of eighteenth-century architecture – elegant entry pillars, a sweeping staircase, sunny bedrooms for the children, a large garden with small shallow ponds and rows of espaliered apple trees; there was room in the mid-1930s for a squash court and loggia, under which was built a room where Naomi might write. The roof of the house, a balcony with a balustraded parapet, was a perfect setting for the Mitchisons' annual Boat Race Party.

Naomi's writing desk was located on the river side of the house, dappled by sun, surrounded by tall view-taking windows, backed by a long sitting-room. Naomi has always been able to write surrounded by people. Mid-way through this long room were drapes which, when pulled, made effective curtains for children's theatre, especially remembered for the practice of Naomi's play, *Kate Crackernuts*.[12] In the back recesses were soft, cosy couches.

Naomi gave birth to her fourth child and first daughter, Lois, in 1925. Naomi remained in London for this birth rather than return to her mother in Oxford as she had for each of her other children.

As had been Naomi's lot in childhood, Geoff, Denny, Murdoch and Lois, and later, Av and Val, were tucked in bed before 8 o'clock by their nanny. Sometimes Naomi read to them, as Maya had read Kipling to her. They did not see much of Dick. He would arrive home after 7 o'clock; he and Naomi in evening dress dined in adult solitude when they were not entertaining.

The dining-room had space to sit fourteen easily, and it often did. For several years they were in the habit of giving two or three dinner parties a month. Naomi describes them as rather formal affairs where women were accompanied to the table on the left arms of men, where one was expected to talk with the person on the right until after the main course when one was expected to turn to the person on one's left, and where the women abandoned the men to cigars and brandy after dinner.

At first their social life was the usual round of family and friends. They visited Dick's parents often, Dick to play bridge, Naomi to read. Later, this filial connection waned in favour of people nearer their own age. Aldous and his wife Maria were continuing friends, although they were less and less likely to be in London as they were drawn increasingly to Southern Europe, to France and Italy. New friends emerged, including Dominick and Margery Spring Rice, whose Liberal Party politics appealed to the young Mitchisons, as did their coterie of Liberal friends. Margery was the secretary of the League of Nations Society. The Spring Rices had several children the same ages as Naomi's and Dick's. There came a time when the two couples would share dinner once or twice a week; during holidays they rented cottages together in France. A photo of all of them together displays a small mountain of children; Margery and Naomi nestle in their midst, both with hair parted in the centre and arranged in soft braids, both in comfortable flowing peasant dresses, both smiling at one another with clear affection.

Besides a full social life and a large family, Naomi devoted time to one of the first birth-control clinics in London. After her second child Denny was born, she had been fitted for a Dutch Cap, a form of contraception. Soon Naomi was on the committee that oversaw the North Kensington Clinic which was modelled on one begun by Marie Stopes (whose *Married Love* had proved so helpful) earlier in another part of London. Naomi's involvement in the birth-control movement would profoundly influence her thinking about women.

The idea behind the North Kensington Clinic was largely political: the birth-control movement was 'mainly thought of as family spacing and helping in the emancipation of women, not as population control, still less as allowing general "permissiveness" '.[13] Naomi had come to believe that a woman could not be politically independent until she had political control of her own body, including the choice of fathers for her children. By the end of the 1920s, Naomi would be publicly defining the ramifications of this controversial point of view. Her political novel about the Labour Party Left published in 1935 was thought disreputable by some because it expressed feminist ideas regarding autonomous sexuality.

Busy as she was, Naomi always made time to write. We know that she wrote parts of her first book, *The Conquered*, while pushing Murdoch in his perambulator. She wrote in the River Court house with neighbourhood children swarming under foot. At times, as her notebooks attest, children scrawled on the opposite page as she wrote. But usually, Naomi wrote in the morning when the nurse would be responsible for the children.

Naomi was writing largely out of her dreams, those nightmares that had not abated. Partly, she wrote because it was her habit and her skill; partly, her writing quietened her terrors. She wrote plays utilising her dreams, one of which Dick suggested might have happened in the sixth century AD. Naomi, who had always claimed to hate history, was first drawn into Volume IV of Gibbon's *The Rise and the Fall of the Roman Empire*; from there she read backward into Mommsen's *The History of Rome*: 'Then I was on the Cresta Run, no stopping'.[14]

You May Well Ask provides accurate, but frustratingly generalised, information about Naomi's life during her early period. She asserts that this memoir 'will try to show honestly how I grew up and changed into the woman I was when the next war came'. It is true that Naomi grew up during the twenty or so years between the wars, and her passage was not smooth. But *You May Well Ask* does not tell us how or when or why she changed. Instead, Naomi presents a series of thematic categories arranged in chapters devoted to medicine, education, politics, sexual mores – scattered pieces of a jigsaw puzzle, sociologically and historically fascinating yet obscuring the chronology of Naomi's private life. How she grew up in her early thirties must be quilted together from odd sentences in the memoir, from bits and pieces of our conversations, from issues at stake in her fiction and from letters that have survived.

In the early 1920s Naomi continued her efforts to understand and shape herself, primarily, it seems, through the fictions she was creating. Despite the trappings of adulthood – house, husband, children, social life, travel, a promising start as writer – some dimension of selfhood was missing, although she seemed unaware of it at the time. We might note that even her fiction, set as it was in remote history, seemed unconnected to her visible life, although it was very much connected to her inner turmoil. Besides performances in plays, writing had been a creative outlet encouraged in her childhood. Now it had become an activity about which she was fully confident. What poured out of her imagination was distress.

Naomi's early fiction was about the despair of women. *The Conquered* is about a sister's despair in relation to her brother, and *Cloud Cuckoo Land* is about a wife's despair. Of course, all the despair is muted, softened by its integration with other types of knowledge – with history and philosophy, for instance, and with conventional thematic conflicts.

She chose to situate *The Conquered* on the Celtic edge of the Roman Empire during Caesar's invasion of Gaul. Perhaps her Scottish and Celtic heritage brought her to this theme; perhaps it appealed to her own psychological resistance to authority. In *The Conquered* the conflict is between loyalty to personal relationships against loyalty to nation – an issue that had emerged most painfully for Naomi during the First World War when so many of her friends were killed in the name of patriotism. Should Meromic, the young Gaul, be true to his friend and owner, a Roman, or to his nation in rebellion under the leadership of Vercingetorix? As might be expected, Naomi has her hero choose love, but unexpectedly honest to her own psychological experience – and herein lies her ultimate power as a writer – she then has him languish in profound depression for his betrayal of Celtic nationalism. There are no easy answers for Meromic, though Naomi eases her way out of the novel's dilemma by invoking a magical resolution: Meromic becomes his atavistic totem, a wolf, and returns to his homeland where he, presumably, will roam as a beast.

The relationship between Meromic and his sister, Fiommar, tells us something about Naomi's continuing intense involvement with her brother, Jack. In *The Conquered* she melodramatically has the sister kill herself and thrusts the brother out into the world to roam and have adventures; according to Fiommar, Meromic must live in order to reproduce the male line of his family. Naomi hardly needs to confess, as she does in her memoir *You May Well Ask*, that Fiommar

and Meromic are herself and Jack. In her brother's arms, Fiommar
stabs herself:

> Meromic, with his eyes shut, warm against his sister's soft heart-
> beating, felt her suddenly quiver all over; he looked up; she smiled
> at him with all the colour ebbing out of her cheeks; her hands
> fluttered for a moment over his face; she fell on her side. From
> the slope below, the wild goats bleated faintly together; a tuft of
> thistle-down blew across Fiommar's hair; she seemed to sink lower
> into the turf. He bent over her, looking at her closely; he had
> never seen before just how her lip crooked up at the corner, nor
> how the fine downy hairs joined her eyebrows in the middle:
> well, he would remember. He picked up her hand where it lay,
> palm upward on the grass; but it was heavy, it dropped from the
> wrist; he shivered: this was not his sister. He put his arm under
> to drag her over to her place, and he felt the hilt of the knife
> driven in by a firm hand; the blood was sticky on her dress, he
> folded it under her; at first he could not make her lie straight,
> she was all tumbled by the fall, but at last he got her lying along
> with her arms at her sides and her hair over her shoulders like
> a princess in a fairy-tale. Slowly he brought the turfs from the
> pile; he laid them on, covering her face last; it was like a game
> – surely she must jump up soon and scatter them, the turfs they
> had cut together![15]

Once in a conversation with me about this first novel, Naomi said: 'I
made a mistake in that book. I killed off the love interest too soon'.
She smiled at me. She likes to keep curious people mystified about
her relationship with her brother.

But there is not much mystification regarding the passions of sister
and brother in *The Conquered*. We feel the impact of incestuous
tangle even if the intent was beyond Naomi's knowing control.
Indeed, Naomi's writing, as in later works, achieves power by
unselfconsciously plunging us into her inchoate inner life. Her
fiction loses force when she seems too much in control of her
intentions.

In her memoirs Naomi proposes in the light of hindsight that
the major love of her life had been Jack. What does she mean?
Certainly, and perhaps foremost, she is referring to the admiration
she felt for her keenest competitor. When it came to capping verse,
or anything else for that matter, Jack had been her equal and
sometimes better. Her love for Jack was mixed with jealousy; he
would usually win their competitions, although not all of them, and
some competitions were hardly intellectual. She, for instance, would

have children and he would not, much to his torment, reports his biographer, Ronald Clark.[16] Although later in the 1920s Naomi and Jack would quarrel and not speak to one another for long periods, the two were boon companions in the first years of Naomi's marriage and before Jack left Oxford to teach in Cambridge.

Early in the 1920s, they shared holidays together. For instance, while Naomi was writing *The Conquered* and *When the Bough Breaks*, she yearned to see the country that she was describing. Jack accompanied her on a walking tour of the Auvergne:

> It was very hot. On those mountains covered with blaeberries three times the size and juiciness of Perthshire ones, I took off my thick hot-weather wear, quickly slinging on the skirt again if we met anyone, which we seldom did. Once we came down hungry to a village, ate well, washed it down with red wine and staggered into an old quarry full of wildflowers to sleep it off. And turned dizzily towards one another. And suddenly Jack was shocked to his respectable Haldane soul. I wasn't. But that was all.[17]

So Naomi's love for Jack was erotic as well as sisterly. After his death and her own ageing, she shared her feelings about him. But early on, it was difficult for Naomi to know exactly what she was feeling. Nevertheless, her fiction of the 1920s and early 1930s records her tacit psychological life with Jack.

Whatever the relationship between them – and the details will never be entirely known, screened as they have been through Naomi's predilection for titillation and perhaps her own confusion – we do know that it was intense. So far there are no records of Jack's feelings for Naomi. The significant words, in my estimation, are in the throw-away line at the end of Naomi's description of her dalliance with Jack on their walking tour. She wrote: 'But that was all'. As I have matched Naomi's ruminations in *You May Well Ask* with external evidence, it has been my experience that she does not lie about important matters. What she has to say about her life may be unclearly arranged without chronology and context, her confessions may be highly fragmented by an enigmatic organisation, but she does not tell big lies. If Naomi says 'that was all', then it was.

Mixed with Naomi's half-hidden feelings towards her brother were half-hidden intellectual drives: Naomi was trying to invent a fictional form for the questing woman. Just as she strove to be her brother's equal, she strove to send her heroines out to adventure, to quest for ideals. Her task was not simple. The quest-romance had been the province of male heroes who act upon and within a world characterised as female; the medieval Lancelot and the twentieth-century Stephen Daedalus, alike, require a female environment in which to enact the values of their culture. There were few female literary models for Naomi's endeavour. Perhaps there might have been one if she had read Elizabeth Barrett Browning's *Aurora Leigh*, but, although Maya had read this long epic poem in her youth, it was out of fashion, and out of print, in Naomi's day.

Naomi, in her fiction, explores brother–sister relationships and, at the same time, she explores the literary possibility for female questing. These were alive issues for young middle-class women who were told in the 1920s that they now had the same privileges as young men. If so, why did not more women venture bravely forth in science, in professions, in the arts? During this period, Virginia Woolf was asking the same question in *A Room of One's Own*: what would have happened if Shakespeare's sister had been a genius desiring to be a poet? If boys could quest and girls could not, a sister might well want to know why.

While Naomi was fielding rejection letters on *The Conquered*, she continued writing; she worked on short stories that she would gather together in a volume entitled *When the Bough Breaks*. Finally Jonathan Cape accepted and published *The Conquered*; he would publish all of Naomi's fiction for the next ten years, until they parted company over an issue of censorship. *The Conquered* was published in 1923, *When the Bough Breaks* in 1924, followed by another novel, *Cloud Cuckoo Land*, in 1925. The novels were well-received in both Great Britain and the United States. *The Conquered* was honoured with the prestigious French award, the Palmes de L'Académie Française. *When the Bough Breaks*, her volume of short stories, received mixed critical response. However, by the time *Cloud Cuckoo Land* appeared reviews were headlined 'A Brilliant Novel' and reviewers were consistent in their praise. An anonymous reviewer in the *New Statesman* wrote: 'Mrs Mitchison succeeds. She not only succeeds, she has that ease, that definiteness of success, which shows that failure was unthinkable: she does not *make* a book, it is there, real, solid, intimidating'.[18]

Naomi does not allow Fiommar, the sister-heroine of *The Conquered*, even to live, let alone wander. In *When the Bough Breaks*, a set of short stories that follow the rise and the fall of the Roman Empire, Naomi begins by probing into issues of female adventure-questing. One story poses the anguished question: why should boy-children have more potential choice and power than girl-children? The answer: girl-children have the freedom of boys until they become mothers. With motherhood their freedom to adventure ends. Naomi seems to be concluding that women are biologically rather than culturally restricted.

Another story in *When the Bough Breaks* links slavery and the status of women. The heroine, raging about her unfair treatment in comparison to her brother's, suddenly perceives that she and her interlocutor, a slave, are alike:

> Then all of a sudden it was like something inside me giving way, and I said, 'It's so hard being a girl! Here I am, just the same as a man really, and no worse than my brother anyway – I've got all the same eyes and hands and ears and everything that matters! But just because of two or three silly little differences I have to be treated as if I was an animal, ordered about, not allowed to decide anything for myself! I'm shut up, I'm watched, I have to do what men tell me – nothing's my own, money or husband or religion – I have to take what they give me and say thank you! Oh, it is unfair – haven't I got a soul every bit as good as theirs?'[19]

Woman and slave commiserate: 'And then it came to me that perhaps he did understand, perhaps he felt a little like that too, and oh, I was sorry for him!'[20]

In another story of this 1924 collection, a northern barbarian, Gersemi, disguises herself as a man and joins the invading armies that sweep down into the crumbling Roman Empire – first to Athens, then Spain and finally Rome. Battling by the sides of men, gaming and jousting, she is safely hidden by her armour until she saves a beautiful young maiden, propriety herself, to whom she promises sisterhood. Stupidly, the maiden loses Gersemi's magic bear skin. It follows that Gersemi loses her head, falls in love, and has a short week of love-making before her soldier-lover disappears to die in battle. Gersemi's adventuring days are abruptly over; she is pregnant, then a mother – encumbered. Unless women can control procreation, they cannot adventure, and without the ability to roam and meet obstacles and tasks, how can there be quest?

In her next novel Naomi takes up the thread of biological control that ties Gersemi to home and ends her adventure-questing days. She paints a hopeless picture of possibility for both women and for humankind. *Cloud Cuckoo Land* is set in fifth-century Greece at the end of the Peloponnesian War. Naomi has Moiro, her soft and gentle heroine, kidnapped during a scene of raping chaos in a brushfire revolution on an unimportant Greek island. She is carried to Athens where her kidnapper marries her, although Naomi makes it amply clear that, as a woman and possession, Moiro is lucky enough to be married at all. Moiro's adventure into the wide world, an adventure that she has not chosen, is limited to the four walls of her Athenian dwelling and to the limitations of her husband's lack of courage and wit.

Naomi's writing is direct and sensual, full of distanced description of violence. She does not pull punches in this novel; the lot of wives is grim. Moiro is allowed by her husband to keep her first-born, a boy; her second-born, a girl, she must kill. The baby is left to die in a jar on the corner of an Athenian street:

> It was such a thin, long, heart-breaking cry that came from the pot. . .
> Some people didn't notice; a few did, and passed on quickly, with a
> glance perhaps at Thrassa, pitiful and angry. No one stopped. By
> evening the little thing had finished crying.[21]

If Moiro's plight is not sad enough for the reader, Naomi goes a step further. She has Moiro die from self-inflicted abortion:

> Any woman could tell you it went wrong sometimes when you did
> – that. If it wasn't just right. But what was the God who would
> help now? Again she felt her mistress' burning skin, and smelt the
> horrible breath of spent fire coming from her mouth. . .[22]

Naomi is brutally forthright about abortion. I can think of no other fiction in the 1920s that is as vivid about the unspeakable. Nor was this lost on reviewers who remarked on the book's feminist intention. It was a short step, wrote one, to asking if the lot of modern women was much better.[23] Birth-control was a political hot potato, and Naomi's experience in the North Kensington Clinic was reflected in her fiction.

Despite being one of Naomi's more sympathetic characterisations, Moiro is a heroine with neither courage nor intelligence; she is buffeted about by historical forces which are beyond her comprehension. Not so the character of Nikodike, a young Athenian woman who speaks out in the Agora against on-going war. Still, for all her bravery and understanding, Nikodike's destiny is no better than Moiro's. Whereas her brother can adventure out of Athens to organise a band of rebels against the tyrants, Nikodike must marry, and when she attempts to join her brother in the hills, she is physically assaulted. Her fate? 'Hagnon saw in his mind's eye a little picture of his sister shut up there in her house, sitting disconsolate with her hands in her lap, and her heart closed against him forever.'[24] So sits Nikodike until old age and death.

The narrator's opening words about Nikodike had been accurate: 'she thought about things perhaps three times as much as any of the other women, which was unfortunate for her, being a respectable Athenian'.[25] Surely Nikodike is like Naomi then, another sister who felt abandoned by her brother.

What began to happen in Naomi's personal life in the year she published *Cloud Cuckoo Land* is folded on yellowing sheets of paper, now stuffed in large brown envelopes in the lower drawers of her bedroom desk at Carradale. Some of the seven envelopes are misleadingly labelled: 'Clem Brown and a few others', 'Part I: "Happy Hampstead"', 'Part II: "Hampstead"'. Other envelopes are more or less accurate to their contents: 'Dick', 'H. T. W. G.', 'Margy Spring Rice', 'John Pilley', 'Letters from children, 1935–36'. In each packet there are batches of letters, most of which are undated, but usually folded in clumps into a single letter-sized envelope that bears a postal date. Roughly, these letters fall into three time frames beginning in the mid-1920s, gathering again after 1927, and then again in the first half of the 1930s. Warm, passionate, searching, sincere, they document the self-conscious beginnings of Naomi's lifelong personal quest.

Naomi made two major decisions in 1925, one regarding the direction of her writing, the other the direction of her marriage. In her writing she decided to shape her fiction through the heroic journeys of women. In her marriage, she and Dick decided it was all right to take lovers, in trust and respect for one another, fully committed to marriage and family. This decision, mixed as it no doubt was with mutual disappointments and unmet expectations, became part of a larger agenda that took as its purpose nothing less than inventing a better, less violent, more communal world. The letters in Naomi's drawers are particularly fascinating because they record the search of earnest, word-conscious people stretching to articulate their new experiences of intimacy.

4

Loves and Losses
1925–1930

Even before Naomi and Dick had agreed to the terms of their new marriage pact, Naomi had begun to write her massive opus, her quest novel, *The Corn King and the Spring Queen*. In 1925 she wrote part one and most of part two of what would be seven sections, then put aside the manuscript for three years. The opening portions of her novel survey the hills and dales of another brother–sister saga, well-mapped landscape reconnoitred in previous fiction. Then she shelved it. Before writing more, Naomi began a risky venture in her own life. She began to explore new territory as if in search of fresh possibilities for a woman hero.

When Dick began a love affair with Margery Spring Rice, Naomi supported the relationship. Several months later Naomi, whose face Margery had thought troubled, brightened. Naomi and H. T. Wade Gery had fallen in love. Wade Gery was the classical scholar teaching in Oxford who had played a part in her amateur 1920 production of *Barley, Honey and Wine* and from whom she had sought information while writing historical fiction. Nicknamed 'Widg' by Naomi, Wade Gery was unmarried, in his mid-thirties, his photos presenting him tall and lean, with dark, waving, unruly hair; his letters display a finely tuned, sensitive temperament, sometimes cruel. In the beginning, they were emotionally and sexually passionate with each other, the two of them talking non-stop for days at a time on walking holidays together, finally sitting silent over wine, in love, or so one of his letters reminded Naomi when several years later their relationship became more difficult.

Naomi and Dick helped each other throughout their respective relationships, Naomi propping up Margery with continued trust and confidence, Dick sending Naomi daily letters of affection and encouragement when she was on a walking holiday in Somerset with Widg. In one, he wished he could join them, but adds that Margery and he had been happily picnicking with the children.

While Bloomsbury in the 1920s acquired a reputation for experimental living, it was also characteristic of the Hammersmith crowd. These Hammersmith young people had survived the First World War, but they continued to suffer from that traumatic loss of brothers and friends, a loss that had shocked them out of any complacent sense of stability. In their minds these loved young men had been killed by the wrong-headed values of the generation that had preceded them, and some, like Naomi, felt a moral obligation to invent a new way to live. If she made a good invention, perhaps, just perhaps, she might stave off another devastating war. It sometimes seemed that she thought the future of Western Civilisation depended on her habits of loving. In a letter to Aunt Bay, Naomi defended her behaviour in a cogent analysis of the ethical motivations marking her generation of intellectuals. Stung by some reprimand from Aunt Bay, she replied:

I don't believe you realise how much the war has upset our generation – mine and the one immediately after it. Liz Belloc, for instance. The first wave of disturbance was the one at the time, and now we're in for the second, after the period of calm and exhaustion immediately following the thing. I think this is much what happened after the Peloponnesian and after the Napoleonic Wars. Our's was worse than either. You have still a balance in your life: all that incredible pre-war period when things seemed in the main settled, just moving solidly and calmly like a glacier towards all sorts of progress. But we have had the bottom of things knocked out completely, we have been sent reeling into chaos and it seems to us that none of your standards are either fixed or necessarily good because in the end they resulted in the smash-up. We have to try and make a world for ourselves, basing it as far as possible on love and awareness, mental and bodily, because it seems to us that all the repressions and formulae, all the cutting off of part of our experience, which perhaps looked sensible and even right in those calm years, have not worked. Much has been taken from us, but we will stick like fury to what is left, and lay hold on life, as it comes to us.

I am an artist; it doesn't matter to me whether I and mine stick to the rules or not; I can't be hurt economically, and when one has economic freedom that's a great deal! I would prefer not to compromise at all; I hope my children won't choose 'respectable' professions.

I believe I am right in saying that I have rather a large influence over a good many people my own age or thereabouts. Like Queen Victoria I try to be good. But my good has to come ultimately from my own conscience, not from any other person or any book, though either may influence us. We do, among us, consider the good rather a lot and on the whole try and act on it. Sometimes we get into tangles and sometimes we don't. . .We suffer ['my generation of intelligentsia'] perhaps from spiritual shyness (the two things often go together) owing to the hurt the war has given us. A few people produce parts of the doctrine, usually disguised as rather difficult fiction – to take the first few names that occur to me: D. H. Lawrence, Wyndham Lewis, Aldous Huxley, Robert Graves – these are all of my profession, of course. I am less obvious because my stuff is disguised!

However I doubt whether all this is at all convincing; we should like a few miracles and things! So don't bother about it. And don't worry about me; I wouldn't be a Haldane if I didn't butt into things and get into rows and think for myself.[1]

By the time Naomi wrote this letter to her Aunt Bay in 1928, she had a right to consider herself influential. Even before *The Corn King and the Spring Queen*, her books had made her famous. Arnold Bennett, the most powerful literary critic in England during the 1920s, wrote that she was the only British novelist who knew a novel from a bon-bon.[2] Any well-read person in Great Britain who grew up during the 1920s and 1930s will have read Naomi Mitchison. Not only was history factually accurate in her historical novels, which pleased the scholarly critics, but she was a good read for fast moving adventure and for complicated, erotic love. Naomi's letter to her beloved and respected Aunt Bay also makes it clear that behind and beside her craft she had moral intentions.

But Naomi's motivations are never singular. In addition to moral dimensions she could articulate for her aunt, Naomi may have been impelled to experiment because of the despair and uncertainty her writing had brought to consciousness. According to Naomi, the sexual part of her marriage with Dick had never been completely fulfilling for her or for Dick. Devoted to one another, they, nevertheless, wanted something more. In her memoir, Naomi described in generalised terms the overall nature of their love affairs. In a chapter entitled 'Patterns of Loving', she wrote:

I think each of us realised that the other needed new channels of communication to other lives, other ideas. Perhaps too we needed the touch of a stranger, the exploration of another mind and another body. This mattered to me over my writing, to Dick over his political and perhaps his social life as well. One may be able to get this communication in other ways, for instance through shared and intense religious or political experience; but it is quicker in bed, sometimes even too much of a short cut. Yet I still believe that this did not spoil our basic relationship with one another, our deep affection, respect and loyalty, even when the other partner was doing something very much out of the pattern.[3]

Several years into their marital experiment Dick's letters continued to demonstrate his affection, respect and loyalty towards Naomi. There are many instances in which he expressed support and comfort in the vein of the following quotations excerpted from letters he wrote from Durban, South Africa, where his legal work, his practice now flourishing, had taken him in 1930. He wrote:

No, I won't be your ballast, if it's to prevent the balloon going up. I only ballast in order to put the balloon on its mettle and make it go higher.[4] . . .Nou, I do love you so. I feel I'm going back to court you – with chastity and the intellectual affections, if you like it so – but to court you more deeply than I'd court anyone else. I don't know that that's conventional marriage but it means more to me than anything else.[5] . . .I suppose I laugh at you a little sometimes and, more often, I'm rather jealous of you for being so successful – but I do think you're fine stuff and generous beyond measure and, though *you* may laugh, rather a great woman. It's difficult to feel small about you.[6]

We can see that Dick was devoted to Naomi; we will have to wait for Naomi's letters to surface before we can assess her reaction to him. However, we may glimpse Naomi through Margery's eyes in a long letter she wrote in 1928. Margery describes Naomi's apparent strength and her encompassing love for both herself and Dick; she is grateful to Naomi for having held them in close circle, attributing the success of the 'experiment' to Naomi's good will.

Although she writes a couple of paragraphs about their love relationships in her memoirs, Naomi does not name their lovers. Partly, she is being discreet, exercising a code of honour which disapproves of kissing and telling.[7] Partly, she is keeping to her conception of her life as sociological data. Naomi would have us know that if she and Dick negotiated an experimental marriage it was not primarily motivated by romantic up-welling or personal trouble. No. It was the result of a play of social forces begun, in this case, by technological innovation – the discovery of effective contraception for women. Coupled with the new status of women after the war and with their new political equality, birth-control changed the social pattern of the British upper middle class: 'Several of our friends were, like us, behaving in ways which I think would have been utterly unacceptable even twenty years before'.[8] Some of Naomi's behaviour was motivated by her feminism. She and nobody else owned her body. Even though it was still difficult to have children by different fathers, she hoped that it would be different for her daughters.

Naomi spices her discretion with coy allusions to her lovers:

> Yet looking back on it now, I remember the pain almost more clearly than the delight, whereas with the relationships which did not include love-making – for instance with Lewis Gielgud or Angela Blakeney Booth or Aldous or Zita Baker, the only remembered pain is at their death.[9]

How much Naomi implies! She suggests that she might have made love with hosts of people – men and women – whom she has not named. Elsewhere in her memoirs she writes that she had 'one main lover and then others'. That is all she publicly divulges. Nevertheless, despite her teasing, the story that emerges from the packets of letters in Naomi's drawers is not titillating; it is a profound testament to humane idealism, to desire for a world in which ever-enlarging circles of love, sex, intimacy and loyalty are possible.

In 1926 Naomi and her father testified on Jack's behalf in front of Cambridge University's Sex Viri, a faculty committee that had found Jack guilty of 'gross habitual immorality'. He had fallen in love with Charlotte Burghes, a married woman, who, given the mortifying and restrictive divorce laws of the day, had to be witnessed sitting in a hotel room with Jack so that she could be accused of adultery in order to be released from her first marriage. Even though Charlotte received her divorce and married Jack, university officials deprived Jack of his Readership when he refused to resign. Jack's successful appeal against the Sex Viri's decision doomed that venerable committee's power forever, a watershed moment in Cambridge history. In matters of love, as in politics, both Naomi and her brother were complex renegades.

Willing as Naomi was to take on life – in her loving, in her writing, in her philosophy – it was death that shook her to the depths of her being. In 1927 her oldest child, 9-year-old Geoff, died of spinal meningitis. His death touched Naomi's guilt as a mother, although there was, in truth, little she could have done to keep him alive. Penicillin had not yet been discovered. There is no way around the pain: spinal meningitis is both a horrible way to die and a horrible nightmare for a mother whose child is dying of its ravages. Naomi's close friend Aldous Huxley described the unmitigated suffering of Geoff's death in *Point Counter Point*:

> Next day, instead of whimpering with every return of pain, the child began to scream – cry after shrill cry, repeated with an almost clockwork regularity of recurrence for what seemed to Elinor an eternity of hours. Like the scream of a rabbit in a trap. But a thousand times worse; for it was a child that screamed, not an animal; *her* child, trapped and in agony. She felt as though she too were trapped.
>
> Trapped by her own utter helplessness to alleviate the pain.[10]

Naomi was offended that Aldous had used her tormented experience as fodder for his fiction. In time, she would forgive Aldous and she would forgive her brother for his reaction. But both had to wait for the distance time would bring.

In conversation with me, Naomi recounted her memory of Jack's rejection of her in the wake of Geoff's death. She began her story *in medias res*: in the night darkness returning from Cambridge she crumbled her roadster into a stone wall bordering a country lane and sank her head to knuckles which were white from gripping the wheel. She was not weeping; she was numb. Eight-year-old Denny's presence beside her on the seat reminded Naomi that she had to pull herself together. She had to ferry this son safely back to Oxford. Murdoch and Lois were waiting for their mother to return from Jack in Cambridge, to whom she had gone for comfort in her despair.[11]

Geoff had just died, dreadfully. Her first thought had been to seek help from her beloved brother. Margery stayed with Dick. With Denny beside her, Naomi had driven madly for Cambridge where Jack now lived with his wife, Charlotte. However, it was a mistake to ask for help from Jack at this time, because, as Naomi would be able to say over fifty years later, he, too, was suffering and reacting in shock. Instead of folding Naomi in his arms, Jack attacked with words she would never forget. He blamed her for Geoff's death.

Perhaps Jack had also been influenced against Naomi by Charlotte, who, besides finding highbrows to be show-offs, rude and artificial, had just published a book in which she took to task modern young women who value careers instead of traditional mothering. In *Motherhood and Its Enemies* Charlotte assails women who use birth-control devices, enabling them, she wrote, to compete with prostitutes. Women with careers in music, drama, and film are 'female parasites'; women who choose not to have children are 'sub-normal'; lesbians, an 'intersex', are 'abnormal'. In an author's note, Charlotte wrote that her husband had read and approved her book.[12] In many ways, Naomi was the sort of woman against whom Charlotte railed; she was flourishing in her career as a writer and a noisy proponent of birth-control.

Whatever the reason, Jack had profoundly failed his sister – loss upon loss for Naomi. She was on her own.

The record of letters in Naomi's bottom drawer goes blank for several months after Geoff died. What remains are letters of condolence preserved in the Haldane Collection in the archives of the National Library of Scotland. Naomi did not write fiction during this period. We can assume that she slumped into grief and depression.

As if to underscore the nearness of death and human fragility, another tragedy overwhelmed the Mitchison household. In 1928 the Thames tide overflowed its banks, crashing with door-tearing force into the River Court basement apartment, drowning two servants in their sleep. Their deaths have become part of Hammersmith lore, proving that the River could be unpredictably dangerous. It was just more grisly distress for Naomi and Dick.

Seeking respite in their grief over Geoff's death, in the early summer of 1928, together with H. T. Wade Gery, Margery Spring Rice and Liz Belloc, the poet Hilaire Belloc's daughter and Naomi's close friend, Naomi and Dick rented a yacht on which they toured the Greek Islands. Naomi was two months pregnant with Avrion. She kept a diary, a manuscript now entitled 'The Yacht Avrion' in her private files, in which she painted blue surfaces of water and sky. In her memoirs she describes a moment of the trip:

> Wade Gery found a new inscription on Thera. Here the volcanic plug bubbled with hot sulphurous springs and the sea swam with strange floating pebbles of pumice that knocked against the sides of the boat all night as we slept on deck.[13]

In all of *You May Well Ask* it is the sole reference to Wade Gery, save for this poignant acknowledgement of his scholarly influence:

> And always there was H. T. Wade Gery, my main influence on the Hellenic world. Later I worked as a gentle critic with him and Maurice Bowra, who had been my brother's most brilliant New College undergraduate, on their Pindar translations, and Maurice was there when Wade Gery went suddenly out of my life and I felt that for me Hellas was finished.[14]

It was several years beyond 1928 before Wade Gery was completely out of Naomi's life, for it was much more difficult to end this affair than either one of them imagined. No surprise. It is clear from their letters that they were deeply, passionately in love. What seemed to have happened is this: after the cruise of the Greek Islands, Widg travelled by himself to Athens where he courted and won the hand of Vivian Whitfield, who reluctantly gave over her professional work as a trained archaeologist to return to Oxford with her new husband. Widg had told her about his intimate friendship with Naomi the afternoon he proposed to her, a scene he described with dramatic detail in a long letter to Naomi. During the next year Naomi and Vivian exchanged letters, in good faith, wanting to know and like one another. One letter from Vivian is rhapsodic about the birth of her first baby. It appears that in the beginning Vivian had thought it possible to share Widg's affection and loyalty with Naomi, but this changed as she began to have children, finding herself house-bound in what Widg considered academic poverty. But before Widg and Naomi agreed to stop seeing and writing to each other, their spouses and intimate friends all lent themselves to Naomi's idea of love. Naomi writes to Julian Huxley of the effort:

> Did you know, Wade Gery had a son last Friday? I'm in such a marvelous tangle about that, far worse than when I saw you last. You see, I have fallen rather deeply in love with his wife (if one dares to say such a thing in these days, but you know I'm in practice rather hetero-sexual) and I think she is, at least, extremely fond of me. And I am not any the less from time to time simply tortured by being in utterly hopeless love with him! And in the meantime he and Dick spent a weekend walking together. Well, well.[15]

Naomi's love for Vivian, as for many of her women friends, was intense, displayed most playfully and erotically in her fiction and poetry, finding full expression in the science fiction novels she wrote in her seventies.

Naomi willed herself to forget Widg. They decided they would not even write letters.

She was discovering how much there was that she could not control. Her forming idea of the Just Society – a community of people loyal and nonpossessive, generous and unrepressed – worked well enough when she was its linchpin, embracing Margery, enabling Dick to embrace Widg. But her arms were not long enough to close the widening circle: Widg's wife Vivian was eventually beyond her reach, and so was Dominick, Margery's husband; the Spring Rices separated. When Dick began to expand the circle with his new lovers, she could not easily comfort Margery. She did the one thing in her power to control.

She held tight to her own principles; in matters of the heart Naomi was always generous and unpossessive. This quality of character is documented in Naomi's letters to Vivian, to Dick, to Margery, to Margaret Cole and to many others – as well as substantiated by her conduct, welcoming Dick's special women friends into her home for the rest of their lives.

Naomi had lost her son and, in less absolute terms, her brother and her lover, and, in a way, Dick. In response, her writing intensified; whereas she had always written copiously, she now took up new themes and, although it hardly seems possible, wrote even more. Also, the pattern of her relationships changed; some old friends faded; her new friends tended to be younger. Moreover, she began to speak out publicly and more courageously, first on issues of birth-control and sex, then mixing these women's issues with politics more conventionally construed.

5

The Corn King and the Spring Queen
1928–1931

Naomi grew up. At the age of 31 the person she pulled together was no longer a dependent daughter, sister and wife, no longer a girl. Now, when Naomi Mitchison returned to her massive historical novel *The Corn King and the Spring Queen*, her writing was infused with a maturity and courage that came from overcoming terrible loss, loneliness and rejection. And she was writing more than ever. In 1928 alone, she produced three books: a biography, *Anna Comena*; a volume of short stories, *Black Sparta*; and four plays for children, *Nix-Nought-Nothing*; she also started writing regularly for *Time and Tide*. In 1929 she wrote two volumes of short stories, *Barbarian Stories* and *The Hostages and Other Stories for Boys and Girls*. She produced a feminist tract, *Comments on Birth-Control*, in 1930. She wrote all this while writing *The Corn King and the Spring Queen*, her 700 page novel published in 1931.

As if this literary flood were not enough, Naomi wanted more children. She was pregnant twice again, giving birth to Avrion in 1928 and to her second daughter, Valentine, in 1930. Books and babies, familiar comfort. But nothing was the same.

In her memoirs Naomi embeds two descriptions of a shift in her social alliances that occurred in the late 1920s. The first comes at the end of a paragraph describing family vacation retreats on the Continent: 'By this time we were no longer sharing with the Spring Rice family but with the Coles and their circle'.[1] Another more lengthy passage describes the political implications of this shift: the Spring Rices were political Liberals, whereas Margaret and Douglas Cole were political Labourites. Douglas Cole was an influential teacher and writer in Oxford, drawing under his wing aspiring left-leaning intellectuals – Maurice Bowra, for instance, and Hugh Gaitskell. Douglas, with Margaret's capable help, had taken over directorship of the Fabian Society from Beatrice and Sidney Webb. Naomi, to some extent, and Dick, especially, began to dream of finding purpose in their lives through commitment to socialism.

This shift of allegiance from the Spring Rices to the Coles also had implications in the private lives of the Mitchisons, for Dick and Margaret Cole were romantically drawn to one another. Many people in their circle knew about it, including Douglas Cole, Margaret's husband; letters discussing the entanglement went back and forth for years between Margaret and Naomi, between Naomi and their other friends, between Dick and Naomi. What to do? For, as it turned out, Douglas had asked Margaret to remain sexually monogamous, even though, perhaps because of his diabetes, he was 'undersexed', or so Margaret noted in her late-life autobiographical essays. Margaret was devoted to Douglas, unwilling to hurt him, and Dick shared her consideration. Margaret's biographer suggests that Margaret and Dick actually consummated a sexual relationship. Of Margaret she says in reference to Dick's company, 'self-confidence radiated from her happiness'.[2] However, when the letters in Naomi's drawers stopped discussing the issue of 'what-to-do' in 1932, Dick and Margaret were still honouring Douglas's interdiction. Meanwhile, Dick had started a love relationship with Leticia (Tish) Rokeling, a congenial companion for travel, his friend for life.

Although Margery Spring Rice continued to be invited as a single woman to dinner parties throughout the 1930s, she and her children stopped taking holidays with the Mitchisons. Naomi was grateful to Margery for introducing her to the writer Stella Benson. Their correspondence lasted until Stella died in China in 1934. Liz Belloc disappeared as well from Naomi's circle in the early 1930s. While debating religion, they ended up on the floor wrestling, violent and unhappy. (Naomi had a tendency to physically lash out at people: here with Liz, soon with Hugh Gaitskell and then her brother, and later in Scotland collaborating over writing with one of the local fisherman.) Liz never returned, to Naomi's dismay, as she recalls in her memoir.

Aldous Huxley returned and stayed in Naomi's life, their loyalty recorded in countless letters, mainly those she saved of his, hers presumably destroyed along with all of his private papers in a fire that engulfed Aldous's Los Angeles home in the 1950s. She and Dick visited Aldous and his wife Maria in Southern France at one of the several places the Huxleys lived before settling in California in the late 1930s. Dick's fluent French and Italian suited the Huxley social circle. Aldous, like Dick, had sexual relationships with many women and was often helped by his wife when courting them. Maria's reason for aiding Aldous was mirrored by Naomi's generous reception of Dick's women friends. According to Sybille Bedford, Aldous's biographer and lifelong friend, Maria thought that as a man Aldous needed relationships with women to fuel his creativity. As a creative woman, Naomi assumed the same prerogative for herself.

Along with other women, Naomi pioneered what would become that characteristically twentieth-century search for new language to express the experience of women as separate and perhaps different from men. At least, this is what she and Margaret Cole did in their letters, and what she reports doing in conversation with Angela Blakeney Booth and Elizabeth (Harman) Pakenham, who was Lady Longford in 1984 when she and Naomi confided in conversation with me that they had mainly talked about sex in the late 1920s and early 1930s, although they are not sure they used the word 'sex' and are absolutely certain they did not use 'sexual'; theirs was more a search for language to describe all aspects of private human conduct.[3] In her letters Naomi began to use the word 'fuck', more daring than articulate. These women had much to talk about, there being no existing language, according to Virginia Woolf, with which women might express the responses of their bodies and passions. So Naomi and her women friends talked, wrote long and subtle letters to each other and defined new creative boundaries.

The artist Gertrude Hermes, for instance, spent an afternoon experimentally placing her body and Naomi's in various and sometimes improbable positions of sexual intercourse. The result? A series of delightful etchings, men frolicking after women, not unlike figures on Grecian vases, but erotic and definitely from a woman's point of view, the male figures pointedly promising what pleasure they might give. In a note still attached to the etchings, Gertrude asked Naomi not to display them, an interdiction that was obeyed. Alas, they are lodged in a desk drawer with a trove of Naomi's unpublished love poems.

Toward the end of the 1920s, Naomi's younger cousin, Christine Willams, blew on to the scene trailing strings of student friends from her studies in Oxford. Most of these people were ten years younger than Naomi. Key among them was Elizabeth Harman, a beauty with flair for flamboyant dress, a special friend of Hugh Gaitskell's, having been introduced by him to the group of students and young dons who gathered for study and discussion at Douglas Cole's. Through Hugh, Elizabeth met other Oxford intellectuals some of whom overlapped Naomi's world: Maurice Bowra, for instance, and H. T. Wade Gery, and soon W. H. Auden and Stephen Spender. In her autobiography, Elizabeth describes falling more and more under Naomi's 'seductive influence'.

Through Elizabeth's eyes we glimpse the Mitchisons' social life in 1929 and 1930. Their dinner parties had become considerably less formal. Elizabeth remembers sitting under the supper table with Adrian Stephen, brother of Virginia Woolf, discussing Freudian psychology. At River Court she found the 'Bloomsburys' in more human shape than in Cambridge. Another time at one of Naomi's parties she went on a walk at dawn with A. P. Herbert to his favourite shrine, an electrical generating plant, where she remembers laughing hysterically over the illusion Herbert created that his arm was the generating piston itself. Not only were Dick and Naomi's parties less formal; they had become larger. They had big parties on Midsummer's Eve where guests jumped over a bonfire in a ritual of wish fulfilment and fertility. Their Boat Race parties expanded to at least a 100 invited guests and many more who were uninvited, it being the pattern in Hammersmith for passersby to be welcome in any merry-making house on this special day, when the Oxford and Cambridge rowing teams competed on the Thames for London's pleasure.

Elizabeth came to know Naomi during the years when Naomi was struggling hardest to cut her emotional ties with Widg. She recalls Naomi claiming that nothing increased creative production like pregnancy and an unhappy love affair. In another vignette from a weekend in Bledlow Ridge in 1930, after pointing out that Naomi did not wear a wedding ring 'on feminist grounds', Elizabeth describes having once tried to comfort Naomi's heartache. Naomi responded:

'Listen to the larks.' Scores of them were rising in spirals from the ridge. Naomi made a face. 'I hate the sound. It's like a little screw.'[4]

In 1929 Naomi had hired W. H. Auden, then a young and penurious student at Oxford, as her son's Latin coach. Soon he was a member of her family, helping to decorate the Mitchison Christmas tree, following them to holiday retreats. Naomi recognised his poetic genius, taking pains to present his poetry to Arnold Bennett, who was chairman of a short-lived literary journal, *The Realist*, on whose board she sat with her brother Jack, Julian Huxley, Bronislaw Malinowski,

Rebecca West and Gerald Heard, among others. The journal failed before Auden's poems were published.

In *You May Well Ask* Naomi quotes several letters from Auden that she received at different times over the next decade, the letters dwindling after Auden moved to the United States just before war broke out in Europe. These letters suggest that, aside from Naomi's financial patronage, she and Auden met primarily on literary grounds, often reading and criticising one another's work while it was still in manuscript. Auden dampened Naomi's confidence in her poems; she, on her part, stopped liking his after 'For the Time Being'.

Soon Auden joined the coterie of mainly homosexual men surrounding Gerald Heard. When Heard's friend Joe Ackerley moved in 1933 from Hammersmith to Maida Vale, so did Auden, along with his friend from university, Stephen Spender.

Although Naomi's published writing had brought her new friends, some of these relationships did not deepen until later in the 1920s. A note from E. M. Forster about *The Conquered* glowed with praise; there ensued a relationship of progressive closeness that continued through the Second World War. It was helped along by the neighbourly proximity of Joe Ackerley who lived in Hammersmith Terrace housing. Here he brought together Bloomsbury highbrows with local workers. Forster was a close friend of Ackerley's. Moreover, Forster's circle of friends included Gerald Heard, who was a uniquely influential and intimate friend of Naomi's.

Now nearly forgotten, Gerald Heard was a self-made historian-philosopher. Naomi claims in her memoir that he influenced her more than any other writer at the time. In 1930 she reviewed his *The Ascent of Humanity* for *Time and Tide*. Gerald persuasively wrote about the push of humanity toward a higher form of consciousness. It is hard to understand Gerald Heard's startling influence on a generation of intellectuals for his books are turgid and obscure, relying heavily on nineteenth-century anthropology, mystically suggesting a route for certain élite intellectuals to rise above the masses. Perhaps his personal charm helped; his mind was encyclopaedic, sharp, and witty. He was an apt companion for Aldous during those decades of self-imposed exile in California.

In 1930 Naomi made a friend of Wyndham Lewis through a review she wrote of his novel, *Apes of God*. She praised its satire.[5] She was an approving reader, while many others saw his book as a savage attack on Bloomsbury personalities towards whom he was hostile. Naomi chose to review the book as if she did not recognise the personal objects of its satire. It was the beginning of a curious relationship between Lewis, a bitter, unwelcome critic of the liberal Left, and Naomi, a more and more committed socialist.

Naomi and Dick were not particularly political during most of the 1920s. True, Naomi was active in the North Kensington Clinic which exposed her to a brand of feminism that treated the female body politically. And she was a participant in the Women's International League, which was interested in promoting the League of Nations and, too, was partly feminist. But neither Naomi nor Dick participated in the major political events of this decade, although they would join the Labour Party in 1930 and spend the rest of their lives in political activity.

Meanwhile, Naomi missed the Labour Convention described by Dora Russell in *The Tamarisk Tree*. In 1925 in an emotional debate, the Labour Party voted to exclude issues relating to birth-control from its platform. Birth-control was a touchy issue. If women were to be equal to men, according to the tenets of Marxism, they must earn money as workers, which, logically, meant encouraging birth-control. However, the issue was not so clear. The dominant view of socialist men in the 1920s and 1930s insisted that only class issues counted. Many socialists disapproved of feminism because it sapped energy from consensus about the hegemony of class struggle. Moreover, socialist men were opposed to the birth-control movement because they were contemptuous of its class bias. Rightly, they claimed that the birth-control movement was infected with eugenicist notions that wished to limit the procreation of the 'lower orders'. The issue of birth-control brought socialist men and women into sharp conflict.

Neither Dick nor Naomi sympathised particularly with workers in the General Strike of 1926, another indication of how removed they were from political radicalism at this time. Naomi even envied her strike-breaking friends who had the fun of driving railway trains. All this would change in 1930 when Dick and Naomi joined the Labour Party.

The years Naomi spent writing *The Corn King and the Spring Queen* spanned the period in which she and Dick made their decision to participate in Labour politics. Naomi's novel actually charts her metamorphosis into a socialist Labourite. *The Corn King and the Spring Queen* traces her imaginative progress into self-sufficiency and produces hard questions that had to be answered – not in private dreams but through social action. Although Naomi sets the novel in the remote past, third-century Hellas, she confronts issues which plagued her historical present. As the liberating forces of the 1920s in England were replaced by repressions that made Mosley's fascist cadres attractive, and as the economy nosed-dived and crashed, driving working people to hunger and despair, Naomi wrote. While writing, Naomi read Marx – all of *Capital*. She read Freud, reviewing *Civilization and Its Discontents* for *Time and Tide*. She had already read Frazer's *The Golden Bough*. The outcome was an extraordinary work of fiction.

If Naomi Mitchison had written but one book, *The Corn King and the Spring Queen*, she would deserve a significant place among twentieth-century writers. However, the opening chapters of the *The Corn King and the Spring Queen* give no inkling that Naomi's book is a major work of literary achievement. These were the pages written before Geoff's death. They rely on tried and tested formulae, and the tones are faintly condescending, signalling another children's tale. When, after three years, Naomi decided to continue the novel, her voice and vision had changed. Characteristically, Naomi lets the beginning of the book stand unrevised. But the rest of *The Corn King and the Spring Queen* cuts to the bone, ruthlessly weeding through available ideological systems, relentlessly scraping at nerves rubbed raw by death of children and loss of lovers – all contributing to the novel's poignant, understated lament about loss of faith in the old virtues of duty, decorum and repressed sexuality. *The Corn King and the Spring Queen* grippingly describes the brutality and the dignity of human experience, as in the execution of Philylla, a Spartan revolutionary, who straightens her skirt and folds her hands in order to die with propriety while those in a street mob laugh at the desperate grief of her comrades.

In league with D. H. Lawrence and T. S. Eliot, Naomi was fascinated by visions of primitive blood rituals of regeneration. Also, like many other modernists she was taken by the Russian revolution with its promise of a just world. However, Naomi is not counted among the paragons of modernist literature. She eschewed the language experimentation of the works of Virginia Woolf or James Joyce, and she wrote historical novels, a literary form seldom in academic favour. Naomi, in addition, was a feminist maverick during a literary period that was predominantly masculine; some ideologies of modernism adopted Frazer's anthropological theories which sanctified phallic worship and Freud's theories of the unconscious which sanctified the penis. Naomi could not bend to those ideas. In fact, her very intention of inventing a female hero forced her to ask what there was for her, for her woman hero, and for women in general in primitive king worship, in socialist revolution and in theories of the unconscious. These were dangerous questions with unwelcome answers at a time

1 Naomi's father, J. S. Haldane, inspecting a mine for his experiments in physiology.
(*Courtesy of Naomi Mitchison*)

2 Naomi and her brother, 'Boy', wading in tide pools at Sennen Cove.
(*Courtesy of Naomi Mitchison*)

3 Maya with Naomi and Jack.
(*Courtesy of Naomi Mitchison*)

4 Naomi with her Dragon School friends climbing a tree. (*Courtesy of Naomi Mitchison*)

5 Naomi with her mother, father and brother. (*Courtesy of Naomi Mitchison*)

6 Naomi Haldane. (*Courtesy of Naomi Mitchison*)

7 Naomi and Maya, her mother. (*Courtesy of Naomi Mitchison*)

8 Naomi, aged 14, and her brother Jack, who is Captain at Eton. (*Courtesy of Naomi Mitchison*)

9 Cast of *The Frogs* produced in 1914: Naomi, age 17, is seated on the grass directly in front of Lewis Gielgud, central in the chair as Dionysus. Frances Parkinson is directly to Naomi's left. In the back row standing from the left are: Aldous Huxley, bearded and wearing a hat; Naomi's brother Jack, swaddled as a corpse; and Gervas Huxley, with crossed arms. (*Courtesy of Naomi Mitchison*)

10 Naomi, aged 18, showing off her engagement ring, with her future husband, Dick Mitchison, a friend, and her brother during the First World War. (*Courtesy of Naomi Mitchison*)

11 Naomi in Greece in 1928 while she was writing *The Corn King and the Spring Queen*. (*Courtesy of Naomi Mitchison*)

12 Naomi in her twenties. (*Courtesy of Naomi Mitchison*)

when intellectuals were committed to androcentric theories in anthropology, psychology and politics.

The Corn King and the Spring Queen links all stages of Western history with the curve of female *Bildungsroman*. Women are not absent in history; they generate it. To Frazer Naomi says that women witches and magic are powerful cohesive agents networking all communities. To Freud she says that daughters develop psychologically by coming to terms with their mothers, not their fathers. To Marx she says that women have less to gain from a class revolution, having little to give away in the first place and being so similar to one another from class to class and culture to culture.

While Naomi Mitchison may have had all of cultural development in mind – that is, development stages that articulate the speculative ages between savagery and civilisation – she restricts the female hero, Erif Der, to the geographic boundaries of the decaying Hellenic world, a region bounded by Scythia on the north and Egypt on the south. As a wayfarer, Erif Der's mission is to find herself, be cleansed, in order, it turns out, to become conscious of herself in history and to return to her Scythian homeland, Marob, where she will enable her community to negotiate the shift from one stage of civilisation to the next.

Each region through which Erif Der travels is a stage in a progressivist vision of cultural development. Marob, her barbarian homeland on the fringes of Hellenic influence, is ordered by the worship of vegetable cycles, the growing of flax and corn; magic is key to this unselfconscious agricultural worship. Marob, however, is not the most primitive stage in human development. An earlier stage, the savage, is represented by the hunting and herding Red Riders, whose teeth are filed to carnivorous points, and who periodically ravage Marob. Between Marob and Sparta, Erif Der seeks help from the oracle at Delphi where she encounters the bureaucracy of organised religion before she receives her prophecy. Erif Der goes next to Sparta, the context of a later stage of cultural development, a community based on philosophy rather than magic or religion. Stoicism, with its notion of world harmony, enables the martial Spartans to enact a series of revolutions – revolutions that extend citizenship to helots, who are slaves, and equalise the rich and poor by property redistribution. Later, she is in Alexandria, a city marked by social artificiality and sexual extravagances. It is Naomi's view of her contemporary world. Her vision is sour and biting. The consumable ideologies of magic, superstition and philosophy welter there, none with sufficient force to galvanise the mass of people, whom Naomi presents as mindless followers.

Although the title of the book, *The Corn King and the Spring Queen*, would suggest that the story will be about the parallel adventures of King Tarrik and Erif Der, his queen, it is Erif Der's progress that dictates the thrust of narrative organisation. Tarrik crumbles under the pressure of cultural shock when he encounters Sparta; he returns to Marob where he remains for three-quarters of the novel. Erif, on the other hand, begins to change under the stress of a new culture. First, she binds herself in sisterhood with Philylla, representative and dutiful woman of the revolution; then she leaves her class position behind in order to merge with a community of helots. From there, the narrative travels with her to Egypt.

Erif Der changes from alienated individuality to conscious acceptance of her responsible role in her community of origin. Appropriately, her name read backwards becomes Red Fire, which is integrated reason and passion in the novel's image system. She is able to quest, as none of Naomi's previous heroines have been able to do, because she controls her body through the use of magic, using primitive forms of birth and mind control. Each geographical shift through spatialised history corresponds with a step in a woman's quest for self in community.

At first Erif is unconscious, fructifying nature itself, a successful and ritual spring queen:

> Then to the squealing of pipes he threw his hands up like a diver and all his body curved and shot down towards her. She did not feel his weight because of the tension in her own skin from head to heels. In the convention of the dance and in the solid noise of the drums the Corn opened the Furrow, broke into Spring, and started the year.[7]

In Marob as a girl-wife she confronts her first task: she must choose between her patriarchal family of origin and her patriarchal marriage, a losing situation. In either case her personal power, her magic as a witch, is threatened by male co-optation. Her ambivalent choice of Tarrik, her king-husband, leads to the political murder of her first son. Her baby's death initiates a series of unconscious events: Erif slashes her father's throat during a midsummer corn ritual, a violent act that the people of Marob fear will destroy the seasons; then she equates her husband and king with her father. She no longer can make herself perform as spring queen:

> It was Harn Der who would sweep aside the Corn King's rags and show himself, Harn Der who would plunge down on her, Harn Der who was the image of God and Man and her possessor and master!. . .[S]he

flung up her arms against the rhythm, and jumped clear out of it, off the booth, into the furrow ankle-deep. . .[8]

In this passage Naomi makes it amply clear that Erif Der is reacting to the phallus as an emblem of power, not of sex. Her husband is her father, God and master. Her psychological maturation depends on her rebellion against the political authority of patriarchy. Although she is liberated by rebellion, she is tabooed by her community, left existentially alone, ripe for questing into consciousness.

Exiled, Erif Der roams the Hellenic world accompanied by her brother Berris Der. He, an artist, embodies the powers of creative imagination; she, a witch, embodies the powers of magic and female fertility. For the sake of ego-integration, they must come together.

In Sparta first and in Egypt later, Erif Der completes her development. In order to participate in the Spartan corn ritual, she divests herself of her status as queen. She merges in promiscuous sexuality with slaves, the only class of people who invoke the vegetable deities in Sparta, a godless land. Later, in Egypt, Erif Der gives up her use of magic, at least the kind of magic she uses for merely personal ends. While worshipping the mother goddess, Isis, she unmagicks an old enemy, a character who embodies the sterility of civilised repression and is the censoring aspect of motherhood; by having her woman hero forgive a wicked mother-figure, Naomi frees her to greet a positive embodiment of mother, and in both instances has added a significant step to female questing, an important recognition that female autonomy hinges on a daughter's relationship with her mother and not her father. No sooner does Erif come to terms with her mother than she comes to terms with her brother. She absorbs what he has to offer by erotic merging:

He laughed and suddenly threw his arms round her waist and squashed her softly against him; the heat and excitement passed from his skin to her; her throat and breast and belly began to throb. . .She turned from her brother's arms into the arms of another faun.[9]

After rebellion against patriarchy, family and marriage (all provoked by the murder of her baby) and after abandoning class status and identity, learning to make love with whoever she chooses, forgiving her mother and merging with her brother, Erif Der is fit to become an actor on the stage of world history. She invigorates a new mystery religion that promises to inspire even decadent Alexandria and is a model for the unborn religion that will be Christianity.

Cleansed, Erif Der and her tag-along brother return to Marob where their personal fates go unreported. A narrative gap swallows Erif; she does not reappear; no character mentions her. This conclusion is a weakness in the artistic closure of the novel. Naomi cannot begin to imagine how an autonomous woman would behave in a culture not prepared to offer her scope for action. Who could?

Hope for women was still in the future during the third century BC, as it was in the 1930s. Naomi ends her novel weakly with an improbable future representation in which women witches, but not Erif Der, are both fertile and artistically creative, autonomous and untrammelled. At the very least Naomi had her marching orders; she had more life to experience before she could write about the next stage of action for women who have achieved selfhood.

Because Naomi was situated at the political crossroads of socialism and feminism, because she was an intellectual and a gifted artist, because she was profoundly tuned to her personal experience – to the death of her child and abandonment in matters of the heart – her version of women's history represented in *The Corn King and the Spring Queen* is wide-sweeping, compelling and passionate.

The Corn King and the Spring Queen was an enormous literary success. It stunned reviewers because of its ambitious historical vision. Naomi's intellectual history – that gleaned from Plutarch, Polybius, Pausanias, Epicurus, among many others – was accurately presented. Nevertheless, it requires sleight of hand to reinterpret history to include women. She did it by emphasis, selecting particular events and characters to body forth, dampening others into shadow; she placed women in light. *The Corn King and the Spring Queen* received rave reviews. All praised its erudition; some, like the editor of the *Saturday Review of Literature*, Henry Seidel Canby, recognised Naomi's powerful imagination and intellect:

> In spite of her fine imagination, she writes often as a social historian (though never dully), and that is why I speak of her work not as pure fiction but as a reflection of a powerful intellectual interest sprung of a new and more scientific knowledge of the past.

Hugh Gordon Proteus, in the *New Statesman and Nation*, appreciated her writing style:

> Her descriptions of ritual and magic are superb; no less lovely are her accounts of simple, natural things – water-crowfoot flowers, marigolds and bright-spotted fish. To read her is like looking down into deep

warm water, through which the smallest pebble and the most radiant weed shine and are seen most clearly; for her writing is very intimate, almost as a diary, or an autobiography is intimate, yet it is free from all pose, all straining after effect; she is telling a story so that all may understand, yet it has the still profundity of a nursery rhyme.

Winifred Holtby in *The Bookman* listed six most important novels published in 1931, with *The Corn King and the Spring Queen* triumphing over all, including Virginia Woolf's *The Waves*. *The Corn King and the Spring Queen* was simply 'a great English novel', full of qualities of integrity and wisdom.

However, something was off about these reader reactions on both sides of the Atlantic. Alarmingly from our present point of view and hindsight, reviewers were unable to see that *The Corn King and the Spring Queen* was about more than a king. They focused in glowing terms on Tarrik and screened out Erif Der, relegating her to shadow. Reviewers, mainly men, saw only the masculine elements of the novel and were blind to 'Red Fire's' quest for psychological wholeness and historical adventuring.

As Naomi was becoming more openly feminist, silence about her barbarian queen who lived 2,000 years ago should have alerted her to danger ahead; she was transgressing acceptable limits of fantasised behaviour for women. However, Naomi did not notice that Erif Der was ignored because she was unspeakable; nor would Naomi have altered her thinking and writing one jot if she had.

6

Feminist and Socialist 1928–1932

Naomi sloughed off early patterns of thought about love, possibilities for women and class privilege. She was becoming a public person who was both novelist and woman of letters, a forceful intellectual unafraid to speak and write her mind.

She spoke about women's issues, birth-control and sex; then, as conditions for living degenerated in England during economic collapse and working-class turmoil, she spoke about poverty and socialism. However, her public synthesis of feminism and socialism in the 1930s ran counter to other historical currents, rip-tides carrying women back into the family and home. Naomi's story testifies to the commitment of some post-suffrage women intellectuals as they worked to dismantle cultural and social structures of patriarchy; it also demonstrates the power of backlash against their endeavours. Feminism and socialism did not mix in 1930s' England.

The feminist period of Naomi's life began in the late 1920s, overlapping her writing of *The Corn King and the Spring Queen*, and it lasted until the mid-1930s, when she reframed the woman issue to comply with her changing concerns. Her feminism never completely disappeared, although in later life she would come to disavow the label of 'feminist' itself; nevertheless, the idea of women's autonomy was a foundation upon which she built many of the central constructs of her long life.

In 1928 she shot her opening public salvo, publishing several letters to the editor of *Time and Tide*. Her first letter asserted that women of all classes should have the opportunity to use birth-control if they wished. Male readers heatedly retaliated in letters to the editor: some claimed that doctors could not be found who would advocate birth-control; others asserted that modern women were simply sex-crazed. Naomi's response did not turn from controversy:

> As to this business of our being an over-sexed generation. . .Love is a subject of profound interest to all men and women between twenty-five and forty-five, and always has been. But it is only lately that they have had the courage to write to the papers about it! Different aspects have interested different generations; the facts have been variously disguised. One of the things that interests our generation most is the tenderness, the bodily awareness, the opposite of that hardening of the spirit that had to happen to us during the war; this awareness can be made plain, though it is often not, in honest, thorough, physical love between man and woman.[1]

This run of letters brought Naomi to the attention of the editors of *Time and Tide*. Soon she was a regular contributor of short stories, poems, essays and book reviews; she became the main reviewer for novels written in French. From 1928 to mid-1933 Naomi published consistently in *Time and Tide*. Well known in its day, *Time and Tide* was owned and edited by Lady Rhondda; its editorial intention was to sponsor women intellectuals who wrote about international politics and literature. It published writing by Lady Rhondda, Cecily Hamilton, Winifred Holtby and Naomi Mitchison side-by-side with Wyndham Lewis, T. S. Eliot, Gerald Heard and George Bernard Shaw, among many others. As long as *Time and Tide* was run by Lady Rhondda, it was a first-rate highbrow periodical, advocating a form of equal rights feminism. In it Naomi displayed her intellectual breadth; she wrote lengthy essays about works by Gerald Heard, Wyndham Lewis, Sigmund Freud and D. H. Lawrence, amongst shorter reviews about other works.

As a political movement, feminism in general began fragmenting in the 1920s; it had lost its unifying, single purpose, which had been the attainment of voting rights for women. After attaining these rights, women moved to scattered areas of concern. Some women turned to improving women's working conditions, some to welfare reform, others to women's education, and yet others to writing and publishing, as did those who contributed to *Time and Tide*. By the time Naomi began to write for *Time and Tide*, many feminists of her generation, including herself, were no longer committed to organised political action. Naomi thought the battle had shifted from the public to the private sphere, as she wrote in

1930: 'Apparently, all the feminist battles are gained, or almost all. Actually nothing is settled, and the question of baby or not baby is at the bottom of almost everything'.[2]

While Naomi was heatedly arguing for sexual freedom and birth-control in *Time and Tide*, she was lecturing on the public platform for the World Sexual Reform League. In 1929, Norman Haire, the famous sexologist, organised a Sexual Reform Congress where literati such as Desmond McCarthy spoke about the censorship of literature and Vera Brittain about the failure of monogamy. Naomi spoke about birth-control, ending her speech enigmatically:

> I would look forward, rather, to a time when people's sensitiveness and awareness is raised to such a pitch that every man or woman shall lie with the lover that is loved best at such times as desire is at its height, and between these fires practise an unusual and excessive chastity, not allowing such a thing as a man to enter their love life. During these periods of chastity their powers would go to other ends, they would work with complete and unswerving forces. And in this time that I look to there shall be no laws nor customs nor evil tongues to stop any pair of lovers from making the child they dream of.[3]

Naomi's concluding remarks about sexual liaisons should be understood in their political and social context. One scholar has noted that the majority of speeches at this congress were devoted to establishing heterosexual hegemony.[4] It was a sign of an ideological backlash against feminist autonomy; women were being urged to abandon separatist ideologies in favour of marriage or 'free-love' with men. Whatever the expectations of any group, one could rely on Naomi to puncture assumptions with which she disagreed. In this case, Naomi did not fully recognise the League's implicit agenda nor the anti-feminist mood spreading throughout England. Almost nobody did at the time. Nevertheless, in her speech she rubbed against the heterosexual grain by advocating chastity when passion was lacking; she also implied that women might choose to love whom they wished, perhaps even each other. No individual man, she suggested, should interfere with art and the generation of children conceived in passion.

Naomi's speech, with its hope for children born outside of restrictive patriarchal codes, became the basis in 1930 of a long essay for Faber and Faber's *Criterion Miscellany*, a series of sociological tracts published in the form of small, hardcover books. In this printed version, Naomi dropped the passage cited above. Her intended audience was what she called the professional class of women, by which she meant educated women who might wish to pursue careers. Although the tone of 'Comments on Birth-Control' was of reasoning common-sense, many of Naomi's ideas were radical. Low-keyed irony would always be one of her favourite literary devices. For women who are dependent on their husbands, she advocated accepting 'domestic prostitution'. She envisioned contraception as a mere stop-gap measure; she imagined that in the future women would control procreation by exercising a higher form of consciousness, a process of mind over matter; she advocated expanding the nuclear family to include sexual mates who would nurture both tired working husbands and their professionally busy wives. The style was droll, the intent, serious.

Behind these public statements was Naomi's hard thinking about women in culture. A typed page of notes buried in a Texas archive opens a small window into Naomi's private discussions with her intimate friends. Attached to a manuscript copy of an essay entitled 'Breaking Up the Home' when it was finally published in a magazine called *Twentieth Century* in 1932, these notes record her conversations about the issue of women; in parentheses after each statement she tells with whom she was conversing. When she suggested to Dick that 'the best women are better than the best men', he replied, 'pure romanticism – try again'. In another conversation she observed that the Western attitude toward women needed 'exploration'. With Wade Gery, Bronislaw Malinowski and Margery Spring Rice she decided that there must be 'some way of assuaging the almost universal feeling among women that they would rather have been men and certainly that they are getting the worse out of life'. In the same conversation she asserted that she wanted to reaffirm the 'she-values', by which she especially meant 'the physical values, which have been lost and laughed at – laughed at by men so that civilised women have ceased to believe in their value'. Typically, Naomi turned on her own assertion, it being her habit to be of two or more minds about almost every subject. She contradicted: 'It seems a bit of a tory policy!'[5]

During the approximate time that these conversations took place, Naomi bewails in a letter to Stella Benson her progress writing a book about feminism for which she had been gathering information:

Goodness knows if I shall ever get it written because I want it to be history and philosophy and political discussion and that may be more than I can do. But I don't want to write another novel for a long time, if ever again. I get more and more interested in events and I am quite sure that the feminist position wants to be restated every few years. There are a whole lot of new problems since the last statement which must be dealt with. . .[6]

Naomi began to write but did not finish her book on feminism. Two chapters plus a detailed outline are among the Haldane papers in archives at the National Library of Scotland in Edinburgh. Her book on feminism begins:

If one is in this curious position of being a woman, one cannot unquestioningly accept the ordinary historical point of view about the values of civilisation. Why not? Because up to the last few years all historians have been men. In some branches of knowledge it does not appear to make any difference whether men or women practise the search for truth. The most bigoted feminist would not mistrust the findings of a pure mathematician who happened to be a man, nor, I think, would even an Englishman mistrust the findings of a pure mathematician who happened to be a woman, though I am less certain of this. But the nearer we get to the human side of truth and especially to art, which is intensely human – a Sabbath made for men – the more we find that the sex of the seeker or researcher or writer makes a great difference to the result. On a given problem in physics or chemistry, a man or woman of equal ability would give the same answer, but take the same type of problem in architecture or biology – the answer might be different. In medicine or history or sculpture – the answer would almost certainly be different. And so far we have only the man's view of civilisation and the trend of human thought and culture.[7]

Naomi was moving intellectually to new territory. Now she clearly perceived the restraints androcentric views placed on all forms of thinking about human values. As a cultural impulse on the part of women in general, this kind of analysis withered, not to flower again until women scholars – in the 1950s, through to the 1970s and 1980s – began to reinterpret Western history and thought.

The project of analysing all culture from a woman's point of view seemed to overwhelm Naomi and in some of its implications to frighten her. In fact, to write a book of the scope that she envisioned would have required an army of scholars plus another fifty years of education and training. The time was not ripe; as the complicated politics of the 1930s took hold, the time was blighting to the spirit of feminism.

The outline that remains of Naomi's projected book on feminism divided the subject into three parts: part one proposed to analyse the historical present, including a statistical account of women in capitalism, an analysis of fiction (especially that of D. H. Lawrence), and an attack on the representation of women in pornography; part two proposed to describe biological and historical possibilities for women, including a final description of the then feminist movement as it was represented by the 'bourgeoise value' of Virginia Woolf's *A Room of One's Own*; part three envisioned solutions such as more self-control based on biological and environmental transformations. Naomi ended part three of her outline with an extensive list of immediate political actions: she advocated, for instance, boycotting consumer products aimed at keeping women in their place, the home.

Naomi had made a radical statement of feminist ideology in the privacy of her unpublished manuscript. She stopped writing when she felt her feet turn cold, and they turned cold when she began to connect Christianity with the oppression of women. Of Christianity she wrote:

> This is all perhaps too controversial to go into now, though I should like to work out what seems to me to be the gradual debasement and oppression of women, from about the third century AD to the nineteenth – and even the twentieth century.[8]

Naomi sensed that her historical survey of the status of women – coupled with an analysis of masculine history, philosophy and politics – would bring her into conflict with the Established Church. She stopped working on the book but not on the intellectual inquiry and discourse regarding women's issues that had been raised in her mind.

The Corn King and the Spring Queen was published in the spring of 1931; its wide success fixed Naomi in the public eye. In the same year she carried her polemic about birth-control into the national press. She was especially outspoken about the current Encyclicals of the Catholic Church which reaffirmed the nuclear family; letters to the editors of newspapers from all corners of England attacked her, some by associating her stand on birth-control with communism:

> Mrs. Mitchison tells us that she and her friends are about to cease to be tolerant, but she does not tell us on what lines they propose to proceed. Of course, according to the principles she lays down, if

anyone gets in your way, and prevents you doing exactly as you like, you are at perfect liberty to remove him forcibly from this world. This is the Russian method. In the Middle Ages, if Mrs. Mitchison had published the article under discussion, she would have certainly met an unpleasant end at the hands of the State. . .As Mrs. Mitchison does not apparently believe she has a soul or a hereafter, let her go right and ahead, and 'wait and see'.[9]

Naomi responded to this letter from a Catholic Rector; she pointed out that the Catholic Church, not being able to burn her as it once had burned witches, proposed simply to send her to hell.

In *Twentieth Century* in her essay entitled 'Breaking Up the Home', Naomi suggested that women, who have started doing the same demanding professional jobs as men, also need someone to replenish them at home. She wrote that D. H. Lawrence's idea of The Couple no longer fits the needs of the modern home, and that, just perhaps, The Couple must expand into a Group. She concluded:

But I can imagine a communist society – but perhaps I had better not talk about that. It was after all, the peasant women rather than the peasant men who so liked the idea of communal farms under the Plan, who so cheerfully forsook the traditions that women are supposed to like so much. I am afraid women are rather dangerous people. I am afraid they are responsible for the cracks in the plaster of the home. I had better not say anything more about it.[10]

Naomi agreed with her detractors: women, potentially, are culturally dangerous people.

Together with Margery, Widg and Dick, Naomi had already attempted, and failed, to fashion her family into an extrafamilial group. Naomi and Dick finally settled on something that looked more like a conventional extended family than it did an exotic new kind of community. Their family extended to include Maya and Uffer, Naomi's parents, who took over the caretaking of Dennis in the year after Geoff died and then a year later, Murdoch. The boys were attending Dragon School in Oxford as day-students living with their grandparents at Cherwell.

In London during the late 1920s and early 1930s Naomi again settled in for a round of pregnancy and lactation. She remembers reading novels by John Dos Passos and Winifred Holtby while feeding Avrion and Valentine. In *We Have Been Warned* Naomi described her heroine's ambivalent reaction to yet another pregnancy, her decision to have an abortion overturned by an up-welling desire for another baby. In her private copy of this novel Naomi has pencilled in the margin that this passage describes her reaction to being pregnant with Val.

Naomi continued to organise portions of her life around the young children at home despite her prolific writing and marital independence. Lois remained a senior citizen of the nursery until 1933 when she left home at the age of 8 for progressive St Christopher's on her way eventually to Badminton. One of Av's first memories is of fairies on rope pulleys, the stage effects accompanying a play, *Kate Crackernuts*, Naomi wrote for her children to perform with the children of friends; Livia Gollancz, the daughter of Victor Gollancz, warmly remembered play-acting as a child with the Mitchison children, and she also remembered big, jolly birthday parties.

After Geoff's death, Naomi's relationship with her parents, particularly her mother, became increasingly tense and distant. They mourned differently. Naomi hid all reminders of Geoff, any of which would open afresh the wounds of his passing, an agony which she would endure throughout her life into old age. Maya, on the other hand, kept photos of her first grandson displayed on sitting-room tables.

While sending her sons to her mother's care, Naomi was herself trying hard to separate from her mother. Ostensibly the language of disagreement was political, her Left politics taking her further and further from her mother's Tory embrace. In the letters folded in packets in her drawer, however, she confessed to her friend John Pilley that what she feared most was becoming like her mother as she became politically committed to socialism. Uffer told Naomi she was becoming just like Maya. Naomi quailed at the thought. She went on to write that she feared political passion would distance her from real relationships with people as she believed it had distanced her mother. Nevertheless, Naomi's separation from Maya was difficult and guilty:

> I think I simply must go down to Oxford this Sunday. I felt very guilty coming away last time, after a real row with my mother; I ought to be able to manage that, I ought to be able to feel contact with her too. It was like hurting someone defenceless, I must try to make it up.[11]

Both Denny and Murdoch remember their grandmother with grateful affection. They experienced Maya as a warm, attentive and tactful grandmother, who gave motherly care, reading long hours to each of them every day, as she had with Jack and Naomi. They recall Uffer as much more remote, a figure who emerged occasionally from his study where he was refining his philosophical views. When he came out, he brought with him the magic of science – memorable multicoloured light shows in the pitch black, for instance, when he was doing work on perception. Although Uffer no longer maintained a working laboratory, its rubber tubes now cracking and breaking, dust gathering on flasks, he kept some apparatus in place for boy-experiments, for concoctions and glass blowing. Uffer's three grandsons became scientists.

In the 1930s Naomi took her children to Cloan at least once every year, usually when Uffer was there. In the late 1920s Granniema – transparent, bed-ridden, alert – had died after celebrating her 100th birthday. Soon thereafter Uncle Richard died. Aunt Bay continued to welcome visitors at Cloan, Naomi finding it less formal than she had in Granniema's day. Naomi roamed the glens with her young sons and more slowly with Uffer, who was now suffering from sciatica and lumbago.

Naomi, Dick and the children took family holidays in Scotland at Craignish in Argyll. Dick and Naomi invited friends to join them wherever they went. Margaret Cole recalled that Dick and Naomi introduced her and Douglas to the 'baronial' style of life, for which she remembered their generosity, nostalgically reminiscing about holidays the Mitchisons regularly organised in Scottish castles. She can recall Hugh Gaitskell enjoying 'very much the talk and miscellaneous collection of "radicals" of all kinds and occupations that gathered there – even if he did once write indignantly to me, "I *will not* be a character in one of Naomi's novels" '.[12] Douglas Cole and Elizabeth (Harman) Longford were with Naomi on one occasion when, angry with puckish Hugh Gaitskell, she threw a half-plucked partridge at him, knowing full well that he detested blood and birds. In the lore of the group it was said that Naomi was infatuated with Hugh. Of Hugh, on her part, Naomi wrote in *You May Well Ask* that they had had an 'unfortunate flirtation and had left one another angrily'.[13] Perhaps she is also referring to Hugh when she remembers that 'there was a curious tripartite mini-affair involving Douglas Cole, me and a rising young Labour politician, unsatisfactory for all of us'.[14]

While the family continued to be a consuming experience in Naomi's life, she began from 1930 onward to travel extensively without husband or children.

After Val was born in 1930 and as she was ending her affair with Widg, Naomi took a walking tour of Sweden by herself, where she sought the remote home of Selma Lagerlöf, an older woman writer:

> I was suffering from emotional wounds and had to get rid of them. So I went on to Sweden and walked for whole days on roads between snowbanks and called on Selma Lagerlöf whose books I had enjoyed so much. She had a beautiful wreath of evergreens on her door and must have been rather surprised at her walking admirer with thick shoes and rucksack.[15]

Selma Lagerlöf was a Swedish feminist and pacifist who had been awarded the Nobel Prize for Literature in 1909. Her *Ring of the Lowenskolds* trilogy had invoked folk themes about peasant life. The evergreens on her door, symbols of regeneration and continuing life, would have comforted Naomi.

With her artist friend Agnes Miller Parker, who was married – in wifely martyrdom, from Naomi's point of view – to another artist, William McCance, she travelled by ocean liner to the Canary Islands, coming back by herself through Morocco, where nightly she shoved a protective bureau against her hotel-room door.

Alone, she went to Paris in 1931 where she met Lewis Gielgud. They wrote a play together, resuscitating the giddy pleasure of their adolescence in Oxford. They worked hard and laughed a lot, producing *The Price of Freedom*. After working to exhaustion each night, they would adjourn to a café or Chez Louise where she remembers occasionally dancing with 'lesbian prostitutes', in Naomi's words.

It was a time of journey and self-searching for Dick as well as Naomi. In his letters to her from South Africa in 1930, Dick yearns to find meaningful purpose in his life and expresses anxiety about pleasing Margaret and Douglas Cole – both socialists – with whom he has discovered hope. Dick is not yet certain he is a socialist; he 'thinks' he is. He asks Naomi if she is. As the 1920s tipped into the 1930s and economic hard times, Dick and Naomi began increasingly to discuss whether or not they would be socialist in addition to being Labour. Commitment to socialism meant embracing ideologies downplaying individuals in favour of collective well-being and it meant, as well, adopting an egalitarian ethos.

In 1931 Douglas Cole, discovering he had diabetes, asked Dick Mitchison to take his place standing for Parliament in King's Norton in Birmingham. Dick accepted Cole's invitation. However, he lost the election, the political tide washing parties from the Left, both Labour and Liberal, out of power in favour of the Conservative national government.

Naomi was less certain of her socialism than Dick. Before she could make up her mind she needed more personal contact with working people – which she got in Birmingham trying to get Dick elected. Particularly influential was Dick's political agent, Tom Baxter, who spent long hours describing the difficulties of growing up working-class. Naomi struggled alongside Dick, gathering impressions of politics and life which she was recording in a daily journal, exhilarated by the work and the community of workers. She found she liked the people she met in King's Norton.

Nevertheless, Naomi still had to settle for herself what socialism meant. Tom Baxter was committed to socialism by class and experience. Along with his intellectual commitment, Dick's political ambition was his motivation. In 1931 he joined the Coles in organising the Society for Socialist Inquiry and Propaganda (SSIP), then in bringing the New Fabian Research Bureau (NFRB) and its *Quarterly* into existence. Dick and the Coles intended the NFRB to give theoretical direction in the 1930s to the routed Labour Party. It was a small but effective force within the Labour movement, having by 1938 published over forty pamphlets which presented fresh ideas for scrutiny and discussion, and it was a socialist think-tank, a crucial force in British history. However, Naomi was not a significant figure in this group; she often played truant.

Naomi and Dick attended weekend political workshops held by Fabian and non-Fabian socialists in Lady Warwick's vast and rambling Easton Lodge, now demolished but memorable in Labour history. The SSIP, largely owing to Margaret Cole's tenacity, took shape in these surroundings. Ernest Bevin was chairman of its executive committee, Margaret was secretary and Dick was treasurer. While these committed people – together with Douglas Cole, George Lansbury, Clement Attlee, Stafford Cripps, Hugh Gaitskell, among others – hammered out policies that would shape British socialism in the twentieth century, Naomi spent her time swimming in the great lily pond, grateful that Margaret was sympathetic and refrained from scolding her.

In her bones Naomi was a writer of fiction, not a politician, political propagandist, or organiser. Still, she could be a politician's wife if need be.

All the while, stewing in doubt, Naomi helped Dick's campaign in King's Norton; she canvassed; she spoke at meetings; she stood at his side, a conventional wife – wearing her wedding ring again. Her experiences as the wife of a candidate, first recorded in a diary, found their way into *We Have Been Warned* in vivid descriptions of electioneering in the 1930s:

> The Council estates were well planned and looked prosperous; people prided themselves on keeping up appearances. But inside, behind the white curtains, there was abominable poverty. It was worse in the Carisbrook Road district, or at least it looked much worse. She paid a visit to ex-Councillor Finch's elder daughter Dorothy, who was married and living down there – and on the Means Test. She was a jolly, intelligent girl, with a young baby. When Dione came in she apologised for the smell – Dione had always hoped you didn't notice it if you lived there – saying it usedn't to be so bad, but they'd had to sell the lino off the floors and now there was nothing but the bare quarries, much worn from earlier tenants. 'I scrub and scrub,' the girl said, 'but I can't seem to get the smell away. The suds go down the cracks between the quarries, Mrs. Galton; they aren't properly mortared in, and there isn't any foundations, like. And there's always a draught under the door, and they're that cold to walk on. And now there's the beetles.'[16]

Here and throughout *We Have Been Warned*, Naomi attempts the complicated task of describing working-class life from the vantage point of the upper classes. She was trying to write about the contradictions inherent in British socialism as it was lived by herself and those around her. She felt anguish: 'Oh god, John, it is pretty uncomfortable, this business of being thumbed down into clay in the vague hope one may be remade into something different'.[17]

Enter John Pilley. He was a teacher at Bristol University and a communist. With Pilley, Naomi evolved her philosophy of political and sexual conduct. In long, closely typed, hard-working letters, Naomi resisted what she called his sectarianism, although his Marxist materialism made sense to a certain point. She sought a middle road between communism and individualism, a route for individuals to act within community. With Pilley's help, she came to believe that as a socialist gesture she should share her body sexually with others, non-possessive of them, non-possessive of self. She records detached pleasure with Pilley, writing 'The Bonny Brae', a strong, incantatory, generational poem, to commemorate their connection:

> Others have made this nest before us,
> The bonny brae, the brackenny hollow;
> We join the sweet invisible chorus
> To all good couples that ever follow.
>
> This is the dear, the human flesh,
> Over bone and muscle the berry-brown skin.
> The four-eyed vision is bright and nesh,
> The touch is certain of lips and chin.
> Take it for what it is, oh take it
> As sweet and mortal, nor ever make it
> Into god or goddess that cannot bear it,
> This weight of worship. But take and share it
> With us who have passed or with us who follow,
> Who have bent the bracken and filled the hollow
> With our human voices our pulses human.
> Oh friend, oh comrade, oh man to me woman,
> This is the thing that goes on for ever,
> This is the good we dare not sever
> From couples that follow or came before us,
> The earth-sweet chorus that fills the hollow.[18]

Naomi has pencilled John Pilley's name on her typed manuscript to this poem, the original of which is preserved in one of her desk drawers in Scotland. From Pilley, Naomi learnt that she could be sexually kind to men whom she did not love – to 'party' as he called it. She lived her sexual altruism, putting it immediately into practice on her trip to Russia, writing to both Dick and Pilley of her adventure helping one of her travel companions gain confidence in himself, doffing his repressions in the name of good health. Her travel companion wrote Naomi a thank you note for her kindness.

Naomi met John Pilley in 1931 when she was putting together a group of essays about the state of the sciences and humanities written for children by left-leaning thinkers. Victor Gollancz published *An Outline for Boys and Girls and their Parents* in 1932. The essays were written by members of Naomi's close coterie of friends: Dick, Gerald Heard, John Pilley, Margaret Cole, Hugh Gaitskell, Olaf Stapledon and the young W. H. Auden, among others. It was largely a standard statement of liberal thinking; but it also included essays that questioned conventional ideas about the nuclear family.

For instance, one contributor wrote: 'Marriage laws and the unequal treatment of women are therefore only likely to disappear if and when we devise other means of bringing up children which will do the job as well as the family does'.[19] It was then pointed out that Russia under Communist leadership had initiated a system of childcare centres, a model for other countries.

The firestorm that ensued was ferocious, effectively warding off the large audience Naomi needed to provide commission payments for her contributors. An open letter to the press published on 6 October 1932 denounced *An Outline*. It was signed by one Archbishop, two Bishops, the Headmasters of Eton and Harrow, and fourteen other prominent men. They attacked *An Outline* on the grounds that it left out reference to Christ and that it approved the break-up of the traditional family. Apparently the essay describing Soviet crèches and kindergartens had been interpreted by the letter-writers to mean that 'it was possible to remove the rule that a mother and father must go on living together'.[20] In the fray, many leapt to Naomi's defence: Victor Gollancz, George Bernard Shaw, Norman Haire, Harold Laski, Rebecca West, Dora Russell, C. E. M. Joad and especially Lady Rhondda.

Lady Rhondda wrote an essay for *Time and Tide* in which she analysed the religious backlash represented by the open letter to the press. She pointed out that the letter purported to speak for organised Christianity, and yet not a single woman's signature had been included. The issue about omitting mention of Christ in *An Outline*, she went on, was a strategy to mask the real intention of the Church, which in her view was an attempt to 'bracket atheism, anti-theism and the destruction of the family'. These gentlemen, she asserted, were not speaking for Christianity; they were speaking for the threatened patriarchy.[21]

Attack on *An Outline* killed it in the market-place. To Naomi's disappointment it was never published in the United States. Nevertheless, by looking at the debate we may chart the drift of two cultural currents in the early 1930s. One flow, the thinking of women intellectuals, continued but with less and less force. Literary women, at least those who wrote for *Time and Tide* throughout the mid-1930s – women such as Lady Rhondda and Naomi – continued to speak out against patriarchal values. But a flow against thinking women was becoming floodwater; feminist issues became associated in the public mind with communism, a dangerous association in the polarised political situation in England during the 1930s, especially since official socialism in the Labour Party and official communism

83

had both disavowed interest in women's issues. No conventional political organisation backed feminism.

Nevertheless, Naomi studiously practised her socialism, still believing that some version of it was women's best political hope. In 1932 she travelled with a Fabian Society expedition to Russia. Dick joined one group along with Margaret Cole; Naomi participated in another which included her cousin Graeme Haldane, whom she admired and envied because 'he has been among the workers; he has been in danger, and doing things with his hands. He's a craftsman'.[22] The Russian expedition's leading figure was the serious-minded Beatrice Webb, to whom Naomi, flustered and also wanting to seem serious-minded, said she wished to observe Russian abortions and archaeology. After the Revolution in 1917, abortion had been legalised in Russia, as it was nowhere else in the Western world. The archaeology that Naomi had in mind were the objects being collected from the Scythian digs around the Black Sea. She wrote an essay about Russian archaeology which was collected with essays by Douglas, Dick and Graeme in a volume, *Twelve Studies in Soviet Russia*, published by the NFRB.

The abortion she witnessed shocked her. Naomi described it in *We Have Been Warned* where it became one of the passages her publishers wanted censored. True, the Russian government sanctioned abortion, but the abortion she observed happened also to be performed without anaesthetic. Naomi concluded that the lot of women in this regard had not changed appreciably under the Communist regime. However, in other ways Naomi was delighted with what she observed in Russia and much of her delight flows into *We Have Been Warned*. Although she noted that equality for women in Russia meant double labour, the workplace labour and labour in the home, everywhere she looked she saw positive signs for women: they seemed more sexually independent; they could hold jobs in respected professions; their children were cared for in crèches and kindergartens. Unlike even the egalitarian Labour Party in England, official government policy in Russia legitimised women's issues.

This was early in the 1930s, we might remember, and Russian reform was a beacon for reform-minded British. Much of the admiration would be tarnished by the end of the decade, and Naomi would be among the first from the Left to speak out in distress. Even in 1932 she had her doubts about communist Russia:

Some times it seemed to her that the whole place was like one vast school, all becoming more and more imbued with that public school spirit which all sensible women are up against: here was the house spirit, government by public opinion and if necessary public chastisement, the dear old O. T. C. very much to the fore, and Stalin between head-boy and head-master![23]

Nevertheless, by 1932 Naomi was committing herself to socialism both publicly and privately. Elizabeth Longford asserts that not only Dick but Naomi created 'a strong sense of idealism in the party'. She remembers the strong devotion they aroused in their constituency.[24] Privately, Naomi's conclusions about the future of socialism were hard-headed and even prescient:

> I am afraid Russia is more of an experiment than you think or that, perhaps, it should be. I am afraid that there is quite a chance that they will not succeed (on their agricultural policy, chiefly). I do believe that in time capitalism will give way to socialism of some kind, yet it may not be a kind that we would care for or recognise, either of us. If I did not think that socialism would come ultimately I would eat, drink and be merry. But I do not think it likely that it will conceivably be the same here and in Russia.[25]

By the time she wrote *You May Well Ask* Naomi had witnessed forty or more years of revolution and counter-revolution. With the help of hindsight she could observe that her 1930s' conception of socialism, deeply influenced by William Morris, was romantic. She reported that she believed then, along with many others of her generation, that economic liberation would bring other liberations. However, in the 1970s Naomi writes that she never really believed that a socialist society would mean a complete destruction of the values and habits of the life to which she had become accustomed. Never was political change envisioned 'as a boring redistribution, not only of wealth but of other standards'.[26] For Naomi, socialism was an ethical ideal, not an actual goal.

7
Censored
1933–1935

During the months following her return from Russia, late in the autumn of 1932, Naomi met with H. T. Wade Gery. As she described it in a letter to John Pilley, her rendezvous with Widg began their second entanglement. For Widg the tangles were more passionate than ever, albeit more clandestine. To Naomi's expressed consternation, this time Widg decided not to tell his wife. On her side, Naomi could not imagine keeping anything from Dick. In letters to Widg Naomi was stern: although she was 'extremely fond' of him, he had to know that she was through with adolescent intensity and that she absolutely was not in love with him, or with anyone else for that matter. Until the middle of 1934, Naomi and Widg were again 'entangled', her word for intimacy of minds, hearts and bodies. This phase of entanglement took place during a time of continuing malaise in Naomi's life.

Besides being front person for the brutal public attacks on *An Outline*, Naomi's health was bad and continued to be a problem through a debilitating struggle in 1933 to keep her novel *We Have Been Warned* from being chopped to pieces by publishers. In a letter to Julian Huxley, Naomi thought she was suffering from some sort of depression, but she could not be certain:

> I've been rather immersed in these curious local Birmingham politics, making friends with working women and speaking at meetings and that kind of thing. Now I have suddenly decided that I am not at all well; the machine has been breaking down in various places, ending with this filthy business of not sleeping. I went to Obermer, the endocrine man, who proposes to stick enormous doses of pituitary into me, tells me that at my present rate I haven't long to live, and is generally a bully. I like him, though, and think his treatment may perhaps break the circle of mental-physical breakdown I seem to have got into.[1]

The treatment did not help. Naomi's malady remained undiagnosed for its duration, which was off and on for the next two years.

Besides her political work in Birmingham where she was also developing her lifelong friendship with Tom and Bettie Baxter, Naomi was living her busy social and familial life in London:

> Hammersmith was presumably thought in other circles to be very *avant-garde* and we had a good share of love and hate affairs, rushing in and out of one another's lives, having parties and from time to time swimming in the Thames which was surely much dirtier then than now.[2]

The Boat Race Parties continued as annual rituals; dozens of people, sometimes as many as 250, crowded on to the River Court roof to hang over the balustrade cheering the racers. At one, Wyndham Lewis silently listened first to one group and then another. He took his leave abruptly – without having said a word, without even having removed his black hat, without saying goodbye. He was cultivating his reputation as 'The Outsider'.

Motherhood was weighing heavily on Naomi. She was 36 years old and had been at it for seventeen years; with Av, 5, and Val, only 3, she could look forward to another decade of mother-work. Schools had to be found for the older boys. Although both had been registered at Eton when they were born, it no longer seemed a suitable place in the estimation of Naomi and Dick, whose educational leanings now were considerably more progressive. However, for people such as the Mitchisons, who had stepped off the accepted path for success in their class, choosing schools was an ordeal barely alleviated by some fun Naomi had shocking headmasters with her questions – a game of *épater le bourgeois*. Naomi often asked John Pilley for advice. Finally, she and Dick settled on Abbotsholm in northern England for Dennis, finding it less highbrow than Dartington. Winchester College was selected for Murdoch. Lois was at St Christopher's. Av and Val were at home attending elementary schools in London, Val warmly remembering an afternoon on which her mother picked her up from school, a new puppy nestled in her lap as she sat behind the wheel.

Dick and Naomi went on a walking holiday on the Continent with Dennis and Murdoch. Another time, Naomi cancelled her plans for a holiday with the children in Norway; Murdoch was sick. She complained:

> At present I'm having a good typical English holiday. Having come down for the sake of Murdoch getting sea air; now Denny is in

bed with a bad cough & temperature & I am dithering about with
a mild cough & temperature. . .I do envy men who can sometimes
have clear time to work without the ceaseless & intolerable burden
of responsibility. It must be nice being in love with women of 21;
they haven't had to carry the burden till they're all scarred with
it.[3]

Meanwhile, as 1933 wore on, Naomi and John Pilley found
themselves at odds. From their letters it appears that Naomi felt
she had intellectually outgrown him. Pilley, now married, terminated his liaison with Naomi, giving her conventional monogamous
reasons for the break – but not before securing an introduction to
Wyndham Lewis. Naomi and Pilley continued to exchange long,
philosophical letters, and he was a welcome guest in her home well
into the 1940s.

Naomi broadened her circle of friends with more and more homosexuals whom she off-handedly referred to as 'buggers', attributing
her popularity with them to her honest, non-judgemental descriptions
of poignant homosexual love in novels set in Ancient Greece and Rome.
One of the most emotionally moving passages in *The Corn King and
the Spring Queen* portrays a last supper of Spartan men who are about
to commit group suicide; several of the men have loyally loved one
another all their adult lives.

Goldie Lowes Dickinson and E. M. Forster were close friends of
Naomi's, and so were Gerald Heard and Rudi Messel, a left-wing
journalist whom Naomi remembers meeting while swimming in the
middle of the lily pond during the socialist workshops at Easton
Lodge. With Rudi she worked on making a short socialist propaganda
film about the Means Test; she blackened out one of her teeth in order
to play the part of a mother of a young man on the dole. Naomi alone,
or sometimes with Dick, often visited Rudi at Drewsteighton. From
him she received generous friendship and encouragement, especially
when reading aloud her writing in progress, and once, with Dick's
blessing, Rudi nursed her back to health after a miscarriage that had
left her depressed. In Naomi's memoirs as well as in the diary that she
kept during the Second World War, it is clear that she particularly
admired Rudi Messel. Naomi describes their playful, rather trusting,
relationship:

> . . .he asked me to tie and beat him, which I did, making fierce faces
> and quite enjoying it myself but not, I expect, hurting him as much as
> he might have preferred. Why should we insist on certain patterns of
> conduct?[4]

She was not uncomfortable with the company of people whose sensibilities moved well beyond conventional margins.

Along with those who surrounded Gerald Heard, Naomi experimented with mysticism in séances where they attempted to contact the spiritual world, hoping to condition their own minds to higher forms of consciousness, forming an élite cadre of highly evolved minds for future progress. Naomi was not completely persuaded; it seemed slightly hokey to her. Nor was Olaf Stapledon impressed when he was asked to participate. He told Naomi that her belief in magic and community was part of a general sickness of the modern mind, a sickness that was also producing fascism and some forms of communism.

Olaf Stapledon, whose science fiction novels such as *Star Maker* are considered classics of the genre, was a valued friend, offering a serious searching mind that equalled her own. She habitually lunched with him at the Café Royale when he visited London. Sometimes they were joined by Gerald, who others report was attentive to costume, his eyes seemingly made-up with mascara (which, as it turns out, was merely a medicine he used for his conjunctivitis). Hardly so exotic, Olaf and Naomi were of a different ilk – and they had a good deal in common: they both wrote time–space fiction, he about the future, she about the past; both held themselves to high standards of factual accuracy, he about science, she about history; both were idealistically committed to fashioning a better world, and both were extremely involved with their families of children. Between them, they shared a more and more articulated conviction that human beings must develop as individuals within the values of their communities, a theory of 'personality-in-community', as one Stapledon scholar has put it, or of 'Sittlichkeit', as Naomi put it herself. Olaf and Naomi rejected individualism as a capitalistic excuse for exploitation but, at the same time, rejected the suppression of all individualism by communism.

As Naomi writes in *You May Well Ask*, there were others besides her constituency friends at King's Norton who helped to express conditions for working people. One was Walter Greenwood, the proletariat writer of *Love on the Dole*, who wrote novels whilst supporting himself and his family on a small weekly wage as a clothing club director. Naomi acted as a liaison with Jonathan Cape for Greenwood, securing a book advance for him. Naturally, the small payments for writing were extremely important to his livelihood – in a way, we might add, that they never were for Naomi.

Naomi's relationship with W. H. Auden attenuated as the 1930s progressed. Originally, they had established a friendship on literary grounds. She had written one of the first reviews of his poetry in

1930 for the *Weekend Review*. On his side, Auden urged her to stop writing historical in favour of contemporary novels. In the margins of her published copy of *We Have Been Warned*, the political novel she began to write in 1932, Naomi has pencilled, 'this elephant part is in a way the genesis of the book – Wystan telling me to write a book about an elephant at a garden party'. He also disparaged her poetry. Fifty years later, when I asked Naomi if she had unpublished poems, she answered: 'Oh, goodness yes. I have drawers full of poems I felt shy about publishing after Wystan and his friends made fun of my writing'.[5] Some of these have found their way into *The Cleansing of the Knife* (1978); others remain unpublished.

Not all the poems in her drawers are love poems. In one she is angry with young men who hate women. She gives voice to a confident, determined, sexual woman hurling incantatory curses and challenges:

> Young men, haters of women, begetters of no real thing
> Neither of baby sons, gladdeners of full breasts,
> Nor yet of revolutions, hardeners of wild minds,
> Young men from whose loins come only dry, half-light words. . .
>
> We who have laid with men in grass fields, under hedges,
> Hearing the lambs bleat on the hillside, or the twisting water,
> Aware of golden oak leaves or noon-gray apple leaves. . .
>
> To us the dams and the pylons, the fields plowed with tractors,
> To us anode and cathode, to us dyes and test-tubes,
> All delicate adjustments, all new parts,
> The pressing and battering of the half-formed idea,
> To us in silent creation, to us at last
> After centuries freedom. You cannot chain us now,
> You have lost your power, young men. Young men,
> > with freedom we take
> The future also.[6]

Undated, this poem is found among a batch written in the early 1930s, some of which were incorporated into *The Delicate Fire* published by Cape in 1933.

In *The Delicate Fire* Naomi experiments by using poems to glue together descriptions of episodes in historical sequence, successfully creating a finely tuned, exciting tension between expanding feminine consciousness in poetry and hopelessly repeating history in prose. Although at times her fictional portrayals seem psychologically unreal and her poetry seems to struggle for language, *The Delicate Fire* is a brave effort to forge a work fully embracing feminine sensibilities.

In it she lays bare her bitterness towards masculine principles in art, her rejection of marriage as an equitable institution, her own sexual dreams and day-dreams, and even her ambivalence towards women in societies of women. The overall effect is a passionate validation of woman's consciousness breaking out of self-imposed restraint into liberty, creativity and self-determination.

The first short story, set in ancient Lesbos, depicts the generous, intellectually stringent, nurturing culture of women who lived in Sappho's mythical community; one of the last stories describes the twentieth-century censorship trial of a woman's novel about lesbian love – no doubt Naomi's rendition of the 1928 trial of Radclyffe Hall's *The Well of Loneliness*. Another set of framing stories describes ancient slavery and then modern slavery (the latter set in 1897 in South Africa, the year of Naomi's birth), plus a final story in which hunger marchers demonstrate against economic deprivation in the 1930s.

One story, 'The Wife of Aglaos', presents an educated Grecian woman's enslavement and subsequent freedom living with a band of outlaw slaves. Free, self-respecting and happy, Kleta is a lone woman among men, sharing herself sexually with all of them and giving birth to several children whose paternity is uncertain. Naomi's cave-world fantasy rings false until Kleta's husband turns up to claim her in the name of romantic, possessive love: ' "My little Kleta with your soft clean hair and the smile you had for me when I came home, only for me, and the way you put your hands like nesting birds on my shoulders. My own girl. My own wife." '[7] Here, Naomi employs palatable irony.

Interspersed among stories that become progressively more contemporary, poems trace the growth of a woman artist who is finding her voice. She must overcome the restrictions placed on her by men and overcome, as well, the restrictions she has come to place on herself, as 'Two Men at the Salmon Nets' demonstrates:

> Outside, in the rain, on the edge of evening,
> There are men netting salmon at the mouth of the Tweed;
> Two men go out of the house to watch this thing,
> Down the steep banks and field tracks to their
>   minds' and bodies' need.
>
> How can I, being a woman, write all that down?
> How can I see the quiet pushing salmon against the net?
> How can I see behind the sticks and pipe-smoke,
>   intent frown,
> And the things speech cannot help with in which
>   man's heart is set?

> Must we be kept apart always, you watching the salmon
>   nets, you in the rain,
> Thinking of love or politics or what I don't know,
> While I stay in with the children and books, and
>   never again
> Haul with the men on the fish nets, or walking slow
> Through the wet grass in fields where horses have lain,
> Be as sure of my friends as I am of the long Tweed's flow?[8]

The theme of feminine consciousness embracing history passed over
the heads of reviewers, although *The Delicate Fire* was favourably
received. Henry Seidel Canby, for instance, wrote that perhaps Naomi
Mitchison 'does not realise how good her writing is, how important
is the field she has chosen. . .If so', he adds, 'her growing cult of
enthusiastic readers should be a stimulus and a corrective'.[9] Most
reviewers did not mention her poetry, and those who did considered
it bad. Negative reviews attacked her socialist ideologies – not one
review, positive or negative, mentioned her feminist intentions.

Censorship of literature and art was in the wind. As early as 1929, over
Barbarian Stories, Naomi had found herself struggling with Jonathan
Cape who was reacting to the threat of public censorship, as well
a publisher might given the government's regulations. Publishers
were subject to fines and legal costs for publishing books which
were deemed by the Home Office to be sexually explicit; surely
this was meant to encourage publishers through their purses to do
the dirty work of regulating what might decently be said. Cape had
been fined for publishing *The Well of Loneliness* in the previous year, to
say nothing about the bad publicity it had brought his press. There was
a rash of censorship trials from 1928 to 1935. It is not that writers had
become more wanton and wicked than their forebears; rather, books
that were taken to trial tended to be of class insurrection, or of
liberated female sexuality, or of the two mixing, as in D. H.
Lawrence's *Lady Chatterley's Lover*, in which an aristocratic lady has
a sexual relationship with her gamekeeper.

Naomi had been one of the chorus of writers who organised to support Radclyffe Hall's *The Well of Loneliness*. Although not permitted
to testify at the trial, over a hundred British writers were present asking
to speak on behalf of the novel's merits. Soon thereafter Naomi found
herself defending her own writing with one of Cape's agents:

I've just had a letter about the deputation from the combined societies
for the preservation of ignorance in England – and your marked copy
of *Barbarian Stories*. And I'm damned if I'm going to alter one word

for this bloody Jix. I suggest you put off publication until after the General Election, when I trust the little louse will have been kicked out of office.[10]

In the same letter Naomi goes on to say that she will not change her writing because she would be ashamed to do so, feeling as she does that England is losing its liberty.

Joynson-Hicks, the 'Jix' of Naomi's letter, whose Home Office policies were responsible for the splurge of censorship trials, was not kicked out of office as she had hoped, and Jonathan Cape put more pressure on Naomi to tone down her writing, until, over *We Have Been Warned*, she broke her contract with him, ending twelve years of congenial association.

Even in 1933, two years before *We Have Been Warned* was actually on the market, Naomi was anxiously communicating with Jonathan Cape, realising that his conservative politics were not sympathetic with her Left point of view. In fact, she was aware that her novel would be unappealing to most political positions, including that of 'correct' communism. From politics her letter shifted to sex. Naomi writes that she has purged passages regarding homosexual intimacy. She considers *We Have Been Warned* essentially a woman's book:

. . .for of the people who have read it, the women have been much the most enthusiastic. The whole business of contraception is done from the woman's point of view, which is, of course, a new thing in writing. But it's damned important.[11]

Cape's objections to *We Have Been Warned* seemed to have been based on the novel's descriptions of the sexual assertion and sexual straight talk of women. All direct mention of contraception, especially the word 'rubber', had to go. Naomi was asked to purge a passage in which the heroine smells a man's shirt when trying to decide if he would be suitable for sexual liaison. A half-century later in her memoir, Naomi remained puzzled about the offensiveness of these scenes: 'It seems to me now very curious that those two passages which seem to me to show a normal female sensibility, were thought to be obscene'.[12] She was asked to excise a passage in which a woman unbuttons a man's trousers. Later, after Naomi asked Cape to release her from her contract, Jonathan Cape himself relented on this last point. She might write the word 'button' if she omitted the word 'trousers'.

Besides losing Cape as a publisher, Naomi lost the valued criticism and friendship of Edward Garnett, one of Cape's editors. After reading the manuscript of *We Have Been Warned*, he wrote an excited letter – if one is to judge by its length, underlined emphases, and crescendoing scrawl – advising Naomi to change completely the characterisation of her heroine. He found it unbelievable that any woman could be imagined acting like the character of Dione, a woman who uses her mind to think herself into an affair. If only, wrote Garnett, Dione was acting out of sentimentality or passion.[13] But that was the point. Naomi was not invoking the conventional contours of a female character who might be motivated by what men thought motivated women – that is to say, their emotions. She had invented a female hero who was adventuring into the world, questing freely within a historically specific moment, even though that moment was not propitious for free women. Naomi refused to modify her characterisation of Dione:

> You see, I'm more sure about this book than I've ever been about any of the other books. I know that Dione behaves in an odd way, but I'm quite certain of her behaviour. She isn't a completely normal person any more than Erif Der was – or than I am myself.[14]

Naomi, in fact, was writing from her own experience as notations in the margins of her copy of *We Have Been Warned* make clear. In these margins she has noted where dialogues have been taken from her conversations with her husband, with her friends and with her lovers. Along with numerous references to Dick and other friends, the notations indicate that the character of Phil was a combination of experiences with 'H. T. W. G.' (Widg) and 'J. P.' (John Pilley), and Idriss emerges from association with an unidentifiable 'J. B. T. !'

Disappointed with Cape, Naomi turned to her friend Victor Gollancz whose socialist press would be a natural place for this political novel about the Labour Party. Here again she was rebuffed. After acknowledging *We Have Been Warned* as the first piece of genuinely social art produced in England, valuable for its sexual, political and economic contents, he goes on to reject it for publication:

> The two things which have been working in me against my immense desire to publish the book have been 1) a shrinking before the certainty of jeers and abuse from many of my best friends, and 2) the fear that any efficiency as a publisher of Socialist books would be seriously damaged by my association with the publication of a book which will undoubtedly be widely described as 'filthy'.[15]

In this response from Gollancz Naomi confronted a more complicated situation than she had with Cape. As a socialist publisher, Gollancz was sensitive to the prevailing Left opinion that women's issues were, at best, secondary to class issues. In no quarter of Labourite socialism were men accepting Naomi's socialist-feminist tenet that women had a right to possess their own bodies, and to share their bodies with whoever and as many as they might choose or, for that matter, not to share with anyone.

Not only was Gollancz sensitive to the dynamics of socialist politics and ideology, but he felt it was his responsibility to protect his press from the threatening, conservative political atmosphere that prevailed in England after the general break down of Labour and Liberal power in 1931. The situation was deteriorating; under National Government welfare policies – including the Means Test – great numbers of people were starving. Advocates of the Left, embattled, were beginning to band together in what would come to be called 'The Popular Front'; they feared the rise of British fascism and the imminent danger of war. The Gollancz press was central to this enterprise. Women's problems and varieties of feminism, perhaps because they would have been divisive, were the last issues to be considered by those striving to save their vision of a better, more equal world. Naomi's brand of sexual politics may have seemed frivolous in this atmosphere, correct as she was to have spoken up for the right of women to control their own destinies.

Finally, Constable agreed to publish *We Have Been Warned*, including those passages that had run into trouble with Cape. Even then, the novel did not appear until 1935, two full years after it was completed. At the last minute, when the text was in galley proof, Constable asked Naomi to cut the very passages that they had agreed to print.[16] She gave in, telling herself that she did not want her book to harm Dick's chances to win a seat in parliament.[17]

Unable to write fiction until the publishing difficulties with *We Have Been Warned* were resolved, Naomi put her hand to a non-fiction project. So did Dick; he wrote a volume as a political treatise for the Labour Party which was published by Gollancz. Naomi wrote a book historicising the concept of the home which was published by John Lane. Both books appeared in 1934.

Dick's book, *The First Workers' Government*, was a political pipedream. In constructing it, he employed many of Naomi's techniques for writing historical fiction. It purports to be a history of the socialist revolution of 1936 told from the vantage point of a young historian writing in 1985. The historian-persona describes how a socialist government assumed power – abolishing private property, nationalising industry, dismantling the House of Lords, the Church and the military. Dick's story exemplified the kind of broad-brush solutions characteristic of significant portions of the British Left in its struggle to avoid war.

On the woman question, Dick's socialism offered less radical solutions. He does not mention birth-control as an issue; in fact, he hardly writes about women at all. When he does, he asserts that the exploitation of women workers was not as severe as the exploitation of male workers during the economic depression of the early 1930s. However, he does advocate the attachment of childcare centres to work places, in order, he dodged, to allow women more leisure to attend to their household tasks and to be better mothers. His final word on the subject is that the general lot of women will improve only as working conditions improve for all workers.[18] Dick was speaking the party line.

Many of Naomi's ideas for her projected but unrealised book on feminism are incorporated into *The Home and a Changing Civilisation*. It is an ambitious attempt to describe the concept of 'home' from the beginning of primate history – baboon and then cave culture – through Egyptian, Christian, Medieval, Reformation and Victorian history up to modern times. She praises family life in Russia and disparages German fascism for its oppression of women. Finally, she analyses current ideas in England. Naomi asserts that Freud's Oedipal theory may be incorrectly based on the assumption that sex is more important than patriarchal power; she attacks D. H. Lawrence as a misogynist.

Naomi remembers that she had dictated *The Home* in a white heat. She was angry. Her words, seething near the surface of her thinking, came quickly. Naomi was still receiving hurtful communications from publishers over *We Have Been Warned*. She might have thought that her troubles were coming from the kind of suppression creative women had experienced throughout history. According to Naomi in a letter to Julian Huxley at that time, after the trouble over *An Outline*, periodicals, including *Time and Tide*, had become distinctly less interested in her submissions. Then came the censorship of *We Have Been Warned*. She wrote about the bitter possibility of suppression in a review of Winifred Holtby's book *Women* which had been written for the same Twentieth Century Library series as *The Home*. She wrote:

Women like Winifred Holtby and myself who are – well, between thirty and forty – have gone through the interesting experience of finding our deepest ideas and principles being conditioned by the economic position of the section of society to which we belong. We started before the war as good little bourgeois feminists, determined to beat, or at least to equal, men at their own game, which appeared to us at the time to be, on the whole, 'the professions'. The war came and gave us our chance; we took it. During the boom time the professions swung open to women and this was reflected in our attitude of mind. We ceased to be militant feminists, ceased to regard men as enemies, we were doing so well that we did not feel the hand of ownership pressing upon us. We had earned incomes, praise, and a good deal of freedom. But when the slump came, the professions began to squeeze us; capitalism could no longer afford itself the pleasant amusement of a class of un-owned women.[19]

Naomi goes on to suggest that women novelists might be returning to militant feminism in reaction to the restrictions that they felt coming down on them. It was not to be. As a movement, feminism itself was dead in the water. But Naomi, although she had suffered, was not yet ready to give up.

While Naomi suffered in her work, her relationship with Wade Gery was foundering in bitter sniping, adding to her pain. Their feelings for each other were powerful. Widg seemed paralysed by guilt; Naomi was too proud. In one letter he jeered at her Left politics, comparing her to Lenin. She scoffed at him, having just spent a weekend with radicals who had attacked her gradualism. Naomi, in a letter to Widg, declared her commitment to act on her own values, dangerous as they might prove:

My politics is making friends with people and trying to stop them being afraid of one another, trying to stop Labour and communist from hating one another. My politics is speaking and writing openly, and openly being attacked; when the smash up comes, I shan't be one of the ones who escapes.[20]

Her openness was in stark contrast to Widg's secretiveness. That winter they decided to part; it was almost the end. The last strands of the connection frayed a year later when Widg abruptly ordered Naomi to stop writing her chatty, newsy letters. Then it was over forever. They had been intimate friends on and off for fourteen years.

Never again did Naomi write fiction set in Ancient Greece, the area of H. T. Wade Gery's expertise.

Naomi sought adventure to take her mind off her sorrows. A call for help from Vienna gave her an opportunity to put her desire for dangerous action into practice. Not insignificantly, it also gave her the justification to leave Widg completely:

> The moral imperative said I must agree [to the break-up with her lover], not only verbally, but with everything in me. In the novels of an earlier period deserted heroes used to go and shoot bears in the Rockies; I answered a long-distance telephone call from a left-wing friend, quickly collected money including a generous advance from Gollancz, went off to Vienna and was tolerably successful in forgetting my wounds, at least for a time.[21]

In February 1934 the Dollfuss government turned its guns on socialist Vienna, killing workers, imprisoning those who survived, and desecrating the beautiful public housing that had been the architectural pride of socialist Europe. Engelbert Dollfuss, perhaps attempting to avoid German Nazism, had established an authoritarian regime based on conservative Catholic and Italian Fascist principles. Within three weeks of this bloodbath, Naomi was in Vienna, carrying aid from the Labour Party to the crushed Social Democrats. The Coles had organised a small group of people in response to Hugh Gaitskell's plea for help. Hugh had been studying in Vienna for a year; first-hand he had seen the carnage.

Naomi spent a month in Vienna as witness to the early upheavals in the cataclysm that was overwhelming Europe before the Second World War. She describes those experiences, for the most part, in two separate publications. One, *Naomi Mitchison's Vienna Diary*, was published by Gollancz soon after she returned; the other, *You May Well Ask*, is her memoir which was written nearly half a century later when she was no longer obliged to protect the names of her companions.

Having to co-operate with Hugh Gaitskell in Vienna, keeping in constant communication, ready to warn one another of danger, soothed the bad feeling that had been generated by their 'unfortunate flirtation' at Craignish. Her main Vienna companion was Frederick Elwyn-Jones whom she called Glyndwr in the *Vienna Diary* because of his ability to speak Welsh in telephone calls to England; he used it as a code language not easily deciphered. Gaitskell would be Leader of the Parliamentary Labour Party in 1955, while Elwyn-Jones was Lord Chancellor of Britain from 1974 to 1979.

A number of Naomi's friends were journalists whose writing she began to read in a new light:

> So odd, this newspaper world – writer, and yet how unlike highbrow writer! Applied writing. But can writing be 'pure', like 'pure' science?

Perhaps some of the experimenters. Gertrude Stein, Joyce – and at the moment I simply can't feel they matter two pins.[22]

In Vienna Naomi witnessed great suffering. In her diary she described the illegal imprisonment as well as the torture of workers, some of whom were being released to their starving families while she was there; she also described the trial and execution of Koloman Wallisch, the workers' martyred leader, whose wife she interviewed. In her memoirs Naomi summarised her experience:

> Looking back on that time, what I remember is the constant feeling I was deeply one of the second, Social Democrat, International, a European in brotherhood with European socialists: *Freundschaft und Freiheit*, we whispered to one another in the hurrying, anxious streets.[23]

Naomi returned to England with her diary manuscript for publication. Tucked in her 'thick woolen knickers' were pages smuggled from socialists to their British comrades. Her Vienna experience quickened her voice; from the minute she returned to England she no longer needed prepared speeches carefully read. Greeting her at the train, Dick whisked her to a Fabian meeting where she spoke extemporaneously, as she would forever after.

By May the Dollfuss regime had become completely dictatorial, leading to a revolution by the German-backed Austrian Nazis. They assassinated Dollfuss in June.

Naomi could not interest newspapers or periodicals in her articles about what was happening in Vienna, partly she felt because of a general unwillingness at that time to examine too closely the build-up of fascist forces on the Continent; the possibility of war was utterly frightening, better the ostrich stick its head in the sand. Naomi disdained the attitudes she found on her return to Britain:

> These dear little papers that are willing to call one a genius when one's writing fiction – words that they don't need to take action about – but won't have anything to do with one when one's writing something that really matters![24]

Although *Vienna Diary* was published, it did not receive much attention: some reviewers discounted her work because they felt it was biased by Naomi's socialism, others because it presented too freely her own experiences. Naomi felt that she was seen as a dangerous and wicked woman, a wild revolutionary. The depiction puzzled and bemused her, although she did nothing to scuttle it.

8

To London Margins
1934-1939

Despite what she perceived as her reputation, Naomi was not a hardline or even a straightline ideologue. She was more romantic than revolutionary in her search for a better world and she responded personally, politically and artistically to events as they occurred. Over the next several years Naomi would seem to move in disparate directions as the 'tide of war' rose, disturbing long-shared understandings within London's establishment Left circles. It would be a time for the coming together of strange ideological bedfellows and for familiar ones to part company.

Naomi's collaboration with Wyndham Lewis, the writer and artist, on a book in 1934 reflects the ideological cross-currents of 1930s London, filtered, of course, through Naomi's sensibilities. Lewis was a satirically biting critic of the Left. In addition, he was known for his bad party manners, his hateful depiction of strong, independent women in his novels, and his misanthropic attacks on all humankind. Worse still, Lewis was a public supporter of Hitler's early fascism. Castigated as a fascist by many, Lewis was not one himself; he was not a joiner of causes. Far more than Naomi, he avoided all confining ideological commitments. In *You May Well Ask*, Naomi observes that he should not be, nor should he have been, taken at face value. She believes he cultivated a view of himself as Wyndham Lewis, The Enemy. Perhaps because Naomi understood about such creations (Naomi Mitchison, The Revolutionary), she never took his reputation seriously – although others did.

Naomi may have seen a side of Lewis he usually masked. She points to his tender drawing of her daughter, Val, and his perceptive rendering of Av, posed frowning, tricked by the wily Lewis into thinking mice were trapped under pudding bowls at his feet. He drew and painted several portraits of Naomi, brooding, but fully human, unlike the abstract violence for which he became artistically known as a modernist. In 1938 when Naomi was finally writing fiction again, a novel, *Blood of the Martyrs*, Lewis painted her in blue and grey scowling over her book, a crucifix on the wall behind her right shoulder – the cross was an appropriate symbol given the theme of her historical novel about the crucifixion of Christians in Rome during the first century.

Lewis may have met his temperamental match in Naomi. Opening his door a few inches to her knock, glowering under his famous black hat, he was about to slam it closed when she intervened with one thick foot. Imagine her standing her ground, a short woman in a full, unfashionable skirt, her hair bound by a colourful kerchief, in what she calls the style of highbrow. According to Naomi's memoirs, she shoved hard until the door gave way. All was well, as it often had been when he made some outrageous remark, sometimes distinctly fascist, to which Naomi remembers responding by grabbing his lapels and giving him a good shake. 'That's nonsense, Wyndham,' she would say. She was almost certain that he was teasing in the first place. Naomi described her moderating influence on Lewis in their collaboration, *Beyond This Limit*:

> The ticket collector raised his own hands and laid them over hers but did not tear her hand away nor rise on wings out of her grasp. 'Of course if you put it like that,' he answered, 'I'll do what I can. . .'[1]

Here the character of Phoebe, Naomi herself, bullies the 'ticket collector', who is Lewis. Lewis's illustrations depict the ticket collector wearing a broad-brimmed black hat and Phoebe with her hair bound by a kerchief.

The work with Lewis on *Beyond This Limit* was intense and punctilious. Naomi would write a passage which he then illustrated; whereupon she would compose further from the inspiration of his drawing. Among the several people with whom she collaborated in her life – Lewis Gielgud, Richard Crossman and Dennis MacIntosh – she learnt most from Lewis, who would, as she has written, jump on her 'like a tiger' if she chose a word in haste, without considering its reception by the reader as well as its expressive value. The subject of the book is the psychological progress of a woman artist who develops from safe conventionality into courageous autonomy – a dream sequence, precursor to the fantasy of Naomi's later science fiction. This was a curious book for Wyndham, a reputed misogynist and misanthrope, to have encouraged, lending credibility to Naomi's contention that he was often intentionally contrary, masking himself as satirists traditionally do.

While Naomi worked on her book with Lewis, she maintained herself as a player in British politics by writing political essays about Vienna, as well as one entitled 'Sex and Politics' for *Twentieth Century* in which she maintains that sexual licence should not be substituted for political action. She also continued to support Dick in his preparation to stand again for King's Norton. Dick had become a successful and welcome speaker for the Labour Party. Walter Greenwood arranged with the Salford people for him to speak there. On another occasion he spoke at the Manchester Free Trade Hall with Tom Mann and Harry Pollitt, Greenwood finding hope in his 'shirt-sleeved fighting policy'.

Naomi provided a congenial home environment for political mixing. In a green book that she still possesses Naomi recorded lists of guests year after year at River Court, the last entry being a July party in 1939, its marginal notation lamenting that Dick had suffered from sore feet, Naomi from a temperature and 'several people were drunk'. In 1934 Naomi began shorthand notations in her green book, writing 'A No More War movement party' instead of names and appending to a list of names 'plus lots of NFRB' – referring to Dick's cohorts in the New Fabian Research Bureau. She notes that there must have been frequent political differences:

> I see on my lists the Pritts, John and Celia Strachey, the Ewers, Amyas Ross, Laski, Harry and Joan Thompson, the Nevinsons, Jeeves and Darling, Michael Foot, John Parker, Rudi Messel – but he was a peace maker – Fenner Brockway, Barbara Betts, Reg Reynolds, then three together – Ellen Wilkinson, Dorothy Woodman, Madeline Symons – and of course Coles, Postgates, Beales and Horrabins: all lefties, from the Communist Party through to right-wing Labour or Liberal left. It could have been an explosive mixture though perhaps I tried to separate them.[2]

One dinner party stands out particularly. During a visit to England in 1934 in one of those rare interludes during the first half of the 1930s when he was not in jail for conducting civil disobedience campaigns in India, Jawaharlal Nehru asked to meet with Stafford Cripps, the powerful, very Left-leaning Labour politician. Cripps would help to shape Great Britain's economy after the next war as a key force behind the nationalisation of industry. Naomi was elected to set up the meeting, which she did by gathering a dinner party over great platters of raw vegetables and fruit for her vegetarian guests. Julian Huxley was there and so was her brother Jack, who would make India his home in the 1950s. The connection between Nehru and Cripps was fruitful; later in 1942, Churchill chose Cripps to be his messenger to India with a self-government plan.

Jack was still a part of Naomi's life, although they had not resolved personal enmity incurred in the wake of Geoff's death. It might be noted, in the coolness of their relationship, Naomi no longer obsessed over brother–sister doubles in her fiction. She had gone beyond the confines of her family of origin for her literary models, using sisters as doubles for artistic and reproductive creativity in *We Have Been Warned*. Jack would visit the Mitchison household largely through his friendship with Dick, speaking for him in his election campaigns in Birmingham. Naomi's children remember Jack with some trepidation; he impressed them by continuing to converse while he wrote on the pad resting on his armchair. In his early forties he was an imposing man, described by his biographer, Ronald Clark, as bush-browed with a head that resembled a fly. In 1933 Jack and Charlotte had moved to London where he had taken up a position as Professor of Genetics at University College. Politically at this time he was calling himself a Marxist. He would not become a Communist Party member until 1937.

In February 1935, Naomi journeyed to the United States for the first time with her friend Zita Baker, who would soon divorce her husband and marry Richard Crossman. They planned the trip for months. Zita was herself unconventional, keeping a safety-pin stuck through her ear lobe in commemoration of her months living with a Melanesian tribe. They shared a room, laughing, gossiping and anticipating their American stay, Zita persuading Naomi that it was time that she wore a bra. Crossing the Atlantic in ten days, they landed in deep snow in Boston, bought a second-hand Ford in New York and headed south to Memphis where they were introduced to members of the Sharecroppers Union, an organisation of black and white people all equally poor and shackled by the sharecropping system. It was a corrupt arrangement that kept workers in constant debt to landowners. Naomi had not seen poverty like this before, the wretched shacks, the unhealthy children, the hunger.

They were oddities, these two relatively wealthy, handsome British women alone in the South. They were soon picked up by the American press, which gave favourable publicity to the sharecroppers' attempt to organise. Naomi and Zita marched with their new friends, while Naomi made speeches about European socialism and the brotherhood of the Second International. The two of them walked at the front of illegal marches, protecting everyone by invoking their British citizenship like a safety shield. They must have appeared quite bizarre to local officials generally hostile to the Union. Naomi writes about one of her experiences:

> While we were there there was the tremendous excitement of the illegally banned meeting at Marked Tree: Jennie Lee speaking, bare headed, 'wild looking like a colt'; the voices of the prayer leaders singing and pitching, gathering hopes, calling down blessings. Then my turn to face the packed crowd, a thousand desperately poor people, intent but constantly interrupting with 'Amen, Amen!' or 'Pitch it strong, sister!' And afterwards Jennie and I in the middle of a shifting, weeping, laughing crowd and all marching and singing, braving the Mayor and sheriffs of Marked Tree.[3]

Naomi, at age 93, is still a member of the Southern Tenant Farmers' Union, feeling to this day a deep sense of communion with those in the movement. Upon leaving, feeling humble because she would be safe on her way while these new friends were left to fight on, Naomi knelt in the middle of the road for the blessing of Mr Brookins, 'barely recovered from some forty days in gaol and a beating up, very black'.

From sojourning with the sharecroppers, Naomi and Zita drove to New Orleans, and from there across the reaches westward to Taos in New Mexico for a week with Mabel Dodge Luhan. In a note to Julian Huxley upon her return Naomi wrote: 'America was thrilling, it really was, such delicious people'.

Coming back to London, Naomi prepared to face the uproar over *We Have Been Warned* which was finally being published. She even asked Julian to write a review, something she had never asked of her friends, but she was worried. She had reason to be.

We Have Been Warned did not seem to please anyone. Although very much like *The Corn King and the Spring Queen* in its spatialisation of historical stages, it was, however, a novel set in the political present. Its woman hero, Dione, the wife of an Oxford don standing for Parliament in a working-class borough, journeys from group-minded Scotland through communist Russia, industrial Sallington, into modernist London. Her husband and lovers represent a range of Left political options – from Labourite socialism to revolutionary communism. Thick with detail from her experience in Russia and her work beside Dick in King's Norton, *We Have Been Warned* describes the fissures in the British Left. Her socialists are well-meaning but naive; her communists are idealistic murderers and opportunistic rapists. The conservative capitalists, her Tories, are dismally depicted as well. Attending a demonstration of hunger marchers in Hyde Park, Dione, accused of belonging to the 'squawking sisterhood', has her ears boxed by a 'gentleman' wearing a public school tie:

> Dione ducked and staggered, dropping her bag. When she'd picked it up they had their backs turned and were walking away. The things they'd said were a good deal worse than the immediate pain. You haven't time to teach her now, said the words; you haven't time to rape her now said the tone.[4]

In passage after passage of *We Have Been Warned* Naomi associates the suppression of witches in seventeenth–century Scotland with the suppression of women in the 1930s.

Dione, which means 'law-giver' in Latin, decides to give 'a miss' to what she calls 'the dear old revolution'. Capitalism, communism, political assassination, marriage, sexual restrictions all become embodiments of corrupt values that privilege empirical measurement over everything. She concludes there is no pattern to history:

> No, it wasn't really so neat and tidy; it wasn't twopence one way and a packet of chocolate the other, all accurately paid for and cancelled out, something for each side. It was simply the succession of events. Things didn't fit together nicely finished and cancelled, they just went on; and the less one thought about justice, a fair deal and all that, the more freely and interestingly and newly they went on.[5]

Naomi ends her novel with an apocalyptic vision of the future: jubilant socialists win the election, generating a fascist backlash in which all major Labour leaders are shot against a wall and their women raped, including Dione's daughter. It is horrifying.

Naomi's writing, especially her depiction of violence in unemotive and matter-of-fact language, effectively jars her reader. Particularly vivid and disturbing is her description of Dione's rape by her companion Idriss – both those portions which remain in the published version and those which were excised. In examining Naomi's notebooks, it appears that the Idriss episodes were the first she wrote and those around which she constructed the rest of her novel – suggesting she might have experienced such personal violence in her own life.

We Have Been Warned contains exquisitely written passages and it is an invaluable first-hand description of British politics and mores in 1932. But as a novel, it does not quite hold together. There is too much undigested writing from her journals; its detached, observing voice disrupts identification with Dione, the woman hero. Moreover, by way of contrasting verisimilitude, those sections of the novel which are purely invented for didactic purposes – such as free love in communist Russia – seem psychologically flat.

In the foreword to *We Have Been Warned* Naomi reminds her readers that she had finished writing this novel in 1933, a full year before she witnessed the decimation of the socialists in Vienna in winter 1934.

We Have Been Warned received few reviews, none favourable. For the first time, reviewers from all ideological persuasions actually perceived Naomi's female hero. They were shocked. One in the *Times Literary Supplement* refused to comment extensively because the book caused such continuous embarrassment, the reviewer's short summary going on to reveal a fearfulness about Naomi's descriptions of intimacy between middle-class women and working men.[6] Another castigated Dione's fornication and adultery.[7] William Plomer sarcastically dismissed Naomi's glamorising of free love along with her 'great-jolly-chattering-family' vision of socialism; to be feminine, he went on, is to lack 'a strictly disciplined masculine imagination'.[8] T.H. Wintringham, writing for the *Left Review*, deplored the novel's mixture of social and sexual morality as though they were one and the same, which he thought fed the imaginations of maiden ladies who fantasised about rape and the nationalisation of women.[9]

We Have Been Warned was a disaster for Naomi; it went to only one printing. Her Left politics had already limited her readership, and now she had alienated those who remained. Naomi never recovered her literary reputation in England. Nor did she actually try to retrieve it. *We Have Been Warned* was written in 1933; she did not write another novel until 1939 in the months preceding the Second World War. In another historical moment, Naomi might easily have sustained bad reviews on a single experimental novel. After all she was a well-established and respected writer who had already published over fifteen books. But what she had to say about contemporary circumstances was not welcomed by her usual readers, and she was not interested in writing about anything else.

Elizabeth Longford recalls that the Tory opposition printed certain passages of *We Have Been Warned* for distribution in Quaker-marked King's Norton. Dick again lost the election in 1935, passing the post on to Elizabeth Longford, who stood for two subsequent elections without winning. It may not have been a winnable seat for Labour. Not many seats were in 1935.

Naomi, herself, stood for one of those unwinnable parliamentary seats, the altruistic job of many women in the Labour Party at that time. In the 1935 election she was invited to stand for the Scottish Universities. She did, and lost, as was expected.

Although it was not a novel, Naomi produced one other major piece of fiction in this period, a collection of stories and poems entitled *The Fourth Pig* and published by Constable in 1936. It was a barely disguised allegory dwelling on impending war and disaster. The wolf is her symbol for violent evil:

> [The Wolf's] slavering jaws crush down through broken arteries of shrieking innocents, death to the weak lamb, the merry rabbits, the jolly pigs, death to Mother Henny-penny with her downy chicks just hatched, death to Father Cocky-locky with his noble songs to the dawn, death sooner or later to Fox the inventor and story-teller, the intelligent one who yet cannot escape always. So they die in jerking agony under the sun, and the Wolf gulps them into his belly, and his juice dissolves their once lively and sentient flesh.[10]

Clearly, in this volume in which she revises traditional folk tales, Naomi was gloomy about the future of Western culture and liberal freedom of expression.

By February 1936 Naomi was openly sniping at Gerald Heard, her friend and sometime philosopher-teacher; he continued to advocate pacifism in all circumstances. His mystic vision of human history dismissed the horrors of war as necessary flack that civilisations must go through as they pass from one stage of consciousness to the next. His long view no longer worked for Naomi. In a letter to the editor of *Time and Tide* she chided:

> Seriously, Gerald, why did you write this? Must you make us on the Left doubtful of you? Surely you realise that your real friends and allies must on the whole come from us, from the men and women who have had the experience of conversion, of being in some way bumped out of the purely personal and appetetional focus?[11]

Gerald's error had been to lump class war with international war. Class war, Naomi wrote, is economic and happening right now:

> I call it war when people are being physically and mentally crippled, deprived of life either suddenly or gradually, and reduced to a war mentality of distrust and despair, by inadequate food, housing, and education and unnecessary industrial risks.[12]

Naomi was setting a dilemma for herself. If she was willing to advocate class war, then she condoned violence. Would she also support violence in war to protect home and family? Hard questions. She began to write *The Moral Basis of Politics*, a serious sociological, philosophical, psychological and aesthetic treatise in which she examined pacifism and violence from several angles, many of which were feminine, although she cautiously side-stepped the language of feminism. It took her three years to complete her work, which appeared in 1938.

Meanwhile, screws were tightening on the pacifist Left. During 1936, the Rhineland was occupied, Mussolini conquered Abyssinia, the Rome–Berlin Axis was established, the Germans and Japanese signed a pact, and the Spanish Civil War broke out.

The casual pacifism Dick had expressed in *The First Workers' Government* in 1934 was on the line. Several issues of *Time and Tide* in 1935 and early 1936 were devoted to essays written by Left proponents of pacifism and proponents of war preparedness. The ranks were splitting, in this climate each person feeling obligated to declare a position. In a letter labelled 'International Peace Campaign', Aldous Huxley, Cecil Day Lewis, Olaf Stapledon, V. S. Pritchett, Siegfried Sassoon, Sylvia Townsend Warner, Rebecca West and Leonard Woolf declared themselves pacifist.[13] Many of these people were Naomi's close friends. Some of them never, in fact, faced what they would do with their pacifism if England ever were to be invaded. For various and complicated reasons they emigrated to the United States. Aldous and Maria Huxley left in 1937; Gerald Heard in 1937; W. H. Auden in 1939. It was difficult for those who stayed behind. Thinking about Heard's mysticism and pacifism, Naomi observed in her memoir 'it is certainly easier to practice deep meditation and the crossing of psychological barriers for someone who does not have a husband and children and a house and a number of practical commitments'.[14] During one of the last times Naomi had tea with Gerald, they fought over the war in Spain, she taking private pleasure in having procured arms for the Republican side through a friend she had met in the séance group gathered by Heard in the early 1930s.

So when Naomi writes in her memoirs that she became involved with Tom Harrisson's Mass Observation study in the mid-1930s, she is doing more than affiliating herself with Harrisson's idea of anthropologically studying the British as if they were a tribe and doing more than participating in an innovative grassroots literary movement with surrealist ties. She was putting the final nail in the coffin in her relationship with Gerald Heard, whose theory of inevitable social progress was harshly criticised by Tom Harrisson. In *Time and Tide* Harrisson interrogated Heard: 'What is civilisation? What is savage? What is progress? What things are common to all men?'[15] By aligning herself with Harrisson against Heard, Naomi was, for the time, forsaking her faith in the evolutionary idea of a progressively better world. Naomi gave financial support to Mass Observation research which needed volunteers to record their thoughts, observations and even their dreams; later she became an observer-participant, writing essays on subjects ranging from medicines in her bathroom cabinet to attitudes toward anti-Semitism and keeping a detailed daily diary during the Second World War. Sporadically she also kept a dream diary, as did several hundred others, a chronicle of the national unconscious responding to war terror.

In 1936 Naomi's father, aged 76, fell ill with pneumonia; Uffer was dying. Both she and her brother Jack hastened to Cherwell, where they fought bitterly:

> We could only quarrel in whispers because we were immediately under
> my father's bedroom; behind Jack's shoulder the bronze horses on the
> mantlepiece remained unmoving. I bit his arm; he twisted my wrist.
> Crazy unhappiness made us not care. Finally we broke apart and went
> soberly up to the sick room.[16]

Naomi was 39; Jack was 44. They were not over their nearly decade-long disappointment in one another. They were fighting over a trivial incident, Naomi having phoned a newspaper to say that her father was dying; Jack accused her of some bourgeois sin that today she can no longer remember. In any case, Uffer died with 'a look of intense interest on his face as though he were taking part in some crucial experiment in physiology which had to be carefully monitored'.[17]

It was a time of great sorrow. Maya, who had been ill herself with cystitis during Uffer's illness, slumped into depression. Aunt Bay, grieving, journeyed from Scotland to Oxford for her brother's funeral. On the return trip to Cloan with Uffer's ashes, Naomi and Jack fought again. Jack refused to travel with Naomi and Aunt Bay who had first-class sleepers: 'We were told what was what about the capitalist class travelling first'. With the parcel containing Uffer's ashes, Jack went third. Uffer was placed in the graveyard near the old chapel at Gleneagles; a crowd, which had gathered to honour him, sang 'I to the hills' which Naomi remembers as 'traditional comfort from our fellows'.

Aunt Bay died in the following year, ending Naomi's immediate connection with Cloan. Naomi had always loved and respected her aunt, although she feared stepping into Aunt Bay's humanitarian footsteps when she moved to Scotland, anxious that public good works would engage all her time and energy, as it had her aunt's.

Again Naomi and Jack misunderstood one another. Aunt Bay had left Naomi a small amount of money, which Naomi generously shared with Jack, 'perhaps stupidly, hoping this might heal the breach'. He gave it all to the Communist Party; she thought he had slapped her in the face.

Naomi and Dick continued to seek respite in Scotland. During the summers of 1936 and 1937, they rented a house on Vallay, an island reached from Kyle on a boat that was often crowded with livestock. The older boys were old enough to enjoy shooting and fishing with Dick. If the house had been in better shape, if there had been electricity and heating, if the soil had been better for a garden, then the Mitchisons might have bought the place on Vallay. It brought Naomi back to her Haldane roots. As she had during her childhood at Cloan, she could do farmwork there. Once at Vallay she was binding straw; the scything workmen wrapped and tied straw binding around her, telling her she would get her wish if she wore it. Naomi readily interpreted: 'I realised that I was the sacrifice, the harvest queen, the *cailleach*'. She felt at home in the land of Scottish myth.

Right after Aunt Bay's funeral in late 1937, Naomi went with her Uncle Willie and her cousin Archie to look at another estate in Scotland that was for sale. It was a feudal estate being broken up in Argyll on the Mull of Kintyre; it seemed to her to be a small version of Cloan. Naomi and Dick bought it, mainly, according to Naomi's memory, as a fishing and shooting retreat for the men in the family; Naomi, for herself, had reservations about the amount of housework it would mean for her. From Vallay, she brought for employment at Carradale House the Gaelic speaking Lachland MacLean and his family. Naomi had no way of knowing at that time how important Carradale would be in her life.

During Easter 1938 the Mitchisons holidayed at Carradale. They returned that summer; Uncle Willie and Archie and their party came for fishing; lots of salmon were caught. Although Dick and Naomi had inherited many of the servants who cared for the house, gardens, out-buildings and grazing land, there was still a great deal of work for them to do. First a generator for electricity was installed, the only one in the village. Furniture was procured and heavy-weight curtains installed over the high bay windows facing the sea in one direction and gardens in another; a wooden mantelshelf over the fireplace replaced the marble that Naomi inadvertently pulled down; structural modifications were made in the kitchen so that it was brought up to the same level as the dining-room. Eventually, Carradale was to become a comfortable retreat and Naomi's home for the longest period of her life.

In London, socialist hopes for class revolution and prevention of fascism were disintegrating. Britain never officially opposed fascism in Spain and it was becoming clear that the Republicans were losing ground. Moreover, word was beginning to leak out about show trials in Russia; neither socialists nor communists were talking about it, afraid that breaking ranks would weaken the fight against fascism. On all sides, then, both in Tory and socialist strongholds, information was being white-washed for purposes of propaganda. This created a need, Naomi believed, for extra-establishment distribution of information – such as Tom Harrisson's publications out of Mass Observation.

Trying to set thoughts straight in her own head, Naomi wrote throughout 1936 and 1937 the treatise she had begun in 1935. She worked on it for two years after her father died, perhaps using it to align her thinking with Uffer's vitalism, his philosophy of science. Like her father, Naomi decided that final answers about life and living could not be found solely in an organism's physical nature. One might know the physics and chemistry of a dead rabbit, she wrote, but would still not know the nature of any specific rabbit, for a live rabbit is a functioning set of systems that are reacting and interreacting specifically to individual circumstances – environmental, social and psychological. An individual rabbit can only be understood as a member of a community of rabbits.

In *The Moral Basis of Politics*, published by Constable in 1938, in deliberately plain English – perhaps too simple for it becomes bland – Naomi looks for what she believes is good for people, a state of love and well-wishing in which people are free to be themselves. So far in history, she asserts, it is mainly men as opposed to women who have had the advantage of 'good'. This is her reiterating refrain, its feminist teeth pulled. Afraid that material redistribution of the earth's resources will not be accomplished in time to avert international war, Naomi also comes down against class revolution because 'it is an obvious historical fact that counter-revolutions are always more unpleasant and violent than revolutions'.[18] Nevertheless, violence will change the world more surely than passivity. She yearns for the emergence of a leader who will either captivate the disintegrating crowd or, if not so lucky, then at least inspire through his sacrifice – a process of what she calls 'conversion' and 'catharsis' which will reframe systems of belief, ideological mythologies. She is searching for a modern-day Tarrik, her Corn King whose cannibalised body regenerated the seasons of Marob in *The Corn King and the Spring Queen*.

But *The Moral Basis of Politics* is much more than a wish-list. It is also a courageous commentary on the alarming events of 1936 and 1937 and it is Naomi's blueprint for the rest of her life, a useful map as she journeyed away from the London centre to the Scottish fringes, and beyond that into the deserts of the Kalahari in Africa.

It took courage to criticise Russia, that hope for a new kind of community not based on competition. Not many people on the Left were talking about the show trials in Russia. Her friend H. N. Brailsford did, lending fuel to the 'enemies of good' who distorted his criticism; he lost friends on the Left. Communist attacks were especially nasty. In *The Moral Basis of Politics* Naomi supported Brailsford:

> But sane criticism – that is, criticism made without hate, as I believe Brailsford's was – is proof of rationality and morality. It is an attempt to set some series of facts against a measuring-rod of moral standards. Criticism, if it is any use, must come through the imagination, away from the self; it is to do with morality. Because of our solidarity with Brailsford, who criticised, we are all less near irrational hate and fear. A slight catharsis has occurred.[19]

It is clear that Naomi was burning her bridges with the London-based Left. Nevertheless, it came as a surprise to her that her book was not even honoured with negative reviews; it disappeared, a rock dropped in turbulent and confusing water.

The section of Naomi's *The Moral Basis of Politics* devoted to describing 'what people really want' is a sound as well as a provocative social analysis. Not only do people seek security and status, she writes, but they also want to have 'fun'. She goes on to assert that there is a tendency to think that fun is a matter not for society, but for people's private lives and dreams:

> One reason why this has happened is the equation of fun with sex activity. . .We have developed all kinds of new fun-making sensitivities since those days. Yet it remains that sex activity is for many people the only kind of free fun there is. Everything else costs money. In the middle and upper classes sex usually costs money too, but this gets less necessarily so, as one descends the social scale. Such data as I have, at least, tend to substantiate this, but I am waiting for

13 Naomi with two of her children, Av and Lois. (*Courtesy of Lois Godfrey*)

14 Wyndham Lewis' painting of Naomi while she was writing *Blood of the Martyrs* in 1938. (*Courtesy of Naomi Mitchison*)

15   Carradale House, located on the Mull of Kintyre in Argyll.
(*Courtesy of Naomi Mitchison*)

16   Some of the cast in *A Matter Between MacDonalds*, Naomi's play performed by the villagers of Carradale in 1940. Dennis MacIntosh is second from left. (*Courtesy of Robert Paterson*)

17 Naomi gathering hay at Carradale in the 1940s. (*Courtesy of Naomi Mitchison*)

18 Naomi learning to ride a pony at Carradale in the 1960s.
(*Courtesy of Naomi Mitchison*)

19 Naomi surrounded by her children and their families on the steps of Carradale in the 1960s. Dick is located to left. (*Courtesy of Naomi Mitchison*)

20   Naomi reading *African Heroes* to Kgori Linchwe II in Mochudi in 1967.
(*Courtesy of Naomi Mitchison*)

21 Naomi with her mophato age group in Mochudi. (*Courtesy of Naomi Mitchison*)

22 Naomi and Dick in their seventies. (*Courtesy of the* Glasgow Herald,
'Evening Times')

23 Dick at Carradale. (*Courtesy of Val Arnold-Foster*)

24   Naomi, aged 87, and author in California in 1984. (*Courtesy of John Shelton*)

25   Naomi, aged 91, digging salad potatoes in her Carradale garden. (*Courtesy of Jill Benton*)

Mass Observation. I think it will be found that the need for fun is a very overwhelming one, in general intimately connected with the satisfaction of the self, at any rate not spreading beyond a very small circle. When one is secure, that is that, and one may stop thinking about it. But the need for fun repeats.[20]

Naomi was ready to fashion a community in which she could find what she wanted to make her happy: security, fun and status, the latter being connected with loyalties and mythologies. As her Left-leaning companions were turning on one another in accusing anguish, she was giving up on London. Still, Naomi had one last battle to pitch on feminist turf.

In August 1939 a debate emerged in the *New Statesman and Nation* that had, as one contemporary commentator noted, 'a curious resemblance to the bitter pre-War [First World War] altercations on the subject of feminism'.[21] Anthony West had reviewed four novels by women writers accusing them of being 'lady novelists' because of 'characteristic slightness of plot' and 'infatuation with the personal equation in which the private mind has a value equal to the universe and all it contains'. Two women writers, M. E. Mitchell and Daphne Nichol, published a defence; it is men, they argued, who are willing to march to an annihilation for abstractions and who have brought the world to the present pass. Naomi's friend, Cyril Joad, took up the masculine cudgel, agreeing with West. He asserted that he had read with boredom the dozen 'first-rate lady novelists' who have written about intimate relationships between men and women and, when finished, he had allowed his mind to proceed as rapidly as it could 'to disembarrass itself of the psychological lumber with which it has been cluttered'.[22]

Naomi was stung. From Carradale she scolded Joad, reminding him that he 'is too sensible a fellow to join in the anti-feminist game which is being played increasingly in the intellectual world just now. . . for only the very silly want to encourage sex antagonism'. She concluded:

I am no masochist and I am a sufficiently old hand to know that, sooner or later – probably as soon as I have a new book out – this letter will be remembered against me by those men (or should it be gentlemen?) who want to remove women from economic competition with themselves. Perhaps with the increase of Fascism, under whatever name it goes in this country, these men will succeed as thoroughly as they have done in Germany.[23]

Naomi was not alone in her chagrin about the treatment of women writers in the late 1930s in England. The backlash against thinking women which Naomi delineated may have influenced the strident tone of Virginia Woolf's *Three Guineas* in which she advocated separatism for women intellectuals. The novelist and poet Stevie Smith, who had become a close friend during the time Naomi was writing *The Moral Basis of Politics*, complained about not finding publishers for her poems because 'they can't see what anybody means unless it's said in the accepted voice'. She goes on: 'I now address myself to all old pards, including you love, as the great unaccepted'.[24]

When Naomi's new fiction, the novel *Blood of the Martyrs*, appeared in October 1939, her premonition about its reception by some male reviewers was justified; they were nasty, harking to her debate with Joad by calling her a 'lady novelist'. Some of the reviews were critical simply because she was a woman writer:

> She adopts towards her reader a kind of *locus parentis*: her over-simple prose is warm with maternity, and we feel as too-matron-mothered children might feel waiting impatiently for the night-light to be put out – waiting in this case for five hundred pages.[25]

Accusing this particular novel of having a maternal voice is blind mis-reading, indeed. The opening passages, for instance, explicitly depict a rich Roman girl bedding down with her Briton slave, commanding his sexual service. One suspects that Naomi, back again behind the guise of historical fiction, was thumbing her nose at critics of *We Have Been Warned* who had been appalled to learn that a woman might have control of sexual situations.

But *Blood of the Martyrs*, as one might suspect of a woman who had written *The Moral Basis of Politics*, is only peripherally about the lot of women. Its major subject is the persecution of early Christians in Nero's Rome, their martyrdom as scapegoats for the burning of Rome, which is intentionally analogous to the burning of the German Reichstag and subsequent torture and persecution of Jews. In his review of the novel, Aldous Huxley wished that Naomi had less graphically described mutilation and carnage. But she could not deafen herself to the horrifying stories she was hearing from European refugees flooding into England, some with the help of the international writers association, PEN, which was being directed by another friend of Naomi's, Storm Jameson. In deliberate violation of anglicised, although unwritten, literary rules of historical novel making, Naomi declared in the dedication her intention to associate the present with the past:

> And beyond and behind these known and certain and consciously collaborating individuals, there are other men and women whose

names I may not even know; but my thought and imagination fashions and chooses and eliminates because of our mutual participation in events. There are Austrian socialists in the counter-revolution of 1934, sharecroppers in Arkansas in 1935, old friends in King's Norton and new friends in Carradale: and the named and unnamed host of the witnesses for humanity and reason and kindliness, whose blood is crying to us now and whose martyrdom will help to build the Kingdom which we all want in our hearts, and whose temporary manifestations in friendship and comradeship and collaborations give purpose and delight to our lives and deaths.

In her descriptions of early Christian suppers, what she calls love-feasts, Naomi imagines the kind of conversion, catharsis and communion she had idealised in *The Moral Basis of Politics*:

. . .the eating together and feeling together, after the first prayers, when a tide of mutual understanding seemed to flood over the men and women who had met together in the half darkness – for they had usually to meet at night when workers and slaves could get away. . .Sometimes there would be such happiness and understanding, such acute temporary experience of the Kingdom, that one or another must stand up and sing or dance. . .And sometimes several, or all, would be dancing, moving in joy, filled, body as well as soul, with ecstasy, not knowing what they did, only that it was good.[26]

War was declared on 3 September 1939.

9
Scotland in the Second World War
1939–1945

In 1939 Naomi, now 42, was embarking upon a significant alteration of her life, although she did not know it at the time. Personal and historical events were again converging to change her in dramatic ways. Her feminism, her literary disappointments and her disenchantment with the communist Left had edged Naomi to the margins of London socialism, and now she would physically move to the geographical margins of Great Britain. The Kintyre world of Carradale, within which Naomi was to shape what amounted to a 'second life', was as naturally lovely to the innocent eye as Highlanders might seem open and generous.

Carradale is a small village nestled on the rocky shore of the Mull of Kintyre, which is the finger of land forming the western bank of the Strathclyde, west from Glasgow over the Isle of Arran. It was the habit in the 1940s and 1950s for the Mitchisons and their guests to fly in a small plane over the sea from Glasgow to Campbeltown, the largest town in the Carradale region. As they flew towards Carradale, they would have scanned a rugged coastline with rocks offering more protection to seals than to fishing boats; their eyes would have followed hills, some with standing forests, into glens punctuated by small farms, and finally they would have seen Carradale village, a small cluster of houses, a couple of churches, all nestled near a pier jutting ineffectively into the sea. There was not even a pub. A few dairy animals could be seen here and there. Some of the men of Carradale supported their families by fishing for herring and some by farming potatoes and turnips. In 1939 forty or fifty jobs provided by the Forestry Commission were new sources of income to this isolated community on the edge of the Highlands.

There stood Carradale House, the traditional laird's abode. Most of the land adjoining the Big House had recently been purchased by the Forestry Commission, while local farmers had purchased the estate's most fertile land. About forty acres of arable and a few hundred acres of grazing land remained with the house, as did several cottages and Mains, a farm house. Carradale House had been rebuilt from a seventeenth-century dwelling, having been enlarged and redesigned in the baronial manner in 1870. From the aeroplane one would have seen a three storey, rectangular building with slate roofs and round turrets. It was surrounded by several greenhouses and gardens – lawns, fruit trees and large stands of rhododendrons. Inside, arranged around a wide central staircase, were several downstairs sitting areas, a large dining area and numerous upstairs bedrooms, as well as attic accommodations and basement quarters including a room for billiards. House and grounds no doubt needed the care of the large staff that the Mitchisons inherited from the previous owner.

Naomi was determined to practise in Carradale her idea of the Just Society; her writings in the 1930s – *We Have Been Warned*, *The Moral Basis of Politics* and *The Blood of the Martyrs* – all had explored her belief that an egalitarian community, without barriers of class, could be constructed on the level of intimate social relationships. Naomi's belief that socialism could be lived in one's personal life had been ridiculed in London. In Carradale, it was even more disconcerting. The surprise is the degree of success she actually had with her social experiment in this Highland village.

When the Mitchisons bought the Big House, Carradale was near feudal. Naomi or no Naomi, Carradale's entry into the twentieth century would certainly have occurred in the 1940s, prompted by the disruption of living patterns caused by the Second World War. But Naomi had a hand in quickening the pace of development. This middle-aged mother of five, a passionate, independent spirit, a London intellectual, and a socialist at that, created perceptible shock waves of change.

The house and its surrounding acres were just a fraction of what the Carradale property had been. Before the Mitchisons' purchase, it had even included the harbour and nearby hills. Moreover, the previous owner had enforced his feudal rights. The villagers' cats and dogs were shot by his gamekeeper lest they disturb the forest animals kept for shooting; the paths crossing his property were forbidden, forcing the fishermen of Carradale to walk miles out of their way to their boats moored at Waterfoot. Children were still taught by their parents to doff their hats and bow when the laird rode by.

In keeping with her political ideal, Naomi immediately opened the paths to surprised and grateful villagers, especially the fishermen, and she invited her neighbours to her house. Jemima MacLean, who was 15 when she met Naomi, remembers picking fruit for her family from Naomi's trees, so happy that she warbled as she worked. Not all the villagers, however, were pleased with Naomi. Many scoffed. Her costume, eccentric in London, was outrageous in Carradale. She wore long skirts and a grey astrakhan fez. Despite rather careful moderation of her behaviour and that of her guests in this community dominated by two soberly Protestant churches, many associated Naomi with sexual licence and immorality. She further scandalised them by attending neither church. From the beginning, villagers tended to be in two minds about Naomi – cautiously grateful and cautiously disapproving.

In June 1939, tension in Britain running high as Neville Chamberlain pursued his policy of appeasing Hitler, the Mitchison family journeyed to Carradale for a summer holiday. It was almost as it had been the summer before: Denny, who was studying medicine at Cambridge, and Murdoch, who was still at Winchester, brought friends; Lois was on holiday from Badminton and Av from Horris Hill; Val was home with her mother, plus two of Naomi's friends, Tony Pirie with her child and Joan Rendel with her husband; Naomi's cousins Graeme and Archie came to fish for salmon with Dick. Another of her guests, Eglè Pribram, was a young Jewish girl from Austria. In London there had been talk of more refugees making Carradale their home. War seemed imminent and, if so, then Carradale was planned as a refuge for friends and their children.

The summer holiday ended in anxious preparation for war. Dick returned to his barrister work in London. The older children dispersed to their various schools; however, Naomi did not return to London, nor did her youngest daughter, Val, who was placed in Carradale's elementary school. Naomi stayed to establish a more permanent residence in the relative safety of Carradale; there was war work to be done, food to be grown. In September when war was declared, Carradale was designated as a safe place for the evacuation of children from Glasgow. The Big House was readied, as was Mains, the adjoining farmhouse, and a cook was hired. Children began to arrive. As it turned out, this was a false start. German bombs did not begin dropping for several months. Soon the children returned to their mothers, although Betty Gibson, a teenager with whom Naomi made friends, stayed behind for most of the war. It was the only time children were evacuated to the Kintyre, for this region of the Strathclyde was soon designated too dangerous for evacuations.

Naomi describes her experience in a diary she kept for Mass Observation throughout the war. Of the more than 1,000,000 words she wrote, less than 150,000 have been published. Three versions of the diary exist: a typed top copy which Naomi still possesses; a ditto manuscript which is in the Mass Observation archives at Sussex University (Naomi sometimes censored it by deleting pages before she submitted it each month); and Dorothy Sheridan's edited version, *Among You Taking Notes*. The latter, a remarkable source of social history, describes the effect of the Second World War on rural Scotland, as it tells the story of Naomi's immersion in the life of Carradale, of her year by year education as a farmer and of her intensifying commitment to Scottish nationalism and politics.

Settling into Carradale in 1939, Naomi wrote and had published a poem, *The Alban Goes Out*, which was about sea fishing; her friend, Gertrude Hermes, illustrated it. During the war years, Naomi wrote only one play, which she never published, and one long poem that was not published until 1978. Essentially she did not write fiction at all until 1943 when she started a historical novel, *The Bull Calves*, which was about the Haldanes of Gleneagles; it was published by Jonathan Cape in 1947. For Naomi, this was a trickle of her usual creative flow. She devoted herself and her energies to farm work and to the Carradale community. Of course, she wrote extensively in her diary almost every evening. Her urge to write always ran deeper than her desire to publish.

One of Naomi's first friendships in the community was with Jemima MacLean, whom she met stooping over the recalcitrant earth, digging for potatoes. Jemima was a bonny Highland lassie of 15, red-cheeked with black curls, In a conversation with me fifty years later, Jemima remembers how hopeless she felt at that time in her life because her brother had died a year earlier of peritonitis. Her parents had raised him to cultivate their farm in the glen and to care for them in their old age. Now her parents, poor and with no alternative, had turned to her. She had been forced to leave school; visitors to the farm were told that she would not marry.

As she was unearthing potatoes in the summer of 1939, Jemima remembers that another pair of hands appeared by hers grovelling in the soil. The new hands were square and strong, already calloused with farm work. On an impulse Naomi had abandoned her shooting companions to join the Highland girl she had spied toiling in the field. Jemima poured her heart out to Naomi as they laboured side by side. It was the beginning of a lifelong friendship. Always Jemima would be a welcome guest at the Big House, her full voice swelling in Gaelic song; Naomi encouraged her to train as a nurse in Glasgow and sponsored her marriage in 1942.

Naomi burrowed into life in Carradale, content to be alone, thinking herself more accepted across class barriers because she was not surrounded by people of her own background. Her life was taking the forms of her art. In the first months of autumn she was already finding the agape she sought – once, for instance, after helping the MacLeans along with Lachie, her farm worker, and then staying to eat:

> We were all hungry; again, they petted Lachie, who ate lots of scones and lots of bramble jelly and smiled and said Oh Yiss. I kept on wondering whether I was double-crossing myself, whether this meal at which I was so happy, was really in some ways bogus, whether I was just taking refuge among these people out of romantic or sentimental feeling and possibly out of pique at being criticised by the London highbrows or of being the intellectual inferior of various people. Yet I couldn't make out at what point the sacrament was not genuine; I couldn't see myself not loving these people or not being at ease with them.[1]

Naomi was questing philosophically and spiritually for a small community of goodwill; she thought she had found it in the Highlands. Even so, she planned to return to London as soon as the war was over.

She and Dick established a local branch of the Labour Party, Naomi chagrined to learn as time went by that many villagers were more motivated by desires to please the laird in the Big House than they were by political feeling. It was clear to Naomi that the village needed a gathering place separate from the churches; she and Dick promoted the idea of building a Village Hall and they donated land on which to build it; the fishermen chipped in with wood rationed in the first year of the war. The Hall was completed in 1940.

From the beginning the doors of the Mitchisons' Carradale House were open. A couple of the local fishermen stopped to inspect and left with bouquets of rhododendrons. They and several others would become Naomi's coterie of friends: some were the enterprising Galbraiths, a family who had lived for centuries in Carradale and who continued to speak Gaelic; there was Dennis MacIntosh, a fisherman who was to become Naomi's very special man-friend and companion, and his wife, Lilla, a Galbraith; there was Duncan Munro, new to Carradale but Gaelic-speaking and supervisor of the Forestry

Commission, and within a couple of years, his wife, Mary, another Galbraith; there was Robert Paterson, 'Red Rob', a fisherman and his wife, Chrissie; there was Duncan Semple, a farmer, who turned against Naomi twenty years later; and there were others.

Naomi became especially good friends with the fishermen. She, who had been left behind on a salmon fishing expedition a decade before, would now fish, both legally and illegally, for the rest of her life. She joined the ring-net fishermen on their nightly tours of the sea and with her 'mafia' buddies – sometimes with Duncan, Dougie Campbell and Denny MacIntosh, sometimes with just Red Robert and Denny Mac – Naomi fished and poached.

Her first ring-netting nights occurred before the black-out was imposed at the beginning of the war. Thrilled to be going to sea, she described the beauty of the black night, the stars, the lights of the towns dotting the coast of Arran and the Kintyre. The Alban was one of a group of small fishing boats sleuthing together. When shoals of herring were sighted, low shouts from boat to boat drew them into configuration. With loud shouting, the nets were lowered, drawn together, then pulled up, laden with herring, the 'silver darlings'. With boat motor gently throbbing on the homeward journey, Naomi recalls that the fisherman next to her spoke in the gentle accents of the Highlands. He might have said, 'Aye, listen to this, lassie,' before quoting from the long poem she had written about her first outing on the Alban:

> Green to green and red to red –
> How can we tell our neighbour boat?
> Over wet dark acres the lights are shed,
> The moon is hidden, the clouds are high,
> Thirty couples that shift and float.
> But a wife can tell her man in the bed
> By little touchings of hand or thigh,
> And so we tell our neighbour boat
> By the slope of her lights in the blink of an eye –
> Perfect safety, go ahead.[2]

Many of the fishermen appreciated her poem, having listened to her read it nightly as it was being composed. One had memorised it.

Naomi especially loved ring-net fishing, the accepted style of fishing in Carradale. It seemed to her an example of men working co-operatively, warm in brotherhood and intuitive communication, the living centre of her ideal of a just and intimate society.

Late in 1939 Naomi was pregnant again; it was one of her personal responses to the war, an expression of hope for the future. She also thought a baby would 'be a kind of binding' between herself and Carradale. Early in July Naomi gave birth, but the girl-baby died a day later, its heart defective. She was buried at sea, and Naomi grieved:

> The silly thing is that I realise perfectly that much worse things are happening at this moment to thousands of people (and indeed have done so for a long time), but one cannot generalise as simply as that. . .But she was part of me, and wanted, all these months, and warm, and one said what a nuisance, but lovingly, and now the whole thing is ended: the love has no object. I had dreams of the sweet warmth and weight of a baby at my breasts and now my bound breasts ache.[3]

In the poem that Naomi composed about her baby's death she struck a more universal note, hoping desperately that she had clinched a bargain that would save the lives of other members of her family:

> These twenty centuries of bourgeois bargaining,
> Since Jesus, himself a Jew, saw through it, saw there must be
> No scales of corn-growing justice, but only love,
> Have left their mark on me.
> Now I am trying to bargain, to say take her death, my grief,
> But save me the others, from bombs, shells, from pandemic
> Disease, save me children and husband, save Ruth, Dick,
> Taggy and all of them,
> Clutching out for lives on the spread bargain counter,
> clutching them to my heart. . .[4]

Naomi had rationalised living in Carradale rather than London on the basis of the baby she was carrying: 'To some extent, too, I had used this as an excuse to be out of the war, out of destruction, still on the side of creation; now that's over. I wish I could go to the south and get into an air-raid'.[5]

Several times in her diary entries of this period, Naomi longed for her women friends in the south: for Storm Jameson, Margaret Cole, Stevie Smith, Joan Rendel, Tony Pirie, as well as Margery Spring Rice, Elizabeth (Pakenham) Longford and Christine (Willams) Hope. But she was becoming established at Carradale, learning what she needed to know in order to grow turnips and potatoes, becoming accustomed to working side by side with her labourers as an encouraging 'boss-lady', as she called herself in her diary. It was back-breaking work, and Naomi made mistakes as she learnt how to do it. After all, her only experience as a farm worker had been on the sidelines at Cloan in her childhood. Her Carradale farm lost money in the first years.

Besides, Naomi no longer really had a home of her own in London. Dick was living with Margaret and Douglas Cole in Hendon, lending his legal expertise to Douglas who was assisting William Beveridge in the Manpower Survey he was doing. They were assessing the nation's resources for war production. Dick worked with Douglas Cole throughout the war, first in the Ministry of Labour and by 1941 on a project at Nuffield College in Oxford commissioned by Ernest Bevin; their charge was to chart post-war reconstruction, which they did, laying the foundation for the welfare state the Labour Party was ready to implement when the war was over.

When Dick visited Carradale, as he did when he could, he took the train north to Glasgow, then travelled by plane or ferry to Campbeltown. These years marked a change in Naomi and Dick's living arrangements. For the rest of their married life they would live partly together and partly apart, communicating by almost daily letters. This arrangement appealed to both of them, although Naomi was to wish that Dick would take her farming more seriously than she thought he did.

Naomi's oldest son, Dennis, married Ruth Gill, who was also a student of medicine; they shared River Court House with another young couple – with babies and a shared nanny.

Meanwhile, the war that had begun with a false lull drew closer to Carradale. The first blitz of London had seemed distant. Now Glasgow was bombed, and then Campbeltown in November 1940. Local people were killed. Carradale was a haven for people seeking safety: for the Mitchison family members and their friends, for farm workers and for refugees, some German Jewish but mainly the Free French.

Judging from her diary, especially the unpublished manuscript in the Mass Observation Archive in Sussex, Naomi was increasingly depressed as the war years wore on. She had bad patches of disturbed sleep, terrorised by nightmares – many of which are recorded in her dream diary which she kept for Mass Observation. She chewed her nails to the quick. The war was a constant anxiety, food and clothing more and more difficult to obtain, bombings of Glasgow and Campbeltown, the loss of people, the loss of Margery Spring Rice's son in a torpedoed submarine. Fright and loss.

Moreover, the round of farm work was taxing, which made time for writing depressingly hard to set aside. Her published diary *Among You*

Taking Notes attests to her exhaustion; she lost weight and her hands dried and cracked. However, her gusto for life was amazing. She learnt to plough with a tractor; she ran a large household filled frequently with war-needy visitors and, although dinner was called 'tea', a marker of the working class, it was often a formal affair – at least when Dick was home. To help her mother, Val became a first-rate cook. Naomi had community activities as well. She wanted the Village Hall to flourish. She organised a debating society. Then she was elected President of a local branch of the National Farmers' Union.

Naomi may have thought she needed a baby to bind her to a new community of friends, but she did very well on her own. By Christmas 1940 she was at the centre of her group of Carradale friends, having written a play for them to perform in the completed Village Hall, a place for folk to gather away from the sombre Protestant churches. She hoped the Hall would stem the flow of young people away from Carradale – a flow that was draining all the Highlands.

Preparation for her production, *A Matter Between MacDonalds, A Romantic Play*, went on for several weeks. Everybody participated: Chrissie Paterson, Dennis Mac, Duncan Munro, Duncan Semple, Naomi's entire mafia, as she called it, minus Jemima who was in Glasgow. Dress rehearsals were not reassuring; some of the men had never had to memorise parts for a play; others were shy about performing in front of an audience.

Naomi was especially fond of one fellow who was, on his part, distressingly fond of drink. She devoted a good deal of effort trying to keep her Highland cronies from drinking too much. In her diary for Mass Observation she records the extreme measures to which she would go to extract a promise of abstinence:

After a bit he said yes, he would promise from Thursday to New Year, and then he would see; I took out my knife and opened it and said promise on the knife, so he said yes, and he would not break his promise to me. That was the promise in my play, but I said now you shall have the end of the oath as it should be. So I cut my hand across twice with the knife. It was sharp and I must have cut a fairly deep scratch and he put his lips down on it and must have got enough of a mouthful of blood to count. He said You did this for me, why did you do it? I said I could do more for you if I knew what to do. We'll see what comes of this. He held my hand and watched the drops of dark blood trickling over it and under the strap I wear on the sprained wrist, and he said I am seeing a plan for my life in your blood. Then he picked up the knife and shut it and gave it back to me and said The Knife will remain clean to us.[6]

Blood oath or not, Duncan did not leave off 'the drink' at this period in his life (although he did later) and was incapacitated the night of the performance, disappointing Naomi – but giving her grist for several poems about him in her collection *The Cleansing of the Knife*, which was not published until 1978.

Dick and the children were home for Christmas, happy to swell the Carradale audience for the play. Margaret and Douglas Cole and her brother Jack visited as well. Naomi records in her diary that Douglas and Jack sparred often – the one representing socialist Labour, the other representing communism.

Jack was accompanied by his student and eventual wife, Helen Spurway. He and Charlotte had parted ways in the late 1930s, officially divorcing in 1945. Perhaps because of Helen's kindly urging, Jack and Naomi were finally speaking to each other again. At the time, Jack, newly appointed editorial board member of the communist publication the *Daily Worker*, was patriotically performing secret experiments for the military: first, he was at Harpenden investigating the disaster of the submarine *Thetis*; later he worked for the Admiralty. In the best of Haldane traditions, Jack was experimenting on both himself and Helen, as his famous father had experimented on himself during the First World War. They were simulating the kind of oxygen deprivation that occurred in submarines in the deep sea. During this particular visit to Carradale, Jack was mildly crippled; his pelvis had been thrown out of joint by convulsions that had wracked his body during these experiments.

However compellingly close Naomi felt to her family in England, her mother and brother, and to old friends, and they were close enough to draw Naomi southward several times each year during the war, it was not enough to keep Naomi from beginning to consider staying in Carradale for good. On the first day of the new year in 1941, a few days after the community performance of *A Matter Between MacDonalds*, Naomi overheard Dick tell Jack that he might stand for Carradale on the District Council after the war. Naomi approved of the idea as entries in her diary reflect: 'I kept on thinking how much I would like to stay here and have another child and write enormous poems and never go back to London'.[7]

Once a week there was a dancing class at the Big House. Val, who was light and nimble on her feet, learnt to dance the schottiche. Although she was not generally a music lover, Naomi adored listening and dancing to bagpipes. She described her experience in the extensive essay notes that accompany the novel she was researching and then writing during the war. She wrote:

A change in the piper's mind, a slither on the slippery watershed of the emotions, and the laughter and dance follow as the Satyr drama follows the tragedy in the pattern of ancient Greek drama. . .But anyone with any sensibility, who is dancing, say, to a perfectly respectable melodeon record of a schottiche or country dance, will suddenly realise that something is being expressed which, if put into words, would be supposed to make her blush. It is veiled, or should we say kilted, in musical decency, but only just.[8]

There was dancing and singing at the Big House, and games of hide and seek and of sardines. For those who accepted Naomi's play, there was pleasure. Several of the men regularly found their way to the Big House in the evenings. Their wives usually remained at home with children, worn out from the hard work of housekeeping without electricity or readily available hot water.

With the fishermen she discovered the illegal pleasures of poaching, although for Naomi-of-the-Big-House poaching was an instance of having her cake and eating it too. As the major landowner in the vicinity, she held the right to her woods and game, as well as to the Carradale River and salmon. The villagers enjoyed poaching her land, even though Eddie Martindale, her gamekeeper, kept a sharp eye. It would have been difficult for Naomi to repudiate completely her responsibility for overseeing her property. In a sense, poaching, although it was on someone else's domain, was an act against herself. For Naomi, this was quintessential fun. Boundaries, barriers, rules, all experienced as agents of repression, intensified her desire to jump traces. Poaching joined Naomi's renegade spirit with her hopes for friendship in the community.

She and Denny Mac, at times with various others, would row out in the sea, then back again to the shallows where they would lower a net to catch sea-trout. Such goings on must have been a regular competition, or 'ploy' as it was called, with gamekeepers who, on their part, kept watch for poachers until the small hours of the morning. In her war diary Naomi describes these exploits:

We went on across the Bay, Duncan rowing mostly and then Dougie, and I in the bows, feeling shy, not wanting to butt in on the men. Denny M said later that Duncan asked if I was in bad trim, as I wasn't speaking, and he had said no, this was how I was. And as we made for the point, Denny M setting the course, speaking of the rocks by their Gaelic names that are on no map, I began to feel a lovely sense of acceptance: the sparkles flashed out all the time from under our bows, and the men spoke in low voices, and I leant over the friendly sea; there was a jabble in places, but this was such a small and buoyant and unassuming boat, and no sea would hurt us.[9]

Red Robert in conversation with me remembers poaching in the dark of night with Naomi and Dennis Mac, the two men wearing thigh-high waders the better to hide from Naomi the extra fish they caught. She, after all, was the laird and assumed the laird's privilege of doling out the catch. It made a good story, a nice twist in the ploy.[10]

The war continued and Naomi became more entrenched in life at Carradale, sometimes alarmed to find her mind void of abstractions, grinding away on the details of snedding and calving. She ploughed under more land than had ever been cultivated before and began to keep a small herd of cows for milking; she diversified into sheep. Finally the farming operation was beginning to hold its own financially. Her children were growing up: Murdoch gave over his study of medicine at Cambridge to pursue biology before he entered the army in weapon's research; Av began school at Leighton Park and Val started at Kilquanity School in Dumfries, soon to transfer to Badminton where Lois was continuing her studies. Often without a cook, Naomi offered Carradale's hospitality to those who made the journey. Along with family and young friends, with land workers and refugees, among many, many others there were always the Coles, plus visits from Tom Harrisson and John Dos Passos, Eric Strauss, Julian Trevelyan, Rosalind Wrong, who would marry Murdoch a few years down the line, and Tish Rokeling, Dick's special woman-friend from the 1920s.

As Dorothy Sheridan, who edited the war diary for publication under Naomi's scrutiny in 1984, has put it: 'Naomi's friendship with Denny M continued to deepen'. Naomi was writing *The Bull Calves* and Dennis Mac was the model for Black William, the Highland hero of her novel. Each evening she read aloud what she had written that day: 'why his opinion matters to me, why indeed I need it in order to get on. He's the prototype, the image, one I've got to bring alive'.[11] Dennis MacIntosh is uniformly remembered as a handsome man, tall, well-formed, charming, soft-voiced and sweet. Sharing their concerns and hopes, Denny Mac and Naomi day-dreamed about owning a boat together someday. Meanwhile, in 1942 they collaborated on several essays about herring fishing, Dennis Mac providing the knowledge, Naomi the gift for written expression. It was a delicate connection over boundaries of class. For instance, in her diary, she records his reaction after she had hit him in frustration over their writing. 'How could you do this', he wept, 'I'm a poor man, but – '. Naomi was full of contrition: 'It now appears to me as though I had killed a lovely bird, and I'm full of the most wild and painful remorse, especially as I had been considering myself to some extent at least, a superior person'.[12]

When Jemima MacLean was to marry in April 1942, Naomi squabbled with Denny Mac about the role of women in marriage, causing her to muse in the diary:

> I think it all means that my feminism is deeper in me than, say, nationalism or socialism: it is more irrational, harder to argue about, nearer the hurting core. I can write about it from angles, and have, in *We Have Been Warned*, *The Home* and others, but unless people have the same experience, it doesn't get across to them. Denny thinks he sticks up for women, but of course it isn't the same thing, nor can it be until the economic side is cleared up.[13]

Naomi's feminism had become ingrained. She no longer made a political point of it, but after all she was farming and fishing which were jobs for men in Carradale. Still, it was not always a calm feminism. Sometimes she expressed it intensely in moments of eloquent passion. In her diary she reports hitting a fellow on the head when he assumed that the woman nearest him should serve him from the kitchen, and later, as a committee woman talking education, she pulled a fellow committee man's hair over feminist issues.

Dennis Mac and Naomi resumed talking to one another after Dennis's wife, Lilla, intervened, and Jemima married. Wedding guests were bedded down in the Big House and Naomi wrote a nuptial poem for her young Gaelic-singing friend, the jubilant chorus of which went:

> Oh where are we going and what are we doing and which is the
> word that will rhyme her?
> For here is the wedding and here is the singing and here are the
> friends of Jemima!
> Oh apple at top to be reached by the best of us, here is the man
> for it, fortunate climber
> To the black curl of the hair and the red of the lips and
> the cheeks of Jemima![14]

Several decades later, in 1984, Jemima, a middle-aged woman, turned to me. 'Just look at her now,' she said. 'Have you ever seen such sweetness?' She was referring to Naomi, who was plodding toward the Big House from the garden, toting a basket laden with summer vegetables and fruit. Naomi was unaware that we observed her. Jemima was right. In repose, Naomi's soft elderly cheeks and mouth were indeed sweet.[15]

In 1940, for the first time the Scottish National Party came to Naomi's attention when it gained popularity in the Argyll by-election. Unlike the traditional Conservative and Labour Parties, the SNP was vitally committed to Highland problems of fishing, crofting and depopulation. The other parties were London based, a distance away from rural, pre-industrial problems. Naomi tried to interest Douglas Cole and her brother Jack in the SNP politician John MacCormick when she brought them together as house guests during the Easter of 1941. They had no affinity for one another. However, it seemed natural for Naomi to throw her hat into Scottish politics. By 1942 she was actively involved in the SNP, sponsoring MacCormick in Carradale. She helped organise the Scottish Convention Movement, drawn in by MacCormick, who was its first chairman. When the Convention convened in 1943, Naomi was vice-chair, finding the non-political Convention congenial to her Labour affiliation.

Naomi's nationalism had a material as well as idealistic base. Her beloved Kintyre, plus the Highlands and the Islands, were far from the centre of London political interest; their needs for harbours, bridges and roads were being ignored, as was their Gaelic language in the schools and their culture, in general. Politicians in London were unaware of the special needs of crofters and fishermen in the Highlands, nor did it seem that they cared to know. London publishers were uninterested in Scottish literature, finding the Scots-English irritating, if not unreadable. Right in front of her eyes, Naomi could see a way of life, a whole culture, dying.

A literary connection pulled Naomi deeper into Scottish nationalist politics. During the early years of the war, she had written regularly for the Glasgow socialist newspaper, *Forward*, whose former editor Tom Johnston had been Regional Commissioner for Scotland in 1939 and then Secretary of State for Scotland in 1941. Naomi seemed drawn inextricably into political action despite this move to the geographical fringe of Britain.

Naomi's writing and her literary connections mixed with her politics. When she attended the Scottish Convention in 1943, she met Neil Gunn, an important writer identified with the Scottish Renaissance, with whom she had exchanged friendly letters since 1941, a year before he published *The Silver Darlings*. In the flesh they shared their literary thoughts, their love for Scottish culture and their care for one another:

Well then, meeting Neil Gunn in Glasgow, a tall, loose-limbed chap with grand bones, a kind of half squint, might have been Irish, might have been a fisherman, a bit like Willie Galbraith but with sense and ability. But probably as lazy – and maybe as fond of a glass, though he would take it with discretion. In no time at all we were walking hand in hand, laughing, he lifted me from a moving tram and kept his arms round me for that much longer than he need have. We talked mostly about Convention, the Beveridge report, committees, fishing, the film of his book, Alba our mother and the signs of the times.[16]

Affectionate, quick to exchange literary advice, committed to Scottish nationalism, Neil Gunn and Naomi were fast friends throughout the 1940s. However, Gunn was far more reluctant than Naomi to join political groups, eschewing actual membership in the Scottish Convention Movement, although working with Tom Johnston on advisory committees.

Neil Gunn and Naomi disagreed over the politics of Gunn's novel *The Green Isle of the Great Deep* which came out in 1944. Naomi attacked his anarchism and what she took as his criticism of communist utopias. She went on to describe existing conditions in the Highlands:

Underneath, but getting increasingly deep under, there is the remains of the other standard of value, but I see no chance, Neil, none of that surviving without a revolution. If we could organise Carradale with a Soviet (or call it anything else, the name doesn't matter), making people take responsibility and run their own lives which is the beginning of democracy, and discussing every kind of thing with some chance of being effective, then the place would come alive.[17]

In his retort, Gunn claimed that Naomi, 'an incalculably charming woman', had mistaken his intention; he was criticising fascism, not communism. Disagreement did not hinder the friendship at that time, although they began to drift apart in the 1950s.

After several years of war, Naomi's life had settled into a pattern. Farm work was difficult. Running the Big House was increasingly burdensome; Naomi ambivalently welcomed guests for the conversations they brought but resented the work they entailed. She had a hard time saying no to any request – as when a mother wrote to find out why her young son had not written. The son was a camper down by the sea on the edge of Naomi's property, a participant in the Young Communist League's summer camp that started in 1943. Naomi made it her business to find the child, but not without resentment.

Naomi became proud of her muscles, liking to show them off to dressmakers when she visited London. But London was a world removed from the toil of farm work made more difficult by her inexperience. As the war ground on, Naomi laboured, learnt much, but still made mistakes. Once, for instance, she did not call her sheep out of their far-flung pastures in time for lambing; some died. Then nobody had told her about maggots that burrowed into the hide of sheep under their wool, loathsome pests that had to be squeezed to the surface. Naomi did the squeezing, the milking, the snedding, the ploughing, all of it.

After the novelty of dance classes and Big House play-activity wore off, the fishermen came less often to visit Naomi. Some were even caught poaching in her river, reasserting their traditional relationship to the laird. At times Naomi was disconsolate. Belonging to a community with its coherent but narrow values has its underside as well and Naomi was beginning to feel it, as her poem 'Living in a Village' makes clear:

> Living in a village is walking
> Among snare wire, being
> The bulge-eyed rabbit, ware of
> The light heart, dancing gossip-stats, the blood-lipped,
> Biding their time.[18]

Gossip was getting to Naomi. Perhaps she was progressively more twined with her neighbours and caring even more about their opinion. A woman friend, who was teaching in Carradale, told Naomi that people were saying that she was playing at farming. Naomi was wounded:

This just doesn't square with people's actions, but I think there is that much in it, and it may be at least half true, and if it is, then everyone is laughing at me, even my own men. I felt like chucking the whole thing, but yet I couldn't. I've taken on commitments of various kinds. But I was prickly and black with hate and misery and the feeling that I had been betrayed.[19]

Even when she said goodbye to the Free French, young men whom she harboured at different times for months, she feared they were laughing at her, especially when she gave one her thick warm sweater that he had borrowed for the several weeks of his stay. Sometimes she feared that her fishermen pals were laughing at her as well:

And also I felt slightly suspicious, I wasn't quite sure that they [Dennis Mac and Dougie] weren't double-crossing me: for after all, they had obvious benefits of a tangible kind to be got from me, and maybe it was all just flattery and they would laugh at me behind my back. And they said no, no, and they would never let anyone at Carradale say a word against me, and if only they were great capitalists they would do things for me.[20]

However vulnerable Naomi might have felt on occasion, losing her ballast momentarily, she would right herself, concluding: 'Yet what can I do but act according to my faith?' She had faith in generosity – of mind, of body and of material things.

In late 1944 Dick and Naomi sold River Court; Naomi sorted and packed belongings and furniture, sending some to Ruth and Denny and some to Carradale. When her furnishings arrived, she was assailed by swarms of ghosts they brought from another life. She cleaned out her desk drawers, burning most of what she found, unable yet to part with several large packets of love letters. Dick took a small flat in the Temple district of London. Naomi planned to stay on at Carradale. Indeed, there was no decision to be made. Carradale had become finally, if unintentionally, her primary home.

The end of the war coincided with her last years of raising young children and there would be no more; she had moved into menopause. Both Denny and Ruth were practising physicians; Murdoch, having worked for the army in the last years of the war, was a biologist; Lois was a student in Oxford; Av, now 17, had been invited by Jack to be his lab assistant; Val was at Badminton. Naomi hoped that Dick would get back into politics, and he did.

10

Cold War
1945–1962

For the next two decades of her life Naomi lived primarily on her Carradale estate where she farmed while continuing to write. She would become a significant figure in the Scottish literary Renaissance and a public fighter for improving the conditions of her beloved Highlands, bearishly guarding its heritage while fostering its economic participation in the modern world. Then in the 1950s, all the while continuing her life in Scotland, she turned her political attention to a world polarised by Cold War and her adventuring eye to the reaches of what had been the British Empire – Pakistan, Nigeria, Ghana and India. She learnt to 'travel light'.

As Naomi had hoped, Dick went back into politics after the war. In 1945 he stood for Parliament in the borough of Kettering in Northamptonshire. His candidacy had been set up by Tom Baxter, his agent from King's Norton, who was now responsible for the whole north-central region. With some reluctance Naomi dropped her farm obligations for the duration of the campaign, bought a new dress and some stockings and went to Dick's side. She was an old hand now at amicable canvassing and stumping the circuit, enthralling audiences until Dick arrived. Margaret Cole helped as did Naomi's brother Jack, Douglas Cole, Denny Mac, Lois, Av and Clement Attlee, leader of the Labour Party. Kettering, in that election, was an uncertain seat for Labour. Naomi described her mixed reaction to the election results:

> We then heard that Tiffany was in for the next constituency and our own majority of over six thousand made us hopeful of what might be happening all over. But it wasn't till 12 when we listened to the news that we began to realise it. There was a bowl of gladioli in the pub and I stuck two in my hair. . .I began to remember the scene in my own book [*We Have Been Warned*] of the Labour government

getting in and hoped that the succeeding chapters could be averted. I began to feel a weight of responsibility and a depression that was partly reaction, and partly tiredness. . .[1]

Labour's sweep of the 1945 election surprised many people.

In a personal way, the Labour landslide added to Naomi's small resentment about her own political fate, for it meant that one of the two seats open in Dundee for which she had been asked to stand could have been hers. She had been sorely tempted to accept the invitation, reassured by Party officials that she could advocate devolution for Scotland. For Naomi the rub was that Dundee had been viewed as a more likely win for Labour than Kettering. But Naomi anticipated feeling rotten if she won a seat and Dick did not. Moreover, she thought Dick knew more about politics which made him more useful to the Party, telling herself that she did not 'really want to get into Parliament, only to have the fun of the fight'.[2]

As successful as Dick was as an MP for the next nineteen years, Naomi did not feel as comfortable in Kettering as she had in King's Norton, where she had made lasting friendships. She was more cynical and distanced about the role of the candidate's wife than she had been in the mid-1930s, writing:

> Her photograph, preferably with a small child (if over puberty, they are no use) should appear. . .[I]n the minds of the chorus [the women of the 'canvass card ritual'] it must be she who brews his [the candidate's] cuppa, not once but many times through the day and night.[3]

Naomi detested 'cuppa', working-class slang for strong tea. Her writing was not designed to endear her to the 'chorus' of Labour women in Kettering. In retrospect, Naomi was to see that she no longer had the same unquestioning faith in society being able to attain goals of liberty, equality and above all fraternity. It all seemed less certain than it had in the 1930s.

Clearly Dick, who dropped his barrister work in favour of legislating, was not going to have time to take on the Argyll County Council for Carradale; but Naomi did. She won the Council seat, describing polling day in an essay for Mass Observation: it was wild and blustery although 'a romantic touch was added by the fishermen coming in, in the teeth of a gale, to record their votes'.[4] The vote of the fishermen was especially important. When they did not make it back in time for the next election in 1948, Naomi was voted out.

In the year or so after the war ended, Naomi settled into county politics; she also travelled again to beloved European places – to Denmark with Dick to visit friends (as she would yearly for the next two decades), to the Riviera with Dick and 15-year-old Val, to Yugoslavia with Tony Pirie, to Zurich with the writer Eric Linklater for a PEN conference, to Sweden with Sonja Meyer, her Danish friend.

Murdoch, soon to be a Fellow at Trinity College and after that to be a Lecturer in Zoology at Edinburgh University, married the historian Rowy Wrong in 1947. Eventually they added four grandchildren to Dennis and Ruth's batch of four.

The Bull Calves was Naomi's first truly Scottish novel. Written slowly and with scholarly and loving care over six years, it was published in 1947 by Jonathan Cape. It is about a middle-aged man and woman seeking absolution through love and marriage. Louise Annand's sketch of the hero and heroine on the title page of the first edition of *The Bull Calves* is a drawing of Naomi and Denny MacIntosh; it was not reproduced in subsequent reissues. A historical novel, *The Bull Calves* is a richly textured story about Naomi's Haldane ancestors living at Gleneagles in the eighteenth century during the Jacobite rebellions. Unlike her earlier works which sweep through years of history, this one obeys the Classic unity of time, all action taking place within twenty-four hours. A psychological novel, it is heavily influenced by Naomi's reading in 1943 of Carl Jung's *The Integration of Consciousness*. For Naomi, Jung's theory of archetypes explained much of the mythology of Scottish nationalism. In addition, his theory of the 'anima', which is the feminine portion of a man's psyche, and the 'animus', which is the masculine portion of a woman's psyche, gave substance to her idea of the complete, mature and self-forgiving personality, an idea of wholeness that wedded Black William, who was a savage Highlander, with Kirsty, who was a civilised Lowlander.

There is another difference between *The Bull Calves* and Naomi's earlier historical novels. In *The Corn King and the Spring Queen*, for instance, she had selected information from works – such as Plutarch's *Lives* – that had already synthesised historical flux. What was not synthesised, she imagined from the odd object or two she would find in museums; this was not much to go on.

By way of contrast, in her research for *The Bull Calves* she was inundated with heaps of raw material – with periodicals, letters, family stories, agricultural records, and with her own experience learning to speak Gaelic, dancing to bagpipes, farming and loving Highlanders. As if to satisfy an understandable desire to connect her Scottish present with her Scottish past, Naomi appended a set of lengthy notes, some of which were essays, some her ruminations on language, music, morality, politics and history. In all, *The Bull Calves* is a powerful, minutely detailed picture of the Scottish past, built on the creation of fictional text and footnote. Moreover it is profoundly connected to current Scottish life with its disheartening loss of population in the Highlands and its economic woes. Naomi was already being considered an important writer in the Scottish literary Renaissance of the first half of the century; this novel confirmed her place beside Grassic Gibbon and Neil Gunn.

Naomi's nationalism was also characteristic of other writers in the Scottish Renaissance. She thought the myths and symbols of internationalism were as yet undeveloped and shallow; Scottish folk culture provided an alternative, a deep and rich source of numinous symbols from a mythological system that had survived the Protestant Reformation, with honourable roots in the Celtic past. Some of Naomi's contemporaries, such as Hugh MacDiarmid, had already blended socialism with nationalism in their writing. They were aided in their synthesis by the thinking of the philosophical politician John MacLean, who identified the communal structure of the Highland clan system with a primitive form of communism.

The Bull Calves was not received well by London-based reviewers who found its Gaelic rhythms and words unappealing. However, it was this very same experiment with language that secured Neil Gunn's praise:

> It's my boyhood rhythm and idiom, with only one real deviation in phrasing. Some of it sang to me and I laughed often. You're a dear girl to do it so well. . .Your extreme skill in making the vast array of social factors significant to your characters without stuffing them was so admirable that I could have wished you less troubled on the matter.[5]

In having chosen to enact her Scottish nationalism both thematically and linguistically, Naomi was choosing to isolate herself from standards of taste prized by the London publishing world, the central clearing-house to all Commonwealth literatures, be they Scottish, Irish, Nigerian, Kenyan, Indian, or whatever.

Nevertheless, *The Bull Calves* is a fine book and one of my favourites; it is heartfelt because it pertains to Naomi's change into middle-aged sexuality and self-acceptance. She is Kirsty, partially convinced she is a witch, thirsty for love and forgiveness. Structurally, in the fiction proper, Naomi avoided the fractured, multi-voiced narration she could not fuse in *We Have Been Warned*. In *The*

Bull Calves her narrative holds together, refusing to fragment under pressure of having too much to convey about urgent contemporary issues; she has harnessed this impulse in a stroke of inventiveness by writing vivid, opinionated essays disguised as footnotes. The form worked as effective art. However, *The Bull Calves* went to but one printing. Outside of Scotland, no one seemed much interested in Naomi Mitchison or her writing.

Yet, in Scotland Naomi's reputation was growing, partly as a writer, but also as a public-minded person who knew enough about crofting and fishing to speak effectively about serious problems facing the Highlands. In 1947 she and John MacNaughton were invited to represent Argyll on the Highland Panel, an advisory group appointed by the Labour Government to voice the region's special problems. At the time Naomi was thrilled; years later she became somewhat disillusioned thinking that Labour may have created the Panel in order to give a push to plans already formed by the Scottish Office.

Naomi was a member of the Highland Panel for more than twenty years, serving until 1973. At the first meeting she was placed in a group to report on sea-fishing, although on the west coast one could not separate agriculture from fisheries for many families had an interest in both. Her personal hobby-horse, however, was the creation of village halls wherever she went, and she took special pleasure in joshing the ministers of the sobre-spirited churches she found on remote islands.

> They [a deputation of Free Protestant Ministers] were against village halls, the singing of songs other than religious or Gaelic, and promiscuous – that is to say boys and girls – dancing. I asked in a shocked voice if they preferred men dancing together; this was picked up with a few friendly twinkles by other Panel members but not by the deputation, buggery being uncommon in the Islands where, I think, sheep are preferred, or small cows.[6]

One can see in this reminiscence that Naomi continued to *épater le bourgeois* both in the remote Highlands of the 1950s and also in the above retelling of her remarks and perhaps shocking thoughts in a self-portrait she wrote in 1986 for the Saltire Society.

Naomi soon learnt that the Panel's effectiveness depended on its ability as a go-between helping to navigate the bureaucratic waters of British government. She could assist villages with their applications for government grants, in their preparation and in securing a fair hearing for them. With other panel members Naomi would slog through sea-water from her boat to a tiny, remote island village where they would hear of need for a harbour or for ferry service or for money for a home industry such as cheese-making; then they would return to the Scottish Office where they would persuade, if they could, those in authority to respond. They might, on other occasions, go directly to sympathetic members of Parliament; Dick, now an MP, was important in this respect.

But the problems, just with fishing, were difficult if not insurmountable. The traditional forms of fishing, including ring-netting, although more kindly to the environment and more conserving of future generations of fish, could not compete with trawling which was a technologically equipped operation that ripped up the seabed taking everything with it. The Panel could not go against the Scottish Office once it made the decision to support trawling, and it is Naomi's observation that 'today the fishermen who go out from Campbeltown, Carradale and Tarbert know very well that they are destroying the future of their own fishing'.

Naomi knew what she was talking about when it came to fishing. The book *Men and Herring*, on which she and Dennis Mac had collaborated during the war, was published in 1949. In the same year the two of them bought the fishing boat they had dreamed of owning for years. Their boat, the 'Maid of Morven', was a 53 feet long vessel equipped with echo-sounder, wireless and 120 horse power engines. A similar boat was part of the stage setting of a play that Naomi and Dennis Mac wrote together; it was produced in Glasgow in 1951 and was so successful that its run was extended.

The play *Spindrift* was treated by the press as primarily the accomplishment of a fisherman playwright; Naomi deliberately took a back seat. In interviews, Dennis MacIntosh described the play as being about economic hard times and then war prosperity in a west coast fishing village between 1938 and 1948. He went on to say to the reporter 'that *Sprindrift* is the play's third title. It was originally called *Spindrift Against the Women* and later *Spindrift Against the World*'.

Naomi's own fictional account of Carradale life can be found in her novel *Lobsters on the Agenda*, which was published in 1952. It was inspired, in part, by Naomi being voted off the County Council in 1948 when the fishermen returned too late to vote. Hurt in her defeat, Naomi stepped away from the village in an effort to assess her relationship to Carradale. In her book she expressed her disillusionment with Highlanders, portraying narrow-minded, even lying, villagers who finally build a community hall. Amusingly, she tells her story from the point of view of a middle-aged woman doctor and, lest the reader think that this is Naomi, she portrays another character, a Mrs Mitchison, who visits the village as one of the members of the Highland and Island Advisory Panel.

So there she is, 'Mrs Mitchison, short and solid in the leather coat, knitted stockings and heavy shoes'. She speaks about her Carradale humiliation:

> 'Oh, granted. If I was writing a book about the Highlands, I'd try and make people mixed, the way they are. My own crowd at Carradale were dirty enough, when they put me out of the County Council in May. But I see why they did it.'
> 'Why did they, then?'
> 'Oh, by and large, I was a witch, a stranger. I did things out of pattern. I upset people. I wore the wrong kind of hat. Let's not talk about it.'
> 'Yes,' said Kate, 'one's got to go slow about changing the pattern. Even when one's got something new and good to give. Like a Village Hall.'[7]

The book seemed to release Naomi from Carradale's grip of some dozen years, and although she continued to act on behalf of Highland interests, both on the Highland Panel and when re-elected as a County Councillor, she began casting her net in new seas.

In her fairy tale for young people, *Travel Light*, which was published by Faber and Faber in 1952, Naomi's heroic woman combines feminine and bearish qualities of defensive loyalty with masculine dragon-traits of hoarding treasure. Halla lives in a mixed past of Nordic and Christian mythology, disdaining both heroes who want to teach her how to be a woman and, at least until the story's end, the sisterhood of Valkyries who snatch up dying heroes for Valhalla. Once she learns to travel light, Halla communicates in all languages, human and animal; she is a diplomat and saviour. To 'travel light' means to leave behind jewels and gold, all treasure; it also means to leave behind attachments to loved groups of comrade-men and to side-step marriage and domesticity: 'No one can travel light with a house on their back, not even a snail'.[8] Procreation is left to others.

Naomi journeyed to Pakistan in 1951 where her daughter Lois, no longer working in a refugee camp, was now teaching at a women's college in Karachi. From there, Naomi made her way northward alone, travelling light, sleeping on tables in train waiting-rooms, cadging rides on the back of student motorbikes, 'swooping hair-raisingly through crowds and round cars, ox carts and other students on bikes'.[9] In Egypt she rode donkeys out to forage for bricks for a new school site: 'As the donkeys had neither stirrups nor bridle I was always falling off whenever they jumped a small canal of which there were many, but they were quite low donkeys and the sand was soft'.[10]

A year or so later Naomi visited the United States where her son Av was living in Maine doing cancer research on a Fullbright Fellowship, having been a Fellow at Magdalen College, a scientist like his older brothers. In Bar Harbor Naomi made a home for Av where they lived on $1 a day because she could only take £35 out of Great Britain at that time. No matter. It gave Naomi an excuse for learning the language of the working people around her: 'I used to walk along the rocks collecting mussels for boiling and at the harbour I bargained for fish until the fishing boats started giving me free fish from their catches'.[11]

When she was not travelling or at home overseeing Carradale, Naomi lived with Dick in his small flat in the Inner Temple where she entertained, bringing politicians together with a mixture of people of all ages, serving simple food and wine in a very informal atmosphere. To Carradale, Dick would often bring his parliamentary colleagues for vacations where Naomi would set them to work alongside her farm labourers.

In the early 1950s Naomi joined hands with other writers in an organisation called the Authors' World Peace Appeal, a response of over seventy British writers to the threat of war posed by the tension between the United States and the Soviet Union. They intended to encourage an international settlement through peaceful negotiations. Naomi was vice-chair of the organisation. Other participants included such luminaries as Cecil Day Lewis, Doris Lessing, Dylan Thomas, among many others, but not Aldous Huxley, with whom Naomi fought in her attempt to persuade him to join. Not all AWPA signatories were British – Albert Camus was a member.

From the beginning, the AWPA ran into political trouble and Naomi was in the thick of it. In 1953 the Labour Party disassociated from the AWPA by listing it along with some forty other proscribed organisations. Naomi and Cecil Day Lewis published a public letter in which they questioned what the Labour Party meant by 'banning' the AWPA and defended the motives of writers seeking peace: 'We can cool the war, which is hotting up against the real wishes of all but a tiny minority, with irony and laughter and even with that most dangerous thing, truth (or, to use Beatrice Webb's phrase, "a few facts")'.[12]

In the first Cold War decade, any organisation claiming that 'differing political and economic systems can exist side by side on the basis of negotiated settlements' was speaking dangerous heresy. The AWPA was accused of being a dupe of the communists. Of course, some of the sponsoring writers were communists, but most were socialist, Labourite and Liberal – the usual mix of British intellectuals for decades. Naomi had spent the whole of her adult life defining the distinction between her brother Jack's communism and her own Labourite socialism. In an AWPA Bulletin analysis published in 1955 – near the end of AWPA's existence – Naomi wrote:

> A non-communist mixing with communists is told by many otherwise sensible bodies of persons he is a 'dupe'! He is always assumed to be fundamentally silly and unable to keep his position or integrity. . .The communist or near-communist working sincerely in a non-communist peace movement (and this certainly does happen, especially in our own Great Britain, mother of paradoxes) is of course accused of 'infiltrating'.[13]

Naomi was appealing to her fellow writers to help clear up the verbal and ideological mess of the Cold War. She herself was on the front lines of the campaign. She feared the psychological climate was being prepared for another war. She advised writers to be more subtle than politicians, to make their effect on the deeper level of people's minds. She was particularly active in a campaign banning American comic books featuring sadistic gore and violence.

In 1952 Naomi, A. E. Coppard, Arnold Kettle, Richard Mason, Douglas Young and Doris Lessing went as AWPA envoys to the Soviet Union where Naomi recalls interviewing along with Doris Lessing, her room-mate on the tour, several Soviet writers who seemed reluctant to speak openly. Two of these writers returned their visit, expressing surprise when staying at Carradale that they could walk to a nearby point of land without an official escort.

What she envied most about Soviet writers was that they seemed to be in personal and constant contact with their readers, something she felt writers in the West had lost. She wrote:

> I myself try to write for my own race, to write intelligibly for the ordinary man and woman in Scotland, to shake them out of their bad dream of respectability. I get little encouragement either from them or from the highbrows. But what I have tried to do would be encouraged in Russia, and I would be able to talk straight to the workers of Scotland without the unkindnesses and hindrances that come from both sides when there is a class barrier still unbroken.[14]

Naomi was again sympathetic with Russia, just as she had been in the early 1930s. It probably took more courage to sympathise publicly during the freeze of the Cold War.

A good deal of Naomi's writing in the 1950s, from her frequent essays in the *New Statesman* to her books for children, was about Scotland. Naomi had stopped writing adult fiction and now wrote books for young people. Her children's books are not as naïve as she deceptively makes them appear. They usually have a social message, although judging from reviews, Naomi's writing was so sufficiently subtle that her didactic intention was seldom noticed. *The Big House* which was published in 1950, for instance, is about a child from the Big House in a fishing village who becomes heart-friends with a child from a fishing family. Some 'thing' always comes between them and, although the 'thing' seems to be a magical monster, it is actually the barrier of class allegorised. *The Land the Ravens Found*, published in 1954, presents an anti-war theme and is a direct result of Naomi's involvement in the AWPA. Other books she wrote were *To the Chapel Perilous* in 1954, *Little Boxes* in 1956, *Judy and Lakshimi* in 1959 and *Rib of the Green Umbrella* in 1960.

Naomi Mitchison's literary career took a new turn in the 1950s as a well-received writer of children's books; her public seemed unaware that she had ever written any other type of fiction. The reviewer for the *Times Literary Supplement* wrote that she deserved praise 'for the original way in which the author manages to combine fantasy with precise details of everyday life', and the reviewer for the *New Statesman and Nation* wrote that she had written a 'magnificent' and 'terrifying' fairy tale set in the western Highlands.

Many years had passed since Naomi had published her fantasy tale, *Beyond This Limit*, illustrated by her controversial friend Wyndham Lewis. Now in the early 1950s Lewis had come to hard times. Naomi, along with T. S. Eliot, helped Lewis get a Civil List Pension for destitute artists when he was stricken with permanent blindness in 1952. Over the years Naomi had given Lewis her friendship as well as financial support. She purchased his paintings when few others did. On occasion, as in Lewis's 1937 exhibit, Naomi was the only one to buy a painting. (As it now turns out, the market value of Lewis's paintings has soared.) Naomi and Dick successfully prevented the local Council from demolishing Lewis's Notting Hill flat until after his death. A loyal friend, she held Lewis's hand in 1954 in the weeks before he died.

In 1955 Naomi's daughter Val, giving over her job as a journalist, married Mark Arnold-Forster, a correspondent for the *Guardian*;

they had five children. Av, now a Lecturer, soon to be a Reader at Edinburgh University, married Lorna Martin in 1957; they had five children. Lois, continuing to publish contemporary books about China and the Far East, married John Godfrey, an Oxford-based scientist, in 1959; they had two children. All told, Naomi and Dick were grandparents of twenty grandchildren.

In 1957 Naomi's brother Jack, apparently disillusioned with the British Communist Party's adherence to Russian scientific dicta, quietly left his citizenship in England and his membership in the Communist Party to settle with his wife, Helen, in India where he became a citizen. At first he worked in the Indian Statistical Institute just outside Calcutta; then he moved to Bhubaneswar where he established the first Haldane Institute in India.

In the same year as Jack's move to India, Naomi went to Africa – first to Nigeria, then to Ghana where she was hired by the *Guardian* to cover the Independence celebration. Even though she was now 60, the high point of the event for her was stepping off a bus loaded with joyless journalists into a crowd of dancers:

> I slipped out into the High Life, a constant change of partners, dark bright eyes, beaming smiles, a bath of happiness. Some time later a friendly policeman tapped me on the shoulder, to indicate that the bus was starting. Odd to think what pleasure the rest had missed.[15]

In her reminiscences about Ghana, signalling her continuing fascination with magic, Naomi described a fleeting image of a witch doctor, 'bedecked with every kind of object, animal and vegetable, especially necklaces of enormous snail shells'. She noted that he kept the rain away from the celebration, and when he ordered it back, it poured. In Nigeria she noticed similar efficacy of magic. Warned that her photographs of Ibibio wood-carved monuments would not develop because the dead would not like it, she noted that, indeed, these were the very photographs on her developed roll that were fogged.

Naomi visited Jack and Helen in Calcutta, stopping over with Ruth and Dennis who were living with their children in Madras, Dennis setting up laboratories for the chemotherapy treatment of tuberculosis. In the midst of what Naomi called frightening poverty visible in the streets of Calcutta, Jack walked the cool marble floors of the Indian Statistical Institute, happy to live surrounded by sprawling gardens, swimming nightly with Naomi in one of two garden pools. Out of Calcutta Naomi would travel, a woman by herself, on buses and, once alone, she was drawn into homes, such as when her hotel reservations fell through in Lucknow and a strange young man at her elbow in the lobby invited her home, gracing her with food and bed and a 'mujira', a poetry reading at which all the guests sat in a circle, presenting an image of uniform white, sparkling with jewellery against the evening darkness.

Even though her eyes were more and more focused on the international world, Naomi kept diligently to her duties as a County Councillor, re-elected by her Carradale constituency term after term. Then, in 1959, because of her influence in getting matching funds from the national government, Carradale finished building a new harbour, something nobody had ever really thought possible before Naomi brought her vision to the village. Naomi reported its opening in the *Glasgow Herald*:

> Here it is finished at last. The fisherman's pennies steadily added up into thousands of pounds. The Government grant has taken solid shape; steel and concrete. This is an entirely new type of harbour and the result is ugly, but solid enough for centuries of wear and tear, and when the fisherman's nets are thrown over the black steel parapet, it won't seem ugly to them.[16]

However, the survival of the fishing industry in Carradale, despite the construction of the harbour, was tenuous. Naomi and Dennis Mac had been forced to sell their boat two years earlier when the price of herring suddenly dropped.

As a County Council member, Naomi modestly recalls doing three good things: she prevented the use of herbicides on the fringes of the roads in Argyll; she protected a family who wished to educate their children at home; and, most proudly, she started a collection of contemporary Scottish paintings that eventually was carried on tour by Jim Tyre to remote schools.

Naomi's retreat into the Scottish Highlands gradually ended in the 1950s when she began to worry over the wider world. She was particularly concerned about hydrogen bombs as NATO installations proliferated in Scotland. In 1959, the same year the harbour was opened in Carradale, she was a major speaker at a mass Nuclear Disarmament rally, and in 1961 in Glasgow she helped lead a march of 10,000 people against the Polaris missile base planned for the Holy Loch.

Demonstrating and marching against nuclear weapons, she was flying in the face of public sentiment in Scotland where, after all, military bases meant jobs for many who were unemployed. Moreover,

Conservative political forces were building in Argyll, and soon enough these forces would overwhelm Naomi.

Meanwhile, as she had for over forty years, Naomi continued to write about the future of humankind now under the threat of nuclear devastation. From having once written mainly historical novels, then mainly children's tales, she now turned to writing science fiction, among the first of a wave of science fiction by women writers. She broke new ground, soon to be followed by Ursula LeGuin and Doris Lessing, in her deconstruction of dualism and hierarchy, attacking conventional patriarchy, imagining androgynies and alternative modes of life.

In *Memoirs of a Spacewoman*, which was published in 1962, Naomi posits a society of space travellers, both men and women, select guardians of a future world in which the peace of the universe depends on communication with non-human forms of life. Her central character, a woman scientist, ages only when she chooses to return to earth to experience pregnancy; otherwise, time is as eternal for her as it is for the men. In fact, the entire novel is a long meditation on child-bearing and mortality; its central caterpillar and butterfly sequence is an allegory of sexual repression in the name of longevity; its parasite-graft sequence is a claustrophobic description of the sensual pleasure in pregnancy and lactation, the graft is first an externalised foetus and then a dependent, merging baby who, disconcertingly, behaves like a self-grown penis:

> I responded by kissing and even licking and gently biting my graft, just as the Diners had done. Then it would wiggle or ripple all over me, pressing against me. These wiggles seemed to penetrate me and where I had found Ariel's incursions between my lips rather disquieting, this one's were welcome. . .I can only remember the feeling of hidden, but complete satisfaction that they set up in me.[17]

As was true of Erif Der in *The Corn King and the Spring Queen* and Halla in *Travel Light*, Mary, the female hero, is gifted with empathy. She can surmount the biological determinates of her human bipartite structure (two arms, two eyes, and so on) which frame her thinking in mere human, bipolar categories. She communicates with all forms of life found in the universe: with Epsies whose 'brain material spread along their rippling sides, and when answering difficult questions they stiffened in a typical and recognisable way'; with Radiates who never thought in terms of 'either-or' and for whom 'alternative' signified 'not one of two, but one, two, three or four out of five, then action is complicated and slowed to the kind of tempo and complexity which is appropriate to an organism with many hundreds of what were in evolutionary time simple suckers and graspers. . .'.[18] The Radiates are artists and feminine.

Memoirs of a Spacewoman introduced Naomi to an entirely different audience once again, this time to readers of science fiction who now consider her work to be a classic. These readers are largely unaware of Naomi's other literary lives.

Because Naomi's abiding literary interest was in the broad genre of the romance quest, she was able to change her surface form easily, giving her imagination free rein over rich and varied territory. She could write historical, political and psychological fiction, as well as fairy tales and now science fiction. *Memoirs of a Spacewoman* is successful; Naomi's intellectualising tendencies, so much a part of the wit in this short novel, are generically expected in science fiction.

If Naomi had had her way when she left the Highlands, as she was doing more and more in the 1950s, she would have aimed for the far reaches of some universe. Almost 60 years old, she tried hallucinogenic mescalin in a controlled experiment but had a bad experience in which she was terrorised for hours by the kind of nightmares she usually only suffered in her sleep. More inner exploration was not for Naomi. Instead, she settled for the Kalahari in the southern reaches of Africa.

11

'Mma' to Chief of the Bakgatla
1963–1990

It never dawned on Naomi that she might rest on her laurels as a 65-year-old woman of enormous accomplishments. By any standard she was still doing more than enough for anyone of any age. Naomi farmed Carradale and spoke out publicly for causes in Scotland and the world. She wrote essays and newspaper articles while enjoying a resurgence of literary reputation for her children's stories and science fiction. Even her rhododendrons were winning prizes in Glasgow flower shows. She certainly had enough children to dote on her and plenty of grandchildren on whom to dote. None the less, she still maintained her abundant will and wonder for exploration – the basis for Naomi's next 'new life', personal, public and literary. Enter Linchwe, designated chief of an African tribe in what is now the nation of Botswana.

Naomi met Linchwe at one of many British Council parties she remembers giving at Carradale in the late 1950s and early 1960s. Their first meeting, she notes, was unremarkable. Linchwe, who was from the British Protectorate of Bechuanaland, was a student in England. He looked much younger than his mid-twenties; he was fine boned and dark skinned, not revealing in that first meeting his mercurial temperament, capable of sharp joy and sullen distraction. Despite an inauspicious introduction, Linchwe returned often to Carradale where he entrenched himself in one of the upstairs rooms and prepared his exams. His relationship with Naomi was not particularly close. To her he was just another young person among many who were guests at Carradale.

Returning to Bechuanaland in 1962, Linchwe sent a letter inviting Naomi to attend his installation as chief of his tribe, which she planned to do, fitting a few days into her swing through Eastern and Southern

Africa. She was taking a holiday, her first in three years, having stayed near her mother, who, as Naomi had suspected, was dying.

Naomi's aged mother Maya wrote a farewell memoir, *Friends and Kindred*, which was published in 1961. She dedicated it to her granddaughter Lois and to Naomi, although with some ambivalence:

This book is for my daughter Naomi Mitchison – indeed it is hers already, for she has recast much of it and deleted notes on friends which I have enjoyed writing, and which I think most of those still alive would have enjoyed reading if it had come their way to do so.

Maya died in 1963 when she was 98 years old. Naomi was free to leave England.

Naomi, travelling by herself, arrived in the middle of the night at the deserted railway station of Gaberones near Mochudi, which is the sprawling central village of the Bakgatla, a tribe inhabiting the territory just on the other side of the northern border of the Republic of South Africa. She described her experience in *Return to the Fairy Hill* (1966). In the Gaberones train depot she curled up on a chair and slept, uncertain of her reception. When she awakened in the morning, there was not much – just dust, temperatures over 100 degrees farenheit and very few people, even though most of Botswana's population inhabits the narrow strip that borders this single railway line traversing the south-western reaches, connecting what is now Zimbabwe with the Republic of South Africa. The vast other reaches of the country are desert, and then, tantalisingly in the north, swamp. *Return to the Fairy Hill* is punctuated by Naomi's pleas for the funding of water projects to bring this northern water to the parched south.

Feeling somewhat lost and alone, Naomi sought coffee at a small nearby hotel where Linchwe found her. He grabbed her up in his arms, elated that she had come. It would seem socially appropriate to most of us that Linchwe would greet Naomi warmly, that he would embrace her. It also seemed perfectly natural to them. However, a few miles away in the Republic of South Africa, such conduct between a young black man and an elderly white woman was unlawful.

Naomi writes that she had not been prepared for the aesthetic pleasure of Mochudi, which was a maze of dirt roads, a few trees, rondavals (round or square houses, grass-thatched and plastered with a mixture of mud and cow dung) and cattle kraals. There was no electricity in 1963 and, likewise, no running water in the rondavals.

In fact, there is almost no water at all in Mochudi save that brought up from bore holes, whose water levels drop measurably from year to year. When these bore holes dry up during times of drought, women and girls must walk five to ten miles with heavy buckets of water to run their households. There were sevens years of drought in the 1960s; Naomi lost great handfuls of her hair, lacking water with which to wash it. For the most part, landlocked Botswana is a grim place, although one might come to appreciate, as did the botanist in Naomi, the delicate vegetation of the Kalahari, which, when there has been rain, films the plain with green. Adventure hunting, Naomi had arrived in a truly inhospitable landscape for her exploration.

The misery and humiliation of apartheid was brought vividly home to Naomi a couple of weeks after she arrived. She and Linchwe, accompanied by his driver-friend, had crossed the border into South Africa in order to do tribal business in Mafeking, which was the district administrative centre for this part of the Protectorate. Naomi was unable to order lunch in any of the local hotels because she was accompanied by blacks; so they bought fruit and soft drinks and sought the shade of a local unmarked park. Soon a white official appeared to warn them away because it was a 'whites only' park. Even though Linchwe withdrew into safe decorum, Naomi lashed back. Her passport number was recorded; eventually she was banned from travel in the Republic of South Africa. In time her books would be banned as well, which she considered a compliment.

Naomi had planned to attend the installation of her young friend, enjoy the ambiance, make a few judicious observations for future articles, and continue her way through Africa. Linchwe had another idea. He had decided she would become his adopted mother and tribal adviser. He did not share his plan with her. Surprised into a feminine reserve which she fancied disguising, Naomi was interviewed by forty male elders of the tribe. They spoke Setwana, the language of the area; Amos Kgamanyane Pilane, the tribe's historian and soon Naomi's dear friend, translated. They approved Naomi; she became the adopted mother of their chief.

The night before Linchwe's installation ceremony, Naomi was asked to guard his sacramental leopard-skin cloak. In a way, Naomi had been preparing for this part since her first girlhood fantasies about pre-Hellenic life. Here she was protecting the power-imbuing fur, living in real life the role of the ancient woman guardian in the Corn King's hut in Marob, her imagined Scythian community on the edge of Hellas in *The Corn King and the Spring Queen*. Just perhaps, she remembers thinking as she settled into sleep that night, the leopard cloak had been trusted to her so that she could protect it from malicious magic.

Duly, her adopted son became Linchwe II, chief of the Bakgatla, a small tribe whose traditional homeland and population was severed by the South African border. Naomi was constantly at Linchwe's side as he negotiated the confusing and dangerous waters of tribal and national politics, finding herself referenced in history books about the development of Botswana as Lady Mitchison, a key influence on Linchwe II, who was a 'young and able' chief, 'convinced that a bridge could be built between socialism and traditionalism'.[1]

In *Return to the Fairy Hill* Naomi described her delight with the culture she found in Mochudi. It seemed that some of her more ardently held beliefs about early cultures were true. One of her more long-lasting interests had been in communal and agrarian societies. Along with other Western observers, she believed that they advocated magic in order to drive the cycle of the seasons, especially the magical power of a worshipped chief, who was part man and part deity. It was in this light that Linchwe appeared to her. Instead of being a Corn King, he was a Rain King, and she liked to consider herself, instead of his Spring Queen, as his Winter Queen. She loved to be near him:

> Sometimes someone danced towards us whirling a war-axe; once Linchwe caught one out of the air and took it into the car to show me. I don't know how long we stayed; I could have stayed for ever; I knew that for the time I was utterly happy, in all my senses. Even if now I was only the Winter Queen, I was with my Corn King – but no, he was the Rain King. Without rain no corn. But the Fairy Hill was Marob, my place imagined over half a century, now real.[2]

Sometimes Mochudi seemed like Marob, Naomi's barbarian village in her novel *The Corn King and the Spring Queen*; sometimes Mochudi was Carradale, her village in the Scottish Highlands, where an agrarian community had been rubbed out by the lure of money-commerce. In Mochudi she persuaded herself that only a 'small effort of imagination' is necessary 'to overcome any awkwardness' cultural differences might cause.

Naomi perceived her tribe on the brink of exchanging one cultural stage for another. The Bakgatla had a chance, she thought, to exploit science and technology, leaving behind, as chaff, habits and institutions that would weaken its sense of tribal unity. She hoped to help her tribe rework the mechanisms of history and to avoid the pitfalls of individualism and capitalism. She wrote: 'There was, indeed, so much work for me, as much as I could manage, of what they would let me do, myself. It was a transition of 30,000 men, women and children from one bit of history, if you like one technological epoch, into another'.[3] The Bakgatla would give Naomi another opportunity to draw upon her deeply rooted urge to shape the world into a 'Just Society', her Platonic phrase for utopia. She had tried first in London within the Labour Party, then in the Scottish Highlands, and now she had settled in a desert territory on the verge of nationhood. Desiring to help it change wisely, she contributed abundant personal skills accumulated through many years of experience and hard work.

During the 1960s Naomi journeyed to Mochudi twice each year, then once a year until the present, usually going during Britain's autumn. She has made over twenty trips to Botswana – mostly flying from Lusaka but sometimes ferrying across the Zambesi. Her route through Bulaweyo and Rhodesia was cut off when she was declared a Prohibited Immigrant in the mid-1960s. She does not know what provoked the indictment. She simply remembers being politely grilled for three unpleasant hours by officials as her train rolled for the Botswana border. They took away her books and photographs of her grandchildren.

Back in London in autumn 1963, Naomi found her brother Jack hospitalised for surgery on what had been diagnosed as cancer. It was terminal, although the attending doctors decided not to tell Jack or Helen, his wife, or even Dennis, Naomi's doctor son. Nor was Naomi alarmed, advising Julian Huxley to stay clear of Jack because he was 'very weak and very cross', then going on to chat about her planned return to Mochudi: 'I go back to Africa in January. It is very strange suddenly becoming one of another, much loved but very different community'.[4]

Jack returned to India with Helen, beginning a new project rather than winding up the ones in progress. Later in 1964, when he realised he was dying, Jack was furious with his London doctors for having misled him, although he had no scruples about misleading Naomi:

> But if it gets round, I fear my sister will want to do all kinds of things, perhaps even come here. Whereas I wish to die in peace, preferably on an easy chair or even a jointed bed, on my verandah, looking at flowering trees and birds in the sunshine.[5]

Perhaps Jack was right. Naomi might have disrupted his peaceful glide into death by trying 'to do all kinds of things' to prolong his life. On the other hand, he may have been wrong. She, too, was becoming accustomed to old age, having written:

> One certainly becomes less afraid of death. One feels it would be a nuisance and an interruption, but more and more of one's friends have gone through the experience. Yet this point of view has its dangers. An old person may be reckless or may spoil something potentially good by being in a desperate hurry. ... .[6]

Jack dictated his own obituary on a tape for Naomi and posterity; he died on 1 December 1964.

In the summer of 1965 Dick, now 74 years old, moved from the House of Commons to the House of Lords. No one reminded him that he had advocated the abolition of the Lords in *The First Workers' Government*, which he had published in 1934. As an MP, Dick had been front-bench leader on science and technology, then on pensions. Some thought he should have been appointed to a ministerial post.[7] Lord Elwyn-Jones remembers that Dick was always helpful to his colleagues; he was dependable and loyal. Naomi had a similar evaluation: Dick was 'a perfect constituency member who knew every inch of local water supplies and all that, and was endlessly helpful to worried MPs, getting their good ideas into form (very important and only comparatively easy for a lawyer) and getting them out of financial difficulties'.[8] From 1964 Dick was one of the parliamentary secretaries to the newly created Ministry of Land and Natural Resources and, in addition, was considered an important Labour voice in the Lords.

Naomi, who was worried about Dick's health, had urged him to accept Harold Wilson's offer of this life peerage. Nevertheless, rather stridently, she refused to be addressed by her title, Lady Mitchison. It would violate her identity as a writer, she proclaimed wherever she could, including an advertisement she placed in the London *Times*. Although she took this tack and held to it more or less, I have heard her overcome her distaste for this title when making plane reservations.

On her return to Linchwe in Autumn 1964, Naomi remembers being deeply uneasy, experiencing pangs of self-doubt. Well she might. The deaths of her mother and brother and the strain over identity as Dick's new Lady Mitchison took their toll. Naomi began making harsh judgements of herself as she contemplated life in Africa. She doubted her heart and gut connection with her tribe. Perhaps she had led herself astray with fictional pipe-dreams; maybe Linchwe did not love her; maybe she was a doddering old woman whose goodwill was being exploited by desperately poor people.

Once again, Naomi scrambled off the train in Bechuanaland. She fell into Linchwe's embrace. All was well. In *Return to the Fairy Hill* she writes that she was certain again that she belonged to her tribe. In exchange Naomi gave everthing she could – her energy, her time, her expertise, generators for electricity, printing presses, all that she could gather.

Naomi lived an unresolvable contradiction, apparent here in the desert as surely as in Carradale and, for that matter, in working-class Birmingham. With the best of intentions Naomi yearned to be a part of folk communities, sharing her resources. In Mochudi she had the wherewithal to feed dying babies with her gifts. Naomi's largesse paradoxically placed her above the folk from whom she sought acceptance. Her economic and social class – whether she liked it or not, she was Lady Mitchison – did not square with her socialism. And really, short of giving away most of what she owned, there was little Naomi could do to change this basic contradiction in her life, as painful as it was – and is.

In May 1965, Naomi's Carradale constituency voted her off the County Council. A friend from her first years in Carradale spread stories about Naomi, claiming that she had squandered County Council money in Africa. Of course, it was untrue. One villager remembers a scene in the Village Hall: members of the audience were hurling insults at Naomi, who was weeping; Dick scolded them for their conduct and the meeting broke up. Naomi's campaign manager, Lilla, Dennis Mac's wife, fell violently ill the day of the election; Naomi rushed to her side. Lilla died that afternoon from peritonitis.

The election was a bitter pill for Naomi, who could not see from her place in the hurly-burly that the turn against her was part of a larger Conservative swing in Argyll. Her stand against Polaris missile bases in the Holy Loch had made her unpopular with people unsure of employment, and her connection with Botswana, especially ardent appeals to raise money for her tribe, had raised suspicions about her loyalties. Naomi was left with sore feelings about the villagers, believing that she had worked very hard to get them the harbour for their fishing boats and that now they were turning her out just when she was finally to have some official influence as Convenor of the Education Committee.

When Bechuanaland became the independent country of Botswana in 1965, Naomi was there to lower the Union Jack from its pole in front of Linchwe's tribal office, a 'kgotla shelter of black twisted timbers'. As soon as the flag was on the ground at her feet and the new flag of Botswana was flying,

> . . .one man with a spear leapt out of the crowd shouting *'Lefatse, lefatse!'* – The country, the country! And he pointed his spear up towards it. So for want of anything better to do I laid my hand over his on the spear shaft and then – then the crowd burst out at last cheering and shouting and came round us both with loving words and looks and kisses.[9]

Naomi was the only person at the ceremony who had ever lit fireworks, so it was also her job to set off huge wheels and fountains and rockets, flinging herself down to get out of the way: 'This too was much applauded and for days after the children went around imitating not only the whistle of the rockets but Mmarona [mother] lying on the ground'.[10]

Mornings in Mochudi, Naomi would waken to the twitter of birds. She washed in a cup of water; sometimes coffee was brought to her, at other times she did without. Her portable typewriter in hand, she walked to the administrative office where a small area was cleared for her to type committee minutes, memoranda, proclamations and grant applications. It was from the administrative office windows that she witnessed the canings that Linchwe ordered as punishment for wrong-doings, ancient tribal justice that she found difficult to accept. Daily Naomi tutored children, preparing them for their exams, British-style. At night she spent hours talking with Linchwe about the political and philosophical problems of slowly opening a closed society; she recommended that he read Karl Popper's *Enemy of the Open Society*. Later, alone, by lantern light and by flashlight she strained her eyes to do her own reading and writing.

Naomi's bouts of loneliness during the war years in the Highlands were not as bad as the isolation she experienced in Mochudi. She sometimes went stir-crazy. After weeks of little water, little food and little of the restful and soothing aspects of familiar Western culture, she was exhausted. Even her outings were taxing. Once Linchwe took her hunting, during which time they and their fellow hunters shared a single cup for portions of muddy water and fresh milk, the flies politely flicked off. Later in the day, the others stalking game in the intense heat, Naomi scooped hollows for her thigh and shoulder in the shadow under the truck, a place of respite from the sun.

It was a very good thing that this refugee from Edwardian ladyhood was a sturdy creature, for nothing other than superb physical endurance could have taken Naomi through the grind of the Botswanan drought-cycle which killed both old and young – especially those babies who had just stopped drinking their mother's milk. In 1965 over half of the Bakgatla cattle died from lack of water, which meant loss of milk and meat, important ingredients in the tribe's diet. The Bakgatla survived as well as they did during the 1960s' drought partly because of the aid that Naomi organised from her friends and from Oxfam.

As tough as the new environment was, it nevertheless generated a surge of creativity in Naomi. She felt essential and strong. She began writing poetry again. She wrote a novel about her tribe, *When We Become Men* (1965), which she read to a group every night, including Linchwe, for confirmation and criticism. That takes courage; at every turn of phrase she risked misunderstanding. In 1965 she also published *A Mochudi Family* and *Ketse and the Chief*. Her description of Bechuanaland, the Bakgatla, and her experiences in *Return to the Fairy Hill* are written for two audiences – for her tribe, to whom she gives advice, and for the world at large, where she found herself appealing to a new set of readers, many of whom did not seem to realise that she had written famous historical novels in the 1920s and 1930s, Scottish literature in the 1940s, children's books in the 1950s and science fiction in the early 1960s.

Once again Naomi could see purpose for writing. The children of her tribe, like most children in South Africa, had been taught only the history of white colonialisation. She set to work by the unsteady light of her lantern, protected nightly by a praying mantis which perched on the carriage of her typewriter. She first wrote a history of Africa from the African point of view, then a book of stories about African heroes, the latter framed by references to Nelson Mandela, the then imprisoned leader of the African National Congress. The book *African Heroes* (1968), a volume of children's stories, was officially banned in the Republic of South Africa. Other books written by Naomi were banned as well, including a biography of a white lawyer who had defended blacks, *A Life for Africa: the Story of Bram Fischer* (1973). One might say of the South African government that it fully respects the revolutionary power of literature.

Naomi was surprisingly well-trained for the job of helping a tribe through the complexities of becoming a new nation. All those years of committee work on the Argyll County Council and on the Highland Panel, those hours of meetings devoted to roads and health and welfare and so on, had taught Naomi something. She knew how the British bureaucracy worked, where best to apply pressure, where money could be found for grants and loans. Because she could listen carefully to what people said they wanted, she had particular success translating relevant desires into the right bureaucratic language. But she did more than transcribe; even Linchwe's Installation speech had her stamp.

Naomi was influential because Linchwe respected her, and he was a chief, complete with the total privilege of this kind of inherited position. Learning to respect what it meant to be a tribal chief in Africa, Naomi came to face the knotty issue of how to incorporate the governing power of a traditional chief into the newly imposed system of parliamentary democracy in Botswana. If a chief were to be made a chairman of a committee and be paid as a civil-servant, then he would be reduced and tribal cohesion would suffer. If he were a politician seeking votes, then he would be vulnerable to political humiliation and, again, the tribe would be weakened.

It is not surprising that Naomi prized the tribal unit. Through her interpreting lens, she found tribes akin to the Highland clans whose history, she thought, continues to vitalise Scottish consciousness. But in her view the health of the community in both tribe and clan alike depends on the charisma and wisdom of the chief. She perceived that the fate of many of Africa's tribes, especially during periods of rapid cultural transition, depends on the character of the chief himself, and that the Bakgatla were unusually fortunate to have a leader with the commitment and the education to lead his people.

Nor did Naomi content herself with evening discussions with Linchwe and their friends. She found world forums in which to present her opinions about the good of tribalism, finally concluding that democracy in Africa depended upon its merger with positive tribal values, an opinion that ran counter to many in Europe who assumed that parliamentary democracy could be slapped down on any culture without regard for its history. In an 'Open Letter to an African Chief' published in the *Journal of Modern African Studies* (1964), Naomi eulogised the good that comes from tribal cohesion. In the same breath she earnestly tried to tell Linchwe why democratic policies are important; the sharing of power that the vote entails may well prevent unjust violence. Her thinking, which was ambiguous in the 1960s – as it had been all of her life on this subject of aristocratic heroism and communal socialism – became clearer by 1984 when, in 'One-Party Rule in Africa' in *The Round Table*, she attacked the tendency of new African states to institute one-party rule. Naomi was especially critical of one-party states superimposed on tribal traditions of consensus politics – a system for informing a chief of differing points of view. In one-party systems she found that leaders tend to be shielded from controversy and are less able to do what is right for their people.

Naomi revered Linchwe. In mock form she would ask his permission to use land for projects, thanking him with a formal curtsy, one she may have learnt as a young woman presented to the British Court. On his part, Linchwe heeded Naomi. He extended suffrage to women in the new Constitution regulating his tribe; all women in Botswana now have the right to vote.

Nevertheless, Naomi's situation as Linchwe's advisor and adopted mother was not without the experience of inner conflict and trouble. As chief, Linchwe's claim to patriarchal power was complete. In *Return to Fairy Hill* she wrote:

> But make no mistake. Relations with the Chief were not always easy or happy. He could be maddening. Sometimes my loyalty to him came up with a jolt against my main feminist loyalties. . .As for me, part of his teasing was probably that which comes to women in a traditionally male-dominated society and to which the answer is floods of tears. Not that I think he ever really wanted to make me cry with anger and frustration as he sometimes did, especially in the very hot weather. He hated it. He went away, and left me to cry on to my typewriter, alone among the flies and beetles.[11]

Although Naomi was to revise her estimate of the status of women, later acknowledging that many husbands did respect their wives, in 1966 she described a difficult situation for women. Women were the property of their husbands, and even well-educated professional women such as Tshire, Linchwe's sister who was a nurse, believed this to be natural. Women's work was arduous as well. Just securing enough water when the bore holes in town dried up required strenuous effort. Women walked miles to potable water, not easy even when a woman has had a lifetime of practice balancing a full pail of water on her head. Naomi witnessed children dying in their mother's arms in clinics where clumps of mothers sat with their near dead children listlessly lying in their laps. By 1968 the situation was desperate, provoking Naomi to act.

Naomi spoke to women's associations about birth and contraception. Then she asked Linchwe's permission to move officially. Together they raised a rumpus by urging Bakgatla women to use birth-control. Of course, they faced opposition both from within the tribe, although not because of intrinsic cultural objections to birth-control, and from missionary doctors who believed that the only basis for stopping illegitimate births was to educate young people to discipline themselves. The overriding horror of helplessly standing by while babies died because of malnutrition caused by drought spurred Naomi and Linchwe in their successful efforts. As it stood, pregnancy was held against a girl, affecting her status and eventual ability to support herself. If a young girl became pregnant, she was not allowed to continue her education. Birth-control, plus Naomi's and Linchwe's pressure for change in school regulations, gave young girls a chance to become teachers and nurses. As Naomi had learnt in the 1920s in her work in the first London birth-control clinics, women must at least have the right to direct themselves if they are to have the power to direct government.

In a formal fashion, Naomi was made a member of the tribe and assigned to a 'mophato', which is an age group of sisters. Whenever anyone remarked about how much younger she looked than her African peers, she took the opportunity to point out that this was because she spaced her children according to the strength of her body, whereas her sisters had not.

It is well to keep in mind that even though Naomi thought of herself as truly a tribe member, even though she found her standards for beauty had shifted away from pink and white skin to plum and velvety skin, even though she adored the sweet, smoky scent of the people, hers was a part-time, albeit deep, commitment to African life. Mochudi was her home for mere portions of the year; once because of a broken leg, she had to miss a year altogether.

Naomi toured other parts of the world in addition to living in Mochudi. The year after Jack died she visited his wife, Helen Spurway, in India, writing newspaper articles about eating 'bhang', a form of cannabis, in its traditional dish of curds; she experienced nothing but an unpleasant hangover. She was back in India with Helen again in 1968 dancing with gypsies in Hyderabad, and again in 1969, remembering a walk around the garden of the Prime Minister's house with Jawaharlal Nehru, talking politics as they usually did when together. He introduced her to his pandas.

Naomi was with Dick at Carradale when he began to suffer a series of strokes. There she nursed him for several weeks before flying him to a London hospital where he died on 14 February 1970. A memorial tribute was held in the House of Lords, and Dick's ashes were dropped ceremoniously in the sea near Carradale where Naomi's boat was accompanied by the Carradale fishing fleet in honour of their laird. Dick was put to rest near the same spot in the sea that had swallowed Naomi's seventh child. In the year or so after Dick's death, Naomi kept a diary, a comforting activity that was her habit in times of distress.

I once asked Naomi why there was not more about Dick in her memoirs. She answered: 'I suppose it is because we were so much a part of one another'. They had celebrated a Golden Wedding anniversary, having been married for fifty-four years when Dick died aged 78. Theirs had been an extraordinary relationship of intimacy, respect and exploration.

In the year after Dick died, Naomi's daughter Val took her to the Riviera along with her own family and Naomi's artist friend, Gertrude Hermes. Naomi visited Pakistan and Australia, as well as Russia where she was a speaker at the Institute of Foreign Languages. She also went to Washington, DC in 1970 to live with Linchwe's family when he became Botswana's ambassador to the United States.

Naomi continued to write books with African themes, including *The Africans* (1971), *Cleopatra's People* (1972), *Sunrise Tomorrow* (1973) and *Images of Africa* (1980). And she published a variety of other works. She wrote her memoirs: *Small Talk: Memoirs of an Edwardian Childhood* (1973), *All Change Here: Girlhood and Marriage* (1975), and *You May Well Ask: A Memoir 1920-1940* (1979), each devoted to a segment of her long life and each treating her personal self and experience as sociological documents of the historical moment, this her socialist compromise with the evocation of personality usually found in autobiography. In addition she published another science fiction, *Solution Three* (1973), in which she imagined a world culture dominated by homosexuals and lesbians, only regressive 'professorials' practising aberrant heterosexuality. A volume of her poetry, *The Cleansing of the Knife* (1978), added to her reputation in Scottish literature, which was further fuelled by a volume of her short stories, *What Do You Think Yourself?* (1982). She wrote *The Magicians* (1978), another science fiction, *The Vegetable War* (1980), and a travel memoir, *Mucking Around* (1981). Naomi published a novel about neolithic life, *Early in Orcadia* (1987), when she was 90 years old.

Naomi was 73 when Dick died. The next year in Mochudi she asked for a change of mophato, the age group to whom she had been assigned. These women, she maintained, were too old for her. She wanted to be with a younger age group, willing to sacrifice the honour accorded older members of the tribe. She remembers that the two mophatos fought over her: 'I found myself with two old ladies holding on to my arms and a couple of others tugging my feet'. She was finally allowed to join the more junior mophato because Linchwe called her 'Mma' rather than 'Ngoko' (granny). She threw a party for her new group, skinning and roasting goats, brewing great earthenware pots of beer made from fermented sorghum, ritually tasting it first then offering big gourds of it around to 100 guests – and dancing, finally, in circles,

> . . .holding on to one another's shoulders, or breaking when one went into the centre and danced, often a kind of posturing, to the hand clapping and singing of the rest. Then I became aware that we were now singing 'serious' songs, that is a repetition of words which by themselves meant little but which had an esoteric meaning and were part of what we had learned as a mophato.[12]

Mochudi has remained Naomi's spiritual home. She would have been satisfied to die there. It was still the practice in Mochudi to bury the dead under the floors of their rondavals or under the floors of their cattle kraals. In *Return to the Fairy Hill* Naomi left instructions for her death, leaving no doubt about the placement of her imaginative soul:

> But if I die here in Mochudi I want to be buried in the great kraal where Chief Molefi was buried, and let the cattle trample out all marks of where my body lies. And I do not want any religious service; nor yet to have my body put in any coffin, but into the skin of some beast; I would like best for it to be a lion skin. So I am writing this now for Linchwe to know.[13]

12

Winter Queen

Naomi was 85 years old when I first met her in 1982. Her manner was carefully polite, her voice upper-class, daunting. But shyly she put her hand on my arm, spinning an immediate web of intimacy. Although she was a very old woman, she was alert, intelligent and seductive. Her face, which she characteristically rubbed or covered with her hands when thinking, was deeply lined like tortoise skin. She was short and rather round, with sturdy hands and feet and with soft, waving, white hair, chopped abruptly beneath her ears. There was bright colour in her necklace of carved wooden beads, Chinese red, and in her simple dress of paisley challis, orange and blue cloth from Liberty's.

When we met, I was an American graduate student writing a dissertation about her novel *The Corn King and the Spring Queen*. Naomi not only agreed to talk to me, she rented me a room in her small London garden flat at the base of her daughter Val's Clarendon Road home. I lived with her in October and November 1982, returning to visit Naomi in Carradale in 1983 and 1988 – now as her biographer. In 1984, aged 87, Naomi stayed a month with me in La Jolla, California, while she delivered a series of lectures and workshops as an honoured Regents' Lecturer for the University of California at San Diego.

Some of Naomi's earlier writings have been rediscovered in the 1980s and 1990s. Among them *Memoirs of a Spacewoman*, *The Corn King and the Spring Queen* and *Travel Light*. In Scotland her novel about her Haldane ancestors, *The Bull Calves*, was reissued in 1986, and in 1988 there were reissues of *Blood of the Martyrs* and her first two memoirs together under the title *As It Was*.

That first October night when we shared the warm lamp light in her London flat, Naomi spread over her knees the galley proofs of her latest novel, *Not by Bread Alone* (1983), a science fiction about

161

her perceptions of her brother who she maintained had always been an intuitive scientist just as she was an intuitive writer. She set the galley proofs aside when we began to tape our conversation. We talked about her reading Frazer's *Golden Bough*, Marx's *Capital* and Freud, all either before or while she was writing *The Corn King and the Spring Queen*, but, 'Och, it's what you select to use that's important', she added. There was a silence before she went on in irritation: 'How can you expect me to remember who that silly woman was fifty years ago?' Characteristically, Naomi does not enjoy talking about her past, preferring to live in the present. What happened next never happened again.

I asked her to identify the name represented by 'Widg' in her notes appended to a manuscript entitled 'The Break Up of the Home' housed in the Humanities Research Centre in Texas. She started, dropping her face to her open hands. She was weeping. 'Oh,' she said when she raised her head, 'He was my lover a long time ago. I rang him up on Armistice Day to ask if we could now be friends. He said "no" and that he hated me.' She did not tell me who Widg was, and I never asked again. In time, I would make my own discoveries.

That night I was awakened by Naomi's screams; she was having nightmares. In the morning she slumped, haggard, over the refrigerator. She said she had died twice in her sleep. Her frequent nightmares during the next two months kept me on edge. We agreed that we would not talk about Naomi in the evening before going to bed.

Naomi's London day would begin typically with crackers and home-made jam from Carradale, the small portions of which were perhaps conditioned by her experiences in drought-desiccated Mochudi. After breakfast, she wrote letters and worked on her current book. Sometimes she wore her glasses and sometimes not; it did not seem to make any difference.

Naomi kept vital connection with an amazing number of the communities in which she had participated during her long, multifaceted lifetime, including a lively on-going correspondence with one of the American leaders in the 1935 sharecropper crisis in Arkansas where she and Zita (Baker) Crossman had rabble-roused. In London during the first week I stayed with her, she talked by phone to Doris Lessing, with whom she had roamed Russia in 1952; shared tea with Elizabeth (Harman) Pakenham, now Lady Longford, conjuring Midsummer Eves in the early 1930s when Naomi's guests jumped over bonfires in her River Court garden; lunched with her old friend Vera Brittain's daughter, Shirley Williams, who was jockeying for leadership of the

Social Democratic Party as it made its bid for power in 1982; and provided supper for Francis Huxley, another old friend and once a contributor to a volume of essays edited by Naomi, *What the Human Race Is Up To* (1962). This was certainly a full life; but she had another fully peopled life waiting in Carradale, and yet another in Mochudi.

During my visit, Naomi was beginning a short historical novel set in prehistory on the island of Orkney, whose archaeological digs had been turning up surprising evidence of early human agriculture. Knowing of my interests in feminist literary history, she coyly handed me a story she had recently completed; it was about the worship of a female goddess in pre-Celtic Britain:

> At each side the heavy, thick marten and beaver furs brushed softly, intimately, against his arms. He moved closely along them, knowing that the opening would come and he would pass through it. He was used to the almost dark, the deep forest feeling. It was part of his training, as were the whispered repetitions, fur muffled, the continuous hammering of knowledge, the murmur of the great rush-thatched beehive. Happy he was to be back. The fur curtains revealed an entrance; he pushed gently.[1]

Despite this story's sexualised insistence on the worship of women deities and the equal power of men and women, Naomi held tight to her assertion that she was not a feminist.

Whenever the subject came up, she would categorically deny feminist motivations. For instance, two young men wanted to make a film of the caterpillar and butterfly sequence in *Memoirs of a Spacewoman*; in order to make the heroine more sympathetic to their imagined audience they planned to degrade her to Earthbound status from her rank of immortal and rational Explorer. In discussion with me, Naomi insisted that it was all right with her if this character was redefined. In 1988 when I met one of those young men, Mark Nash, he told me a different story. He said that Naomi had fought hard to retain the integrity of her heroic woman. Not that she prevailed; but this is an old story for women writers.

Perhaps over this issue of feminism I was encountering Naomi's temperamental playfulness, both her refusal to be pigeon-holed and her desire to titillate. In the several years I have know her she has flooded me with clippings about women – about women coal strikers in Wales, about women and psychoanalysis, about women and the publishing industry.

Naomi's taste for the 'put-on' must be taken into account even when she makes statements of self-criticism. She once said the best biography of her would be a thorough Marxist scourging. Perhaps, although if one did so, it would have to be in generalised terms for she would be the very last person in the world to open her financial records, more than once reminding me that, like Freud, she thought money seemed excremental – 'shit', she said. When I asked about her views of sex, she answered in her still daunting voice, 'Oh fuck sex!'

Another time, she confided that the history of her relationships with people will demonstrate that she drops those she no longer needs. The record does not support her harsh self-judgement. She remains loyal friends with many people, although many have abandoned her – some by dying. Dennis Mac, for instance, appeared nearly every Sunday for supper at Carradale, as recorded in the diary she kept after Dick's death in the 1970s. But Dennis Mac died in the mid-1970s. While I was living with her in 1982, she rekindled her relationship with Frances Parkinson, her adolescent girlfriend; Naomi was relocating Frances so that she would receive better health care. I sympathised with Naomi's dither over Frances' twenty-three cats. There are many stories of Naomi's continuing generosity with friends of all stripes. Indeed, it is impossible to imagine Naomi giving up on anyone or anything.

Naomi seemed to enjoy teasing me. Once we were at Carradale, nearly alone in the Big House. It was November, grey and chill. Naomi led me to her bedroom on the second floor where she pointed to her desk which was framed in a patch of wintery light, looking out to sea and distant islands. As if she were the magic old woman in one of her fairy tales, she said that I might look in any drawer but the one on the bottom right, 'and you may not look in that one because it contains letters from my lovers'. I did not look there, satisfying myself with troves of unpublished poems and manuscripts, interesting enough in their own right because the name of the significant person about whom each had been written was often pencilled into the margins. Moreover, I was not yet planning a biography of Naomi Mitchison.

When I returned to Carradale in 1983, Naomi again led me to her room and again enjoined me to forbear looking in the drawer that secreted her lovers' letters. Either I was less bewitched or less honourable, but as soon as I was alone, I stooped to the drawer. It contained several fat envelopes, each carefully labelled, ready, no doubt, for some future biographer, but not yet for me. By August 1988, I had become that biographer. For the first time I asked Naomi if I could read the letters. She paused for almost a minute, although it seemed longer, then said 'yes'. That was all. We have never talked about what I read, assuming, as I do, that Naomi prefers to leave me to my own interpretations.

Of the poems in the other drawers, many were about her experience as a woman. Some have been published separately; most have not. Together, they would make a powerful volume, chronicling a woman's life from young womanhood through middle age and later. One unpublished poem entitled 'Nettlebed Road' wryly summarises Naomi's lifetime push to break through inner and outer restraints:

> On this road, this road,
> I reap what I sowed.
>
> Suppose, now, I had been good,
> I might truly have understood
> And accepted the oncoming of age
> Without a heart of rage
> Or if only I had been bad
> – All women wish they had –
> The gold leaves would whisper yes,
> That glory, that success,
> One negation the less.
>
> But, being half bad, half good,
> – Ah love, who thought we could
> Between a yea and a nay
> Tread the classic middle way –
> What switch of taunts and jeers.
> The road twists and sneers
> At an old fool, an old, hurt fool,
> Failed in the final School,
> Nothing, oh nothing to show for all that contriving!
>
> I must watch my driving.[2]

On a November day in 1982 Naomi burst into her Carradale bedroom, startling me from my sleuthing in her desk drawers. She was in a fury over a plan that had gone awry for charging more farm rental money on the Carradale estate. She stamped her foot several times, spraying angry tears in all directions, then pulled me to my feet leading me up the stairs to the attic so that she could assess the damage of last winter's storm. Carradale weighed financially on Naomi. Just as she dreaded, the pink flowered wallpaper of the attic room was damply sprouting mushrooms. The roof really had to be repaired immediately.

Naomi already had another plan in the works. The Carradale River ran through Naomi's land, burdening her with what amounts to feudal rights and obligations. Because she owned a portion of the river, she was not only responsible for its regulation so that its salmon would not be over-fished, but she also had to pay about £500 in annual taxes. She proposed to have the local villagers organise a fishing club, pay the taxes and protect the fishing themselves. It sounded like a simple, reasonable plan. It was not so simple. Carradale came alive with small conspiracies which I observed along with Naomi's visiting friend, Roddie MacFarquahar, who, as a member of the Highland and Island Development Council (once the Highland Panel), was being lobbied in hushed whispers by this group or that group vying for control over the proposed club. After some forty years in Carradale, Naomi was still faced with repercussions of her efforts to mix class and community.

As recounted by Naomi's family and friends, Easter and Hogmanay (the Scottish New Year) are especially crowded times at Carradale, all bedrooms full, the long dining-room table elbow to elbow, children, grandchildren, great-grandchildren, friends, the children of friends, visiting foreigners, all in lively discussion. Naomi presides. One wonders how much the scene has changed since the American Nobel Laureate scientist James Watson described it in his book *The Double Helix*, which he dedicated to Naomi Mitchison because, Naomi explains, she had helped him by editing his manuscript. Watson, who had spent the Christmas holiday at Carradale in 1951 as a guest of Naomi's son Avrion, describes a lively and intellectual scene, highlighted by word games in the living-room in front of the blazing fire and by ping-pong in the library. He wonders at how a family of 'leftish leanings could be bothered by the way their guests dressed for dinner'. Even in the 1980s guests still dressed for dinner, many in long skirts, although it might be noted that at least one distinguished guest in coat and tie dined barefoot.

It was certainly more formal in the early 1950s when Watson visited. Long-time visitors to Carradale remember that meals became considerably more relaxed in the 1970s. In 1969 the kitchen portion of the Big House burned to the ground, destroying its maze of small rooms and pantries. It was replaced by a large room accommodating two freezers and two dishwashers. New manners have been fitted to the modern kitchen; now it is the convention for guests, men and women, young and old, to fill the kitchen after a meal, where they wash dishes before coffee and inevitable chocolates in the living-room, settling into soft couches for quiet conversation and reading.

In her California visit in 1984, Naomi wrote absolutely every morning, sitting in the spring sunshine surrounded by fragrant sage, scribbling in one of her bound paper notebooks, which she would then transcribe on a typewriter, still using ditto paper. Each night she read aloud what she had written, pausing every once in a while to pencil a correction, always with an ear cocked to the rhythm of her sentence.

Busy at the University of California lecturing and giving workshops about writing and her life, Naomi had two requests: she wanted to be put in touch with an anti-nuclear weapons organisation and she wanted to swim.

Her fear of nuclear weapons had increased since her participation in the Authors' World Peace Appeal during the tense time of the Cold War in the 1950s. She had headed political demonstrations against NATO installations in the Strathclyde in the early 1960s, and now, during the enormous American stockpiling of nuclear weapons during the Reagan presidency, her war anxieties frequently welled-up in many situations. The last story in *What Do You Think Yourself?* was about a community of people in Argyll surviving the bombing of the Holy Loch. Her middle-aged heroine is angry as she worries about the health of her grandchild:

It was hard somehow the way we in western Scotland had been loaded up with these things which have brought destruction down on us and we were never even consulted. Defence, they said! When the haze came over the sky and the horizon like hellmouth at sunset – some way I had expected this – I kept in all the beasts from the inbye land and the hens, just as I kept in Fiona. I mind now I slapped her for running out. My heart bleeds for it. . .[3]

It is a brave elder who will set her mind to imagining doom; no wonder Naomi continued to have nightmares. She did not shirk. Ten years later she wanted to amend 'Remember Me'; for it had become clear to her that no human life would survive nuclear holocaust. She became active in FREEZE, an international organisation lobbying governments to promise not to make the first strike, and she lent her support to the women at Greenham Common who lived for months in tents protesting against the placement of yet another cruise missile on British soil. She wrote to me in California:

I was down at Greenham Common today. It really is a grizzly place, one felt it must have been funded by the barbed wire merchants.

Double fencing now and lots of police to keep the little camps of women out. . .I came down with a journalist, thrown out of the *Sunday Times* at the change of ownership, because she had spoken too sympathetically about them. . .Obviously the women can't stop Cruise, nor even stop the exercises when they are taken round the country, but they act as a kind of conscience.[4]

Naomi rejected what she saw as the short-sighted and war-mongering tactics of British and American politics in the hands of Margaret Thatcher and Ronald Reagan; she had become more and more dejected about the future.

Whereas it may have warmed her bones to visit Southern California, it did not relieve Naomi's anxiety about future world destruction. Even in innocent situations she perceived signs of American cut-throat competition and aggression. Daily we swam several widths of the spacious olympic-sized pool at the University of California where single-minded swimmers convinced Naomi that swimming had been turned into contest. This, of course, might have been true for some, but in large part these late afternoon swimmers were simply taking their exercise ferociously, a health fashion of the 1980s.

One can understand Naomi's misunderstanding, for the pool setting and the intense swimming she saw must have differed from her lifetime of paddling. She had learnt to swim in the Cherwell in order to be safe when canoeing in that small river flowing by her parent's Oxford home. Later, as a young matron, she had revelled in the Thames, sometimes at dawn after a night's party, perfecting the skill of keeping her head out of its polluted waters. In the Mediterranean, sailing from one Greek island to another, she swam to land for bread, returning like a sleek seal in the sparkling water holding the loaf aloft. In Botswana the water from the pools of British officials had quenched the thirst of her skin, far different from the chilly sea of Carradale, where she still swims in summertime.

Wherever Naomi has travelled, she has rejuvenated in water. In 1958 she swam with her brother Jack in the gardens of his new home in Calcutta:

The cleaner of the two tanks in the garden had a fair amount of kitchen refuse dumped in it but mostly vegetable scraps, and we felt that the carp would probably eat them so we could bathe happily. That way Jack and I used to swim there at night when the water looked merely black and observe the stars – those outsize Indian stars long ago mapped and named carefully watched by the early Indian astronomers whose solidly built observatory complexes still stand in many important Indian cities. Swimming on our backs for a better view, we did not risk getting the water in our mouths; every now and then the great smooth cool fish bumped into our bottoms or flapped against our legs. It was a happy time, just the two of us.[5]

That was Naomi's last swim with her brother Jack, her 'Boy-dear'.

Naomi continues to swim effortlessly and joyously wherever she goes, even in ever-dry Botswana: 'Yes, I swam this year at Chobe by the river but not in it because of the crocodiles, instead in a pool full of dropped jacaranda flowers, with my two grandchildren'.[6]

She continues also to swim painfully and courageously against the social currents and against the political tides. Violence in South Africa has not abated, even as I write in 1989; twice in 1986 Gaberone, the capital of Botswana located thirty miles from Mochudi, was invaded and bombed by military forces crossing from the Republic of South Africa. Before diving into the eye of the storm for her yearly visit, Naomi described the situation:

> People in Botswana are very angry but not at all frightened. I intend to go back in September by which time the situation may be different. Governments are unwilling to employ sanctions according to their level of trade with S. Africa. It seems rather shortsighted, but money rules everywhere. One wishes it was not so closely related with stupidity (over all matters except the various techniques for doing other people down). . .[7]

Naomi was again wading into the fray, hoping to end the stupidity of apartheid; she continues, as do heroic women in her fiction, to quest for her Just Society.

No doubt, Naomi Mitchison will continue to swim where she likes. And where she must.

Notes

CHAPTER ONE

1   Mitchison, *All Change Here*, p. 52.
2   Louisa Kathleen Haldane, *Friends and Kindred* (London: Faber and Faber, 1961), p. 80.
3   Ronald Clark, *JBS: The Life and Work of J. B. S. Haldane* (Oxford: Oxford University Press, 1984), p. 49.
4   Mitchison, *Small Talk*, p. 9.
5   Gervas Huxley, *Both Hands: An Autobiography* (London: Chatto and Windus, 1978), pp. 71–2.
6   Mitchison, *All Change Here*, p. 68.
7   Mitchison, *The Moral Basis of Politics* (London: Constable and Co. Ltd., 1938), dedication.
8   Mitchison, *Small Talk*, p. 38.
9   Mitchison, *All Change Here*, p. 94.
10 Ibid., p. 94.
11 Mitchison, *Small Talk*, p. 33.
12 Ibid., p. 130.
13 Ibid., p. 123.
14 Ibid., p. 19.
15 Ibid., p. 19.
16 Mitchison, *All Change Here*, p. 10.
17 Mitchison, *Small Talk*, p. 63.
18 Ibid., p. 55.
19 Ibid., p. 81.
20 Mitchison, *All Change Here*, p. 12.

CHAPTER TWO

1   Mitchison, *All Change Here*, p. 69.
2   Ibid., p. 52.
3   Ibid., p. 91.
4   Ibid., p. 9.
5   Ibid., p. 24.
6   Ibid., p. 26.
7   Ibid., p. 32.
8   Gervas Huxley, op. cit., p. 72.
9   Mitchison, *All Change Here*, p. 45.
10 Gervas Huxley, op. cit., p. 72; Sybille Bedford, *Aldous Huxley: A Biography* (New York: Carroll and Graf Publishers, Inc., 1973), p. 45.
11 Gervas Huxley, op. cit., p. 72.
12 Mitchison, *All Change Here*, p. 102.

13 Mitchison as quoted in *Twentieth Century Authors* (1942).
14 Mitchison as quoted in interview by Sybille Bedford, op. cit., p. 56.
15 Mitchison, *All Change Here*, p. 111.
16 Ibid., p. 133.
17 Ibid., p. 132.
18 Ibid., p. 105.

CHAPTER THREE

1 Mitchison, *All Change Here*, p. 135.
2 Ibid., p. 135.
3 Ibid., p. 141.
4 Mitchison, *You May Well Ask*, p. 69.
5 Mitchison, *The Corn King and the Spring Queen*, p. 303.
6 Mitchison, *We Have Been Warned*, p. 299.
7 Mitchison, *The Corn King and the Spring Queen*, p. 304.
8 Mitchison, *All Change Here*, p. 158.
9 Ibid., pp. 158–9.
10 Letter from Naomi to Julian Huxley from Cherwell, Oxford (no date, 1918).
11 Letters from Naomi to Julian Huxley from 17 Cheyne Walk (no date, c. 1920).
12 Interview with Avrion Mitchison, London, October 25, 1988.
13 Mitchison, *You May Well Ask*, p. 34.
14 Ibid., p. 161.
15 Mitchison, *The Conquered*, pp. 85–6.
16 Ronald Clark, op. cit., p. 86.
17 Mitchison, *You May Well Ask*, p. 62.
18 Anonymous, *New Statesman* (December 17, 1925).
19 Mitchison, *When the Bough Breaks*, pp. 133–4.
20 Ibid., p. 134.
21 Mitchison, *Cloud Cuckoo Land*, p. 167.
22 Ibid., p. 275.
23 Samuel Chew, 'Days of Ten Thousand,' *New York Times* (February 12, 1926).
24 Mitchison, *Cloud Cuckoo Land*, p. 237.
25 Ibid., p. 103.

CHAPTER FOUR

1 Letter, Naomi to Elizabeth Haldane (August, 1928?), in MSS. 6028-40, Haldane Collection, National Library of Scotland, Edinburgh.
2 Arnold Bennett, *Evening Standard* (September 6, 1928).
3 Mitchison, *You May Well Ask*, p. 71.
4 Letter, Dick Mitchison to Naomi (September 24, 1930).
5 Letter, Dick to Naomi (October 7, 1930).
6 Letter, Dick to Naomi (no date, c. 1930).
7 Interview, Murdoch Mitchison to Jill Benton, Carradale, August 8, 1988.
8 Mitchison, *You May Well Ask*, p. 71.
9 Ibid., p. 70.
10 Aldous Huxley, *Point Counter Point*, (London: Panther, 1978) Chapter 35, p. 418.
11 Interview, Naomi to Jill Benton, La Jolla, March 1984.

12 Charlotte Haldane, *Motherhood and Its Enemies* (London: Chatto and Windus, 1927), p. 133.
13 Mitchison, *You May Well Ask*, p. 66.
14 Ibid., p. 164.
15 Letter, Naomi to Julian Huxley from Stockholm, Sweden (c. 1930).

CHAPTER FIVE

1 Mitchison, *You May Well Ask*, p. 68.
2 Betty Vernon, *Margaret Cole 1893–1980: a Political Biography* (London: Croom Helm, 1986), p. 71.
3 Interview, Lady Longford and Naomi to Jill Benton, London, November, 1983.
4 Elizabeth Longford, *The Pebbled Shore* (London: Weidenfeld and Nicolson, 1986), p. 122.
5 Mitchison, 'Anna and the Apes' (Review of *The Apes of God* by Wyndham Lewis), *Time and Tide* (June 28, 1930), pp. 835–6.
6 Mitchison, 'The Book and the Revolution' (Review of *The Ascent of Humanity* by Gerald Heard), *Time and Tide* (January, 1930), pp. 79–80.
7 Mitchison, *The Corn King and the Spring Queen*, p. 245.
8 Ibid., p. 316.
9 Ibid., p. 582.

CHAPTER SIX

1 Mitchison, 'Letters to the Editor', *Time and Tide*, (August 17, 1928).
2 Mitchison, 'Comments on Birth Control', *Criterion Miscellany*, No. 12 (London: Faber and Faber, 1930), p. 38.
3 Mitchison, 'Some Comment on the Use of Contraceptives by Intelligent Persons', *Sexual Reform Congress*, ed. Norman Haire (London: Kegan Paul, Trench, Trubner & Co., Ltd., 1930), p. 188.
4 Sheila Jeffreys, *The Spinster and Her Enemies: Feminism and Sexuality 1880–1930* (London: Pandora Press, 1985).
5 Note attached to MS, 'The Break Up of the Home' (no date), Mitchison Collection, Harry Ransom Humanities Research Centre, University of Texas at Austin.
6 Letter, Naomi to Stella Benson from Craignish, as quoted in *You May Well Ask*, p. 137.
7 Mitchison, 'Introduction', *The Intelligent Woman's Guide Through Feminism* (unpublished MS, c. 1930), Haldane Collection, National Library of Scotland, Edinburgh.
8 Ibid.
9 H. Barton Brown, 'Catholic Rector's Reply to Mrs. Naomi Mitchison', *Middlesex County Times* (May 23, 1931).
10 Mitchison, 'Breaking Up the Home', *Twentieth Century*, Promethean Society, 3 (17 July, 1932), p. 3.
11 Letter, Naomi to John Pilley (no date, c. 1932).
12 Margaret Cole, 'Discovering the Labour Movement', *Hugh Gaitskell 1906–1963*, ed. W. T. Roger (London: Thames and Hudson, 1964), p. 42.
13 Mitchison, *You May Well Ask*, p. 194.
14 Ibid., p. 214.

15 Ibid., p. 63.
16 Mitchison, *We Have Been Warned*, pp. 397–8.
17 Letter, Naomi to John Pilley (October 20, 1932).
18 Mitchison, *The Delicate Fire*, p. 276.
19 Charles Skepper, 'The Family or One Way of Keeping Together', *An Outline for Boys and Girls and their Parents* (London: Gollancz, 1932), p. 492.
20 Letter protesting *An Outline*, quoted by Lady Rhondda in 'Mrs. Mitchison and the Bishops', *Time and Tide* (October 15, 1932), p. 1097.
21 Lady Rhondda, op. cit., pp. 1096–7.
22 Letter, Naomi to John Pilley (no date but in July after publishing *Powers of Light* in 1932).
23 Mitchison, *We Have Been Warned*, p. 295.
24 Elizabeth Longford, op. cit., p. 172.
25 Letter, Naomi to John Pilley (no date, after trip to Russia in 1932).
26 Mitchison, *You May Well Ask*, p. 192.

CHAPTER SEVEN

1 Letter, Naomi to Julian Huxley, November 19, 1932?, Julian Huxley Papers, Woodson Research Centre, Rice University Library, Houston, Texas.
2 Mitchison, *You May Well Ask*, p. 80.
3 Letter, Naomi to Julian Huxley, (no date, c. 1932 or 1933) Woodson Research Centre.
4 Mitchison, *You May Well Ask*, p. 79.
5 Interview, Naomi to Jill Benton, Carradale (November 1982).
6 Mitchison, unpublished poem entitled 'New Verse', private papers, Carradale.
7 Mitchison, *The Delicate Fire*, p. 182.
8 Mitchison, 'Two Men at the Salmon Net', *The Delicate Fire*, p. 63.
9 Henry Seidel Canby, *Saturday Review of Literature* (September 30, 1933), p. 145.
10 Letter, Naomi to Mr. Howard (March 11, 1929), Naomi's private papers, Carradale.
11 Letter, Naomi to Ronald Boswell at Cape (no date), Humanities Research Centre, Austin, Texas.
12 Mitchison, *You May Well Ask*, p. 175.
13 Letter, Edward Garnett to Naomi (June 1, 1933), Humanities Research Centre, Austin, Texas.
14 Letter, Naomi to Edward Garnett (no date), Humanities Research Centre, Austin, Texas.
15 Letter, Victor Gollancz to Naomi (July 17, 1933), as quoted in *You May Well Ask*, p. 177.
16 The original manuscript of *We Have Been Warned*, complete with excised passages, is located in the Haldane Collection in the archives of the National Library of Scotland, Edinburgh.
17 Interview, Elizabeth Longford to Jill Benton, London, November, 1982.
18 G. R. Mitchison, *The First Workers' Government* (London: Gollancz, 1934).
19 Mitchison, 'The Reluctannt Feminists', *Left Review* (December, 1934), p. 93.
20 Letter, Naomi to H. T. Wade Gery (c. October 1933).
21 Mitchison, *You May Well Ask*, p. 193.
22 Mitchison, *Naomi Mitchison's Vienna Diary*, p. 153.
23 Mitchison, *You May Well Ask*, pp. 193–4.
24 Mitchison, *Naomi Mitchison's Vienna Diary*, p. 218.

CHAPTER EIGHT

1 Mitchison, *Beyond This Limit*, p. 87.
2 Mitchison, *You May Well Ask*, p. 58.
3 Mitchison, *Mucking Around*, p. 54.
4 Mitchison, *We Have Been Warned*, p. 456.
5 Idid., pp. 458–9.
6 Anonymous, 'New Novels: *We Have Been Warned*', *Times Literary Supplement* (April 28, 1935), p. 270.
7 Anonymous, '[review] Books', *Life and Letters*, vol. 12, no. 64 (April 1935), pp. 98–102.
8 William Plomer, 'Fiction', *Spectator*, vol. 154 (April 26, 1935), p. 706.
9 Thomas Hardy Wintringham, 'We Have Been Warned', *Left Review* (June 1935), pp. 381–3.
10 Mitchison, *The Fourth Pig*, pp. 3–4.
11 Mitchison, 'Letters to the Editor', *Time and Tide* (February 29, 1936), p. 292.
12 Ibid.
13 Mitchison, 'Letters to the Editor', *Time and Tide* (September 5, 1936).
14 Mitchison, *You May Well Ask*, p. 116.
15 Tom Harrisson, 'Letters to the Editor', *Time and Tide* (January 30, 1937).
16 Mitchison, *You May Well Ask*, pp. 211–12.
17 Ibid., p. 212.
18 Mitchison, *The Moral Basis of Politics*, p. 103.
19 Ibid., p. 170.
20 Ibid., pp. 326–7.
21 Anonymous, 'Letters and the Arts', *Living Ages* 357 (October 1939), pp. 188–90.
22 Cyril M. Joad, 'Complaint Against Lady Novelists', *New Statesman and Nation* (August 19, 1939), pp. 275–6.
23 Mitchison, 'Letters to the Editor', *New Statesman and Nation* (August, 1939), p. 311.
24 Letter, Stevie Smith to Naomi, (no date, but between 1938 and 1939), as quoted in *You May Well Ask*, p. 157.
25 Anonymous, 'Fiction', *Spectator* (October 1939).
26 Mitchison, *Blood of the Martyrs*, p. 110.

CHAPTER NINE

1 Mitchison, *Among You Taking Notes. . .* (London: Gollancz, 1985), pp. 46–7.
2 Mitchison, *The Alban Goes Out* (Harrow: Raven Press, 1939).
3 Mitchison, *Among You Taking Notes. . .*, pp. 72–3.
4 Mitchison, 'Clemency Ealasaid', *The Bull Calves*, p. 12.
5 Mitchison, *Among You Taking Notes. . .*, p. 72.
6 Mitchison, 'War Diary' (November 16, 1940), ditto MS, Mass Observation Archives.
7 Mitchison, ibid. (January 1, 1941), p. 235.
8 Mitchison, *The Bull Calves*, pp. 472–3.
9 Mitchison, *Among You Taking Notes. . .*, p. 156.
10 Interview, Robert Paterson to Jill Benton (August 14, 1984), Carradale.

11 Mitchison, 'War Diary' (January 12, 1942), ditto MS, Mass Observation Archives, p. 633.

12 Ibid. (January 22, 1942), p. 635.

13 Mitchison, *Among You Taking Notes. . .*, p. 172.

14 Mitchison, unpublished poem, Carradale.

15 Interview, Jemima MacLean to Jill Benton (August 13, 1984), Carradale.

16 Mitchison, *Among You Taking Notes. . .*, p. 234.

17 Letter, Naomi to Neil Gunn (1944), as quoted by Donald Smith in 'Naomi Mitchison and Neil Gunn: A Highland Friendship,' *Cencratus* (July 1983), p. 19.

18 Mitchison, 'Living in a Village', *The Cleansing of the Knife*, p. 26.

19 Mitchison, 'War Diary' (April 30 to May 4, 1943), ditto MS, Mass Observation Archives, p. 975.

20 Mitchison, ibid. (September 11, 1942), p. 825.

CHAPTER TEN

1 Mitchison, *Among You Taking Notes. . .*, pp. 334–5.

2 Ibid., p. 324.

3 Mitchison, 'The Wells of Ritual', *New Statesman and Nation* (November 10, 1951), p. 526.

4 Mitchison, 'History of the '45 County Council Election' (December 1945), Mass Observation Archives.

5 Letter, Neil Gunn to Naomi, as quoted by Donald Smith, 'Naomi Mitchison and Neil Gunn: A Highland Friendship', *Cencratus* (July 1983), p. 20.

6 Mitchison, *Saltire Self-Portraits 2: Naomi Mitchison* (Edinburgh: The Saltire Society, 1986), p. 18.

7 Mitchison, *Lobsters on the Agenda*, p. 205.

8 Mitchison, *Travel Light*, p. 129.

9 Mitchison, *Mucking Around*, p. 83.

10 Ibid., p. 33.

11 Ibid., p. 58.

12 Mitchison and C. Day Lewis, 'Banned Bodies', *New Statesman and Nation* (March 7, 1953), p. 263.

13 Mitchison, *Author's World Peace Appeal*, Bulletin No. 11 (1955), p. 8.

14 Mitchison, 'Writers in the USSR', *New Statesman and Nation* (September 6, 1952), p. 260.

15 Mitchison, *Mucking Around*, p. 117.

16 Mitchison, 'Carradale Harbour Opened', *The Glasgow Herald* (September 18, 1959).

17 Mitchison, *Memoirs of a Spacewoman*, p. 148.

18 Ibid., p. 27.

CHAPTER ELEVEN

1 Lois Picard, *The Politics of Development in Botswana* (Boulder, Colorado: L. Rienner Publishers, 1987), pp. 155–6.

2 Mitchison, *Return to the Fairy Hill*, p. 52.

3 Ibid., p. 86.

4 Letter, Naomi to Julian Huxley (c. December, 1963), Julian Huxley Papers, Woodson Research Centre, Texas.
5 J. B. S. Haldane, as quoted by Ronald Clark, op. cit., p. 298.
6 Mitchison, 'Ageing from Inside', *The Medical World* (1961), p. 25.
7 Interview with Lord (Frederick) Elwyn-Jones, as quoted by Betty Vernon, op. cit., p. 68.
8 Letter, Naomi to Jill Benton (November 8, 1986).
9 Mitchison, *Mucking Around*, p. 120.
10 Ibid., p. 121.
11 Mitchison, *Return to the Fairy Hill*, p. 127.
12 Mitchison, *Mucking Around*, p. 136.
13 Mitchison, *Return to the Fairy Hill*, p. 212.

CHAPTER TWELVE

1 Mitchison, 'Was It So?', unpublished MS, London.
2 Mitchison, 'Nettlebed Road', unpublished poem, Carradale.
3 Mitchison, 'Remember Me', *What Do You Think Yourself?*, p. 100.
4 Letter, Naomi to Jill Benton (November 18, 1983).
5 Mitchison, *Mucking Around*, p. 90.
6 Letter, Naomi to Jill Benton (November 8, 1986).
7 Letter, Naomi to Jill Benton (June 18, 1986).

Chronological Bibliography: a Selection of Naomi Mitchison's Works

[1910s]

Saunes Bairos: A Study in Recurrence, (play) at Oxford Preparatory School, 1913

[1920s]

The Conquered, London: Jonathan Cape, 1923; rpt. London: Jonathan Cape for
    Traveller's Library, 1927; rpt. London: Landsborough Publications, 1958.
When the Bough Breaks, and Other Stories, London: Jonathan Cape, 1924; rpt.
    London: Bodley Head, 1974.
'Motherhood', *The Woman's Leader*, 16 (29 August 1924), p. 249.
Cloud Cuckoo Land, London: Jonathan Cape, 1925; rpt. London: Hodder &
    Stoughton, 1967.
'To the Future', *The Journal of the Divorce Law Reform Union*, 6 (January
    1925), p. 4.
'Ravenna', (poem) *Literary Digest*, (5 December 1925), p. 34.
The Laburnum Branch: Poems, London: Jonathan Cape, 1926.
'A Little Girl Lost: A Short Story', *The Liberal Woman's News*, (December 1926),
    pp. 155–6.
Anna Comnena: Representative Women, London: Gerald Howe, 1928.
Black Sparta: Greek Stories, London: Jonathan Cape, 1928.
Nix-Nought-Nothing: Four Plays for Children, London: Jonathan Cape, 1928.
'Two Poems: Scottish Renaissance in Glasgow. Child Jason is Brought to Chiron',
    London Mercury, (17 April 1928), pp. 627–9.
Barbarian Stories, London: Jonathan Cape, 1929.
'Back from Achaea', *Time and Tide*, 10 (4 January 1929), pp. 7–8.
'Some French Novels', standing review of Contemporary French Fiction, *Time and
    Tide*, 1929–1931.

[1930s]

The Hostages, and Other Stories for Boys and Girls, London, Toronto: Jonathan
    Cape, 1930; rpt. illustrated Logi Southby, London: Max Parrish, 1964.

'Comments on Birth-Control', *Criterion Miscellany*, No. 12, London: Faber & Faber, 1930.

'The Book and the Revolution', review of *The Ascent of Humanity* by Gerald Heard, *Time and Tide* 11 (January-April 1930), pp. 79–80.

'New Fiction', standing review of Anglo-American fiction, *Time and Tide*, 1930–1932.

'Happy Ending?' (story) *Time and Tide*, 68 (April 1930), pp. 431–3.

'Love Gift Broken', (poem) *New Statesman and Nation*, 35 (10 May 1930), p. 149.

'Pain of Waiting', (poem) *New Statesman and Nation*, 35 (19 April 1930), p. 49.

'Buying a Secretary', (story) *New Statesman and Nation*, 35 (7 June 1930), pp. 274–5.

'Anna and the Apes', review of *The Apes of God* by Wyndham Lewis, *Time and Tide*, (28 June 1930), pp. 835–6.

'Child-Rearing Services Some Day', *Time and Tide*, (19 July 1930), p. 933.

'Two Prophets', review of *Civilisation and Its Discontents* by Sigmund Freud and *Apropos of Lady Chatterley's Lover* by D. H. Lawrence, *Time and Tide*, (26 July 1930), pp. 963–4.

'Two Poems: Wild Swan at Port Meirion; Stamfordics', *London Mercury*, 22 (October 1930), pp. 489–90.

'I Look at the Theatre', *Theatre Arts*, (October 1930), pp. 861–5.

'End and Beginning of Lawrence', review of *The Virgin and the Gypsy* by D. H. Lawrence and *D. H. Lawrence* by Rebecca West, *Time and Tide*, 11 (1 November 1930), 1375–6.

Boys and Girls and Gods, World of Youth Series, London: Watts & Co., 1931.

Kate Crackernuts: a Fairy Play for Children, Oxford: Aldan Press, 1931.

The Corn King and the Spring Queen, With four pictures by Z. Stryjenska, London: Jonathan Cape, 1931; rpt. *The Barbarian*, New York: Cameron Associates, 1961; rpt. London: Virago, 1983; rpt. New York: Vintage, 1989; rpt. Edinburgh: Canongate, 1990.

And Lewis Evelyn Gielgud, *The Price of Freedom*, (play) London: Jonathan Cape, 1931.

'Elizabeth Garrett Anderson', *Revaluations*, Oxford: no publisher, 1931.

'Dr. Florence Buchanan', *The Woman's Leader and the Common Cause*, Vol. 23, No. 12 (10 April 1931), pp. 78–9.

'Dunkerque – Paris Line', (poem) *New Statesman and Nation*, 2 (4 July 1931), p. 13.

'Good News', review of *Social Substance of Religion* by Gerald Heard, *Time and Tide*, 12 (25 July 1931).

'Vase Room at the Louvre', *The Island*, 1 (September 1931), p. 61.

'How to Educate Children', *Saturday Review of Literature*, 8 (14 November 1931), pp. 279–80.

The Powers of Light, illustrated by Eric Kennington, London: Pharos, 1932.

'In the Family', *Scottish Short Stories*, ed. Fred Urquhart, London: Hamish Hamilton, 1932.

'What Dare I Hope', *Time and Tide*, 13 (16 January 1932), p. 62.

'Because We Are Fools', review of *Apocalypse* by D. H. Lawrence, *Time and Tide*, 13 (30 April 1932).

'Breaking Up the Home', *Twentieth Century*, Promethean Society, 3 (17 July 1932), pp. 1–3.

'A Socialist Plan for Scotland', *Modern Scot*, 3 (August 1932), pp. 25–30.

'Pages from a Russian Diary', *Modern Scot*, 3 (October 1932), pp. 229–36.

'Romantic Event', (story) *Time and Tide*, 13 (13 October 1932), pp. 1103–5.

'Comment on the Basis of the Sexology Group', *Twentieth Century*, 4 (21 November, 1932), pp. 19–20.

Ed. *An Outline for Boys and Girls and their Parents*, London: Victor Gollancz, 1932.

The Delicate Fire: Short Stories and Poems, London, Toronto: Jonathan Cape, 1933.

'Archaeology and the Intellectual Worker [in Soviet Russia]', *Twelve Studies in Soviet Russia*, ed. Margaret Cole, London: New Fabian Research Bureau, 1933.

'Anger Against Books', *Contemporary Essays*, ed. Sylvia Norman, London: no publisher, 1933.

'Fascism and War', *Storm: Stories of the Worker's Struggle*, 1 (1933), no place, p 16.

'To Some Young Communists from an Older Socialist', (poem) *New Verse*, (January 1933), p. 9.

'Interlude', (story) *Modern Scot*, 4 (2 July 1933), pp, 100–4.

'Sex and Politics', *Twentieth Century*, (December-January 1933–4), pp. 137–48.

Naomi Mitchison's Vienna Diary, London: Victor Gollancz, 1934.

The Home and a Changing Civilisation, Twentieth Century Library, London: John Lane, 1934.

'The N. U. W. M. against Lord Trenchard', *This Unrest*, (1934), p. 61.

'Matter of No Importance, BC 54–51', *Scholastic*, 24 (10 February 1934), pp. 4–5.

'Chapter from an Unpublished Novel', *New Oxford Outlook*, (February 1934), pp. 274–87.

'Marxist Love Poem', *Lysistrata*, 1-2 (May 1934), p. 70.

'Troubled Europe; Austrian Aftermath', *Review of Reviews*, 85 (May 1934), pp. 19–20.

'Fascism in Austria', *Twentieth Century*, 6 (June 1934), p. 257–61.

'New Cloud-Cuckoo-Borough', *Modern Scot*, (June 1934), pp. 30–8.

'The Reluctant Feminists', *Left Review*, 1 (December 1934), pp. 93–4.

We Have Been Warned, London: Constable & Co., 1935.

Beyond This Limit, pictures by Wynham Lewis, London: Jonathan Cape, 1935.

'Toll for the Brave', *Golden Book*, 21 (January 1935), pp. 28–33.

'White House and Marked Tree', *New Statesman and Nation*, 9 (27 April 1935), pp. 585–6.

'Writing Historical Novels', *Saturday Review of Literature*, 11 (27 April 1935), pp. 645–6.

'In Time of Trouble' (poem), *Programme*, 5 (17 May 1935), p. 16.

'Arkansas through British Eyes', *Living Age*, 348 (May 1935), pp. 278–80.

'The Furies Dance in New York', (poem) *New Statesman and Nation*, 9 (June 1935), pp. 807–8.

'Epiphany of Harlem', *New Statesman and Nation*, 9 (June 1935), pp. 808–9.

'Omen of the Enemy' (poem), *New Statesman and Nation*, 10 (27 July 1935), p. 125.

'White Nights', *Modern Scot*, (3 October 1935), p. 226.

'Woman Alone', (poem) *Time and Tide*, (7 December 1935), p. 1787.

The Fourth Pig, (stories and verse) London: Constable & Co., 1936.

'Dr. A. J. M. Melby', (poem) *New Statesman and Nation*, (11 May 1936), pp. 762–3.

'We're Writing a Book', *New Masses*, (5 September 1936), pp. 15–16.

'An End and a Beginning', (play) *Time and Tide*, (28 November 1936).

An End and a Beginning, (play) London: Constable & Co., 1937.

And Richard Crossman, *Socrates: World-Makers and World-Shakers*, London: L. & V. Woolf, 1937.

'Eviction in the Hebrides', *Left Review*, 3 (1 February 1937), p. 20.

'The Story of Freedom', *Women Today*, (September 1937), pp. 8–9.

The Moral Basis of Politics, London: Constable & Co., 1938.

'What People Really Want', *Forum*, 1 (June-September 1938), pp. 368–2.

The Alban Goes Out, (poem) wood engravings by Gertrude Hermes, Harrow: Raven Press, 1939.

The Blood of the Martyrs, London: Constable & Co., 1939; rpt. Glasgow: R. Drew, 1988.

And Lewis Evelyn Gielgud, *As It Was In the Beginning*, London: Jonathan Cape, 1939.

The Kingdom of Heaven, London, Toronto: William Heinemann, 1939.

Historical Plays for Schools, 2nd series, London: Constable & Co., 1939.

'Lady Novelists', (letter to editor) *New Statesman and Nation*, 18 (26 August 1939), p. 311.

'Beginning of a New Order', *Kingdom Come: The Magazine of Wartime Oxford*, (1 November 1939), pp. 7–8.

[1940s]

'Spring', (poem) *New Statesman and Nation*, 21 (1 February 1941), p. 800.

'Rural Reconstruction', *New Scotland*, Glasgow: no publisher, 1942.

'Forestry Commission', (letter to editor) *New Statesman and Nation*, 28 (23 December 1944), p. 422.

Ed., *Re-Educating Scotland*, Scottish Convention, no place, 1944.

The Bull Calves, drawings by Louise Richard Annand, London: Jonathan Cape, 1947; rpt. Glasgow: R. Drew, 1987.

'British View of America', *New Republic*, 46 (24 February 1947), p. 116.

'The Hunting of Ian Og', *No Scottish Twilight*, eds. Maurier Lindsay and Fred Urquhart, Glasgow: McLennan & Co., 1947.

Nix-Nought-Nothing, and Elfin Hill: Two Plays for Children, London: Jonathan Cape, 1948.

'Writing the Historical Novel', *Scotland*, (March 1948), pp. 59–64.

And Dennis MacIntosh, *Men and Herring: A Documentary*, Edinburgh: Serif Books, 1949.

[1950s]

The Big House, London: Faber & Faber, 1950.

And Dennis MacIntosh, *Spindrift: A Play*, London: Samuel French, 1951.

'Embarkation at Gwadar', *New Statesman and Nation*, 41 (17 March 1951), p. 300.

'Women's Magazine', (letter to editor) *New Statesman and Nation*, 41 (2 June 1951), p. 623.

'Wells of Ritual', *New Statesman and Nation*, 42 (10 November 1951) p. 526.

Lobsters on the Agenda, London: Victor Gollancz, 1952.

Travel Light, London: Faber & Faber, 1952; rpt. London: Virago, 1984.

'Winter Fishing', *New Statesman and Nation*, 43 (15 March 1952), p. 296.

'Writers in the USSR', *New Statesman and Nation*, 44 (6 September 1952), p. 260.

'Wester Ross', (poem) *New Statesman and Nation*, 45 (17 January 1953), p. 69.

And Cecil Day-Lewis, 'Banned Bodies', *New Statesman and Nation*, 45 (7 March 1953), p. 263.

'In the Mirror', (poem) *New Statesman*, 45 (13 June 1953), p. 708.

'Platform Party', *New Statesman*, 46 (31 October 1953), p. 516.

'Childhood in the Other Place', *Twentieth Century*, 154 (November 1953), p. 368–74.

Graeme and the Dragon, illustrated by Pauline Baynes, London: Faber & Faber, 1954.

The Swan's Road, drawings by Leonard Huskinson, London: Naldrett Press, 1954.

'Yes, But', (poem) *New Statesman*, 47 (15 May 1954), p. 636.

'Disloyalty', *New Statesman*, 48 (28 August 1954), p. 229.

To the Chapel Perilous, London: George Allen & Unwin, 1955; rpt. London: White Lion Publishers, 1976.

The Land the Ravens Found, drawings by Brian Allderidge, London: Collins, 1955.

'Lean Harvest', *New Statesman*, 49 (26 March 1955), p. 428.

'Leaning on a Gate', *New Statesman*, 49 (26 February 1955), p. 276.

'Thoughts on Growing Grass', *New Statesman*, 49 (11 June 1955), p. 806.

'Writer and the Child', *New Statesman*, 49 (12 February 1955), pp. 203–4.

'Year of the Good Hay', *New Statesman*, 50 (30 July 1955), pp. 130–1.

'Year's Work Done', *New Statesman*, 50 (22 October 1955), p. 504.

'Maggots and Potatoes', *New Statesman*, 49 (7 May 1955), p. 642.

'Celebrating the Solstice', *New Statesman*, 50 (24 December 1955), p. 853.

'Cautionary Story', *New Statesman*, 50 (10 September 1955), p. 294.

'Big Mill', *New Statesman*, 50 (26 November 1955), p. 700.

'The Writ', *New Statesman*, 50 (1 August 1955), p. 128.

'Young Laird', *New Statesman*, 50 (22 October 1955), p. 504.

Little Boxes, illustrated by Louise Annand, London: Faber & Faber, 1956.

'Loch Ness: The Great Fault', (poem) *New Statesman*, 52 (25 August 1956), p. 218.

'Postscript on Palestine: Around and About Jerusalem', *Twentieth Century*, 160 (August 1956), pp. 155–65.

'Price of a Binder', *New Statesman*, 52 (3 November 1956), pp. 544–5.

'Rough Weather', *New Statesman*, 52 (25 August 1956), p. 212.

'Think of a Number', *New Statesman*, 51 (11 February 1956). p. 144.

'Half-Way to Sodom', *New Statesman*, 51 (7 April 1956), p. 336.

'Home is Over Jordan', *New Statesman*, 51 (28 April 1956), pp. 443–4.

'Cow and the Calf', *New Statesman*, 51 (9 June 1956), p. 648.

'Sitting for Wyndham Lewis', *Manchester Guardian*, (9 July 1956), p. 6.

'Buck Rake', *New Statesman*, 52 (22 September 1956), p. 340.

Behold Your King, London: Frederick Muller, 1957.

Five Men and a Swan, London: George Allen & Unwin, 1957.

The Far Harbour, drawings by Martin Thomas, 1957; rpt. London: Collins, 1969.

'On the Council', *New Statesman*, 54 (31 August 1957), p. 245.

'Remote Area', *New Statesman*, 54 (7 December 1957), p. 772.

'Split Mind of Ghana', *New Statesman*, 53 (23 March 1957), p. 371.

'Summer Work', *New Statesman*, 53 (29 June 1957), p. 834.

'Up-helly-aa', *New Statesman*, 53 (9 February 1957, p. 164.

'Highland Committee', *New Statesman*, 54 (16 November 1957), p. 644.

Other People's Worlds, London: Secker & Warburg, 1958.

'Bird-House of Poets', *New Statesman*, 55 (3 May 1957), p. 562.

'Calves', *New Statesman*, 56 (25 October 1958), p. 554.

'Kangra Painting', (poem) *New Statesman*, 55 (12 April 1958), p. 478.

'Kerala Experiment', *New Statesman*, 55 (8 March 1958), p. 296.
'Four Towns and Inverary', *Reporter*, 19 (4 September 1958), pp. 40–2.
'It Is in Glasgow I Would Rather Be', *Reporter*, 19 (16 October 1958), pp. 40–2.
'Visit to the Western Isles', *Reporter*, 18 (20 February 1958), pp. 34–6.
Judy and Lakshimi, drawings by Avinash Chandra, London: Collins, 1959.
'Danish Farm', *New Statesman*, 57 (13 June 1959), p. 820.
'Parkinson in Paris', *New Statesman*, 57 (April 1959), p. 538.
'Threshing Team', *New Statesman*, 57 (21 February 1959), p. 250.
'How the Scots Make Scotch', *Reporter*, 20 (16 April 1959), pp. 32–3.

[1960s]

The Rib of the Green Umbrella, drawings by Edward Ardizzone, London: Collins, 1960.
The Young Alexander the Great, illustrated by Betty Middleton-Sanford, London: Max Parrish, 1960.
'Golden Year', *New Statesman*, 57 (2 January 1960), pp. 9–10.
'On Writing Historical Novels', *Cairo Studies in English*, ed. Majdi Wahba (1960), pp. 113–18.
And George Paterson, *A Fishing Village on the Clyde*, Oxford: Oxford University Press, 1960.
Karensgaard: The Story of a Danish Farm, London: Collins, 1961.
Presenting Other People's Children, London, printed in Czechoslovakia: Paul Hamlyn, 1961.
The Barbarian [The Corn King and Spring Queen], New York: Cameron Associates, 1961.
Memoirs of a Spacewoman, London: Victor Gollancz, 1962; rpt. London: New English Library, 1964; rpt. 1976; rpt. 1977; rpt. London: The Women's Press, 1984.
The Young Alfred the Great, illustrated by Shirley Farrow, London: Max Parrish, 1962.
'Ghosts', *New Statesman*, 63 (27 April 1962), pp. 594–5.
'Anti-Ghosts', *New Statesman*, 63 (25 May 1962), p. 756.
'Ghosts Go North', *New Statesman*, 64 (21 September 1962), p. 360.
Ed. *What the Human Race Is Up To*, London: Victor Gollancz, 1962.
The Fairy Who Couldn't Tell a Lie, illustrated by Jane Paton, London: Collins, 1963.
'Fortunate Isles', *New Statesman*, 66 (22 November 1963), p. 738.
Alexander the Great, illustrated by Rosemary Grimber, London: Longman, 1964.
'Letter from a Tribe', *New Statesman*, 68 (16 October 1964), pp. 572–4.
'Prayer for Rain', *New Statesman*, 68 (21 August 1964), pp. 242–3.
'The Experience of Death', *Contact: Grief and Mourning*, (October 1964), pp. 26–8.
A Mochudi Family, Wellington: no publisher, 1965.
Ketse and the Chief, London: Thomas Nelson & Sons, 1965.
When We Become Men, London: Collins, 1965.
'Deadly Bracken', *New Statesman*, 20 (27 August 1965), p. 282.
Return to the Fairy Hill, London: Heinemann, 1966.
'Dry Day in Botswana', *Saturday Review*, 49 (22 October 1966), pp. 65–8.
'Scottish Mother for an African Tribe', *Harper*, 233 (September 1966), pp. 86–7.
'Tribal Values in Botswana', *Phylon*, 28 (Fall 1967), pp. 261–6.
'Young Auden', *Shenandoah*, Vol. 18, No. 2 (1967), pp. 12–15.
African Heroes, illustrated by William Stubbs, London: The Bodley Head, 1968.

'Beginnings', *Haldane and Modern Biology*, ed. K. R. Dronamrajer, Baltimore: Johns Hopkins Press, 1968.

The Family at Ditlabeng, illustrated by Joanna Stubbs, London: Collins, 1969.

'Experts and Volunteers', *New Statesman*, 78 (17 December 1969), pp. 884–5.

[1970s]

The Africans, London: Blond, 1970; rpt. London: Panther, 1971.

'Mithras, My Saviour', *The Penguin Book of Scottish Short Stories*, ed. J. F. Hendry, London, Harmondsworth: Penguin, 1970.

'Mary and Joe', *Nova One*, ed. Harry Harrison, New York: Walker, 1970, rpt. London: no publisher, 1975.

'Miss Omega Raven', *Nova Two*, ed. Harry Harrison, New York: Walker, 1971, rpt. London: no publisher, 1975.

'Letter from Botswana', *New Statesman*, 81 (4 June 1971), pp. 766–8.

'Letter from Kampala', *New Statesman*, 81 (26 February 1971), p. 270.

Cleopatra's People, London: Heinemann, 1972.

'The Factory', *Nova Three*, ed. Harry Harrison, New York: Walker, 1972; rpt. London: no publisher, 1975.

'Naboth and Others', *New Statesman*, 83 (14 January 1972), p. 45–6.

Small Talk: Memoirs of an Edwardian Childhood, London: Bodley Head, 1973.

Sunrise Tomorrow: A Story of Botswana, London: Collins, 1973.

Solution Three, London: Dobson, 1973.

'My Brother Jack', *J. B. S. Haldane Reader of Popular Scientific Essays*, Mockna: USSR, 1973.

'Out of the Waters', *Nova Four*, ed. Harry Harrison, New York: Walker; rpt. London: no publisher, 1976.

'What Do you Think Yourself?' *Scottish Short Stories*, Oxford: Oxford University Press, 1973.

'A Harvest Experience', *Folklore*, 84 (Autumn 1973), pp. 252–3.

'An African Doctor', *Blackwood's Magazine*, (April 1974), pp. 312–17.

All Change Here: Girlhood and Marriage, London: Bodley Head, 1975.

'The Hill Modipe', in *Scottish Short Stories*, Oxford: Oxford University Press, 1975.

'The Red Fellows', in *Scottish Short Stories*, Oxford: Oxford University Press, 1975.

'What is the Enemy?' *New Humanist*, (January 1975), pp. 309–31.

'Import-Expert', *African Affairs*, 74 (January 1975), pp. 60–4.

Snake, illustrated by Polly Loxton, London: Collins, 1976; rpt. London: Fontana, 1978.

'Call Me', *Scottish Short Stories*, Oxford: Oxford University Press, 1976.

'The Little Sister', *Pulenyani's Secret*, ed. Mary Kobel, Cape Town, New York: Oxford University Press, 1976.

Sittlichkeit: Haldane Memorial Lecture, London: Birkbeck College, 1977.

The Two Magicians, drawings by Danita Laskowska, London: Dobson, 1978.

The Cleansing of the Knife and Other Poems, Edinburgh: Canongate Publishing, 1978.

'The Sea Horse', *Modern Scottish Short Stories*, eds. Fred Urquhart and Giles Gordon, London: Hamish Hamilton, 1978.

'Botswana Contradictions', *African Affairs*, 77 (April 1978), pp. 230–5.

You May Well Ask: A Memoir 1920–1940, London: Gollancz, 1979.

'Self-Interview (Recollections of Neil Gunn)', *Studies in Scottish Literature*, no place, 1979.

[1980s]

The Vegetable War, illustrated Polly Loxton, London: Hamish Hamilton, 1980.
Images of Africa, Edinburgh: Canongate Publishing, 1980.
Mucking Around: Five Continents Over Fifty Years, London: Gollancz, 1981.
What Do You Think Yourself? Edinburgh: P. Harris, 1982.
Margaret Cole 1883–1980, London: Fabian Society, 1982.
'Aldous Huxley on War and Intellectual Survival', *Times Literary Supplement*, 4131 (11 June 1982), p. 635.
Not By Bread Alone, London, Boston: M. Boyars, 1983.
'One-Party Rule in Africa', *Round Table*, (1984), pp. 38–44.
Among You Taking Notes: Wartime Diary 1939–45, ed. Dorothy Sheridan, London: Gollancz, 1985.
Saltire Self-Portraits: Naomi Mitchison, Edinburgh: Saltire Society, 1986.
Early in Orcadia, Glasgow: R. Drew Publishers, 1987.

Additional periodicals and newspapers in which Naomi Mitchison has published and which may not be included in this bibliography:

African Affairs
Argosy Short Story
Atlanta's Garland
Bias
Blackwoods Magazine
The Bookman
Books and Bookmen
Books in Scotland
Botswana Notes and Records
Cairo Studies in English
Cambridge Magazine
Campbeltown Courier
Chambers Journal
Chapman
Children's World
Clarion
Collins Magazine for Boys and Girls
Cornhill Magazine
Country Fair
Countryman
Daily Telegraph
Draconian
Evening Standard
Fact
Farming News
Financial Times
Folklore
Fortnightly
Forward
Field
Foundation
Glasgow Herald
Golden Hind
Geographical Magazine
Graphic
Guardian

Harpers and Queen
Herald (Melbourne, Australia)
Hindustan Times
Illustrated Weekly of India
Irish Times
John O'Londons Weekly
Journal of Modern African Studies
Kintyre Farmer
Labour Record in Scotland
Liberal Woman's News
Life and Letters
Lines Review
Listener
London Mercury
London Review of Books
Medical World
Modern Scot
Museums Journal
Nash's Pall-Mall Magazine
Nation (& Athenaeum)
New Edinburgh Review
Humanist
New Saltire
New Scientist
New Society
New Statesman (& Nation)
North 7
Nova
Now and Then
Observer
Oxford Outlook
Oxford Poetry
Passing Show
Phylon
Picture Post
Picture Post (Scottish Edition)
Poetry Review
Principes
Punch
The Queen
Question
Radio Times
Radio Times (Children's Hour)
Radio Times (Morning story)
Radio Times (Schools Talks)
Rationalist Annual
Raven
Realist
Round Table
Royal Institute of Great Britain Proceedings
Saltire Review
Saturday Review
Saturday Westminster
Scotland's Magazine

Scots Magazine
Scots Writing
Scotsman
Scottish Agriculture
Scottish Chapbook
Scottish Field
Scottish Journal
Scottish Review
Shenandoah
Snark
Spectator
Strata Poetry Magazine
Strathearn Herald
Sunday Pictorial
Sunday Times
Time and Tide
Times Educational Supplement
Times Literary Supplement
Times of Zambia
Town Crier
Traveller
Trends in Biochemical Sciences
Twentieth Century
Varsity
Weekend Review
Weekend Scotsman
Weekly Westminster
Westminster
Woman Journalist
Worlds of Fantasy

Library locations of Naomi Mitchison's manuscripts and papers:
The Harry Ransom Humanities Research Centre, The University of Texas, Austin.
National Library of Scotland, Edinburgh.

Index

Index